Public and Community Services

Editorial Advisory Board

The Career Information Center includes:

Agribusiness, Environment, and Natural Resources / 1

Communications and the Arts / 2

Computers, Business, and Office / 3

Construction / 4

Consumer, Homemaking, and Personal Services / 5

Engineering, Science, and Technology / 6

Health / 7

Hospitality and Recreation / 8

Manufacturing / 9

Marketing and Distribution / 10

Public and Community Services / 11

Transportation / 12

Employment Trends and Master Index / 13

Public and Community Services

Career Information Center

Seventh Edition

Macmillan Reference USA
New York

Editorial Staff

Project Director: Frances A. Wiser

Writers: Tom Conklin, Suzanne J. Murdico, Judith Peacock

Researchers/Bibliographers: Christopher D. Binkley, Peter Michael Gee

Editors: Jacqueline Morais, Joseph B. Pirret, Meera Vaidyanathan

Copyediting Supervisor: Maureen Ryan Pancza

Photo Editor: Sara Matthews

Production Supervisors: Devan Paine Anding, William A. Murray

Interior Design: Maxson Crandall

Electronic Preparation: Cynthia C. Feldner, Fiona Torphy

Electronic Production: Elise Dodeles, Lisa Evans-Skopas, Deirdre Sheean, Isabelle Verret

Acknowledgments: It would be impossible to acknowledge the many people who gave their help, their time, and their experience to this project. However, we especially want to thank all the people at unions and trade and professional associations for their help in providing information and photographs. We also wish to thank the U.S. Department of Labor, Bureau of Labor Statistics, for providing up-to-date statistics, salary information, and employment projections for all the job profiles.

Developed and produced by Visual Education Corporation, Princeton, New Jersey

Macmillan Library Reference USA
1633 Broadway
New York, NY 10019

ISSN 1082-703X

ISBN 0-02-864915-X (set)

ISBN 0-02-864912-5 (volume 11)

Printed in the United States of America

printing number
1 2 3 4 5 6 7 8 9 10

This paper meets the requirements of ANSI/NISO Z39.48-1992 (Permanence of Paper).

Contents

Job Summary Chart

Job	Salary	Education/ Training	Employment Outlook	Page
Job Profiles—No Specialized Training				
Armed Services Career	Average—$28,000	Varies—see profile	Very good	29
Border Patrol Agent	Starting—$19,400 to $24,000 Average—$35,000	High school	Fair	31
Building Custodian	Average—$15,600	None	Good	33
Day Care Worker	Average—$210 to $320 a week	High school	Very good	34
Electric Power Service Worker	Varies—see profile	None	Fair	36
Electric Power Transmission and Distribution Worker	Varies—see profile	None	Fair	38
Firefighter	Average—$26,700 to $43,300	Varies—see profile	Fair	40
⭐ **Geriatric Aide**	Average—$12,100 to $19,300	None	Excellent	42
Highway Maintenance Worker	Average—$18,000 to $23,000	None	Very good	44
Institutional Housekeeper	Average—$240 to $420 a week	None	Good	46
Postal Service Worker	Starting—$21,700 to $22,900 Average—$34,000 to $36,000	High school	Poor	47
Power Plant Worker	Average—$43,500	None	Fair	49
Refuse Worker	Average—$25,000	None	Good	51
⭐ **Security Guard**	Varies—see profile	None	Excellent	53
Job Profiles—Some Specialized Training/Experience				
⭐ **Corrections Officer**	Average—$26,100	High school plus training	Excellent	56
Court Clerk	Varies—see profile	Varies—see profile	Fair	58
Crime Laboratory Technician	Average—$20,000 to $29,000	2-year or 4-year college	Fair	60
Customs Worker	Average—$37,000 to $42,000	High school plus training	Fair	62
Detective	Average—$25,700 to $45,300	High school plus training	Good	64
Federal Government Worker	Varies—see profile	Varies—see profile	Fair	66
Institutional Child Care Worker	Average—$12,000 to $20,000	High school plus training	Very good	69
⭐ **Legal Assistant, Corporate**	Starting—$28,000 Average—$32,000	Varies—see profile	Excellent	71

⭐ High-growth job

⭐ High-growth job

Job	Salary	Education/Training	Employment Outlook	Page
Parole Officer	Starting—$20,000 to $30,000	College plus training	Good	121
Political Consultant	Starting—$26,000 to $31,000 Average—$50,000 to $75,000	Advanced degree	Very good	123
Probation Officer	Starting—$20,000 to $30,000	College plus training	Good	125
⭐ Rehabilitation Counselor	Starting—$18,600 to $25,000	College plus training	Excellent	127
Religious Vocation	Varies—see profile	Advanced degree	Varies—see profile	129
School Administrator	Varies—see profile	Varies—see profile	Fair	132
School Counselor	Starting—$25,000 Average—$38,500 to $45,000	College plus training	Fair	134
School Media Specialist	Average—$27,400 to $37,900	Advanced degree	Fair	136
Social Worker	Varies—see profile	Advanced degree	Very good	138
Teacher, College	Varies—see profile	Advanced degree	Varies—see profile	140
Teacher, Elementary and Preschool	Varies—see profile	College plus training	Good	143
Teacher, Secondary School	Average—$38,600	College plus training	Very good	145
Urban and Regional Planner	Varies—see profile	Advanced degree	Fair	148
Vocational Counselor	Average—$35,800	College	Very good	150

⭐ High-growth job

Foreword

The seventh edition of the *Career Information Center* mirrors the ongoing changes in the job market caused by new technological and economic developments. These developments continue to change what Americans do in the workplace and how they do it. People have a critical need for up-to-date information to help them make career decisions.

The *Career Information Center* is an individualized resource for people of all ages and at all stages of career development. It has been recognized as an excellent reference for librarians, counselors, educators, and other providers of job information. It is ideally suited for use in libraries, career resource centers, and guidance offices, as well as in adult education centers and other facilities where people seek information about job opportunities, careers, and their own potential in the workforce.

This seventh edition updates many of the features that made the earlier editions so useful.

- A Job Summary Chart, a quick reference guide, appears in the front section of each volume to help readers get the basic facts and compare the jobs described in the volume. High-growth jobs are highlighted and identified with a star.

- Each volume of the *Career Information Center* begins with an overview of the job market in that field. These "Looking Into . . ." sections have been completely revised and updated. They also include new graphs, charts, and boxes providing information such as industry snapshots and the fastest-growing and top-dollar jobs in the field.

- Each volume has a section called "Getting Into . . . ," which contains useful information on entering the particular field. It offers self-evaluation tips and decision-making help; and it relates possible job choices to individual interests, abilities, and work characteristics. There is also practical information on job hunting, using the Internet and classified ads, preparing resumes, and handling interviews. "Getting Into . . ." also includes a section on employee rights.

- Each volume has a listing of all job profiles in the series and the volumes in which they appear, making access to profiles in other volumes easy.

- *Career Information Center* contains 676 job profiles in which more than 3,000 jobs are discussed. Each profile describes work characteristics, education and training requirements, getting the job, advancement and employment outlook, working conditions, and earnings and benefits.

- Job summaries, provided for each job profile, highlight the education or training required, salary range, and employment outlook.

- Volume 13 has been revised to reflect career concerns of the 1990s and employment trends through the year 2006. This volume includes updated articles on benefits, employment law, health in the workplace, job search strategies, job training, job opportunities at home, adjusting to job loss, and identifying opportunities for retraining.

- More than 560 photographs appear in the *Career Information Center,* including many new photos. Profile photos provide a visual glimpse of life on the job. Photos have been selected to give the reader a sense of what it feels like to be in a specific field or job.

- Updated bibliographies in each volume include recommended readings and World Wide Web sites in specific job areas. Additional titles for the vocational counselor are included in Volume 13.

- Each volume also contains a comprehensive directory of accredited occupational education and vocational training facilities listed by occupational area and grouped by state. Directory materials are generated from the IPEDS (Integrated Postsecondary Education Data System) database of the U.S. Department of Education.

The *Career Information Center* recognizes the importance not only of job selection, but also of job holding, coping, and applying life skills. No other career information publication deals with work attitudes so comprehensively.

Using the Career Information Center

The *Career Information Center* is designed to meet the needs of many people—students, people just entering or reentering the job market, those dissatisfied with present jobs, those without jobs—anyone of any age who is not sure what to do for a living. The *Career Information Center* is for people who want help in making career choices. It combines the comprehensiveness of an encyclopedia with the format and readability of a magazine. Many professionals, including counselors, librarians, and teachers will find it a useful guidance and reference tool.

The *Career Information Center* is organized by occupational interest area rather than in alphabetical order. Jobs that have something in common are grouped together. In that way people who do not know exactly what job they want can read about a number of related jobs. The *Career Information Center* classifies jobs that have something in common into clusters. The classification system is adapted from the cluster organization used by the U.S. Department of Labor. Each volume of the *Career Information Center* explores one of 12 occupational clusters.

To use the *Career Information Center,* first select the volume that treats the occupational area that interests you most. Because there are many ways to group occupations, you may not find a particular job in the volume in which you look for it. In that case, check the central listing of all the profiles, which is located in the front of Volumes 1 through 12. This listing provides the names of all profiles and the volume number in which they appear. Volume 13 also includes a comprehensive index of all the jobs covered in the first 12 volumes.

After selecting a volume or volumes, investigate the sections that you feel would be most helpful. It isn't necessary to read these volumes from cover to cover. They are arranged so that you can go directly to the specific information you want. Here is a description of the sections included in each volume.

- **Job Summary Chart**—This chart presents in tabular form the basic data from all profiles in the volume: salary, education and training, employment outlook, and the page on which you can find the job profile. Jobs with a high growth potential are highlighted and starred.

- **Looking Into . . .**—This overview of the occupational cluster describes the opportunities, characteristics, and trends in that particular field.

- **Getting Into . . .**—This how-to guide can help you decide what jobs may be most satisfying to you and what strategies you can use to get the right job. You will learn, for example, how to write an effective resume, how to complete an application form, what to expect in an interview, how to use networking, and what to do if someone has discriminated against you.

- **Job Summary**—These summaries, located at the beginning of each profile, highlight the most important facts about the job: education and training, salary range, and employment outlook.

Education and Training indicates whether the job requires no education, high school, college, advanced degree, voc/tech school, license, or training.

Salary Range is given as an approximate yearly wage unless "a week" or "an hour" is noted. These are average salaries that may vary significantly from region to region.

Employment Outlook is based on several factors, including the Bureau of Labor Statistics' projections through the year 2006. The ratings are defined as follows: *poor* means there is a projected employment decrease of 1 percent or more; *fair* means there is a projected employment increase of 0 to 13 percent; *good* means there is a projected employment increase of 14 to 26 percent; *very good* means there is a projected employment increase of 27 to 40 percent; and *excellent* means there is a projected employment increase of 41 percent or more. The outlook is then determined by looking at the ratings and other employment factors. For example, a job with excellent projected employment growth in which many more people are entering the field than there are jobs available will have an outlook that is good rather than excellent.

For all categories, the phrase *Varies—see profile* means the reader must consult the profile for the information, which is too extensive to include in the Job Summary.

- **Job Profiles**—The job profiles are divided into three categories based on the level of training required to get the job. Each profile explores a number of related jobs and covers seven major topics: description of the job being profiled, the education and training requirements, ways to get the job, advancement possibilities and employment outlook, the working conditions, the earnings and benefits, and places to go for more information.

Job Profiles—No Specialized Training includes jobs that require no education or previous work experience beyond high school.

Job Profiles—Some Specialized Training/Experience includes jobs that require one, two, or three years of vocational training or college, or work experience beyond high school.

Job Profiles—Advanced Training/Experience includes jobs that require a bachelor's degree or advanced degree from a college or university and/or equivalent work experience in that field.

- **Resources—General Career Information** includes a selected bibliography of the most recent books, audiovisual materials, and web sites on general career information, how-to books on such topics as resume writing and preparing for tests, and useful computer software. In addition, there are special sections of readings for the career counselor in Volume 13.

- **Resources**—Each volume also contains a bibliography of books, audiovisual materials, and web sites for specific fields covered in that volume.

- **Directory of Institutions Offering Career Training**—This listing, organized first by career area, then by state, includes the schools that offer occupational training beyond high school. For jobs requiring a bachelor's degree or an advanced degree, check a library for college catalogs and appropriate directories.

- **Index**—This index, which is located at the end of each volume, lists every job mentioned in that volume. It serves not only to cross-reference all the jobs in the volume but also to show related jobs in the field. For example, under the entry LICENSED PRACTICAL NURSE, you will find Home Health Aide, Nurse's Aide and Orderly, and Ward Clerk. In addition, the "profile includes" part of an entry lists other jobs that are mentioned in the profile, in this case Licensed Vocational Nurse and Registered Nurse.

- **Volume 13, Employment Trends and Master Index**—This volume includes several features that will help both the job seeker and the career counselor. A useful correlation guide provides the *DOT (Dictionary of Occupational Titles)* number of most of the job profiles in the *Career Information Center*. There is also a special section on career information for Canada. The updated and revised "Employment Trends" section contains articles on health in the workplace; employment projections through the year 2006; job search strategies; employment trends for women, minorities, immigrants, older workers, and the physically challenged; employment demographics; benefits programs; training; employment opportunities at home; employment law; adjusting to job loss; identifying opportunities for retraining. All articles have been written by authorities in these fields. The articles provide job seekers and career professionals with an overview of current employment issues, career opportunities, and outlooks. Finally, there is a master index to all the jobs included in all 13 volumes.

The *Career Information Center* is exactly what it says it is—a center of the most useful and pertinent information you need to explore and choose from the wide range of job and career possibilities. The *Career Information Center* provides you with a solid foundation of information for getting a satisfying job or rewarding career.

Comprehensive Job Profile List

The following list includes job profiles and the corresponding volume number.

Accountant, 3
Accountant, Public, 3
Actor, 2
Actuary, 3
Acupuncturist, 7
Administrative Assistant, 3
Admitting Clerk, 7
Adult Education Worker, 11
Advertising Account Executive, 10
Advertising Copywriter, 2
Advertising Manager, 10
Aerospace Engineer, 6
Aerospace Industry, 9
Aerospace Technician, 6
Agricultural Engineer, 1
Agricultural Supply Sales Worker, 1
Agricultural Technician, 1
Agronomist, 1
AIDS Counselor, 7
Air Pollution Control Technician, 1
Air Traffic Controller, 12
Air-Conditioning and Heating
    Technician, 4
Air-Conditioning Engineer, 6
Air-Conditioning, Heating, and
    Refrigeration Mechanic, 4
Aircraft Mechanic, 12
Airline Baggage and Freight Handler, 12
Airline Dispatcher, 12
Airline Flight Attendant, 12
Airline Reservations Agent, 12
Airline Ticket Agent, 12
Airplane Pilot, 12
Airport Manager, 12
Airport Utility Worker, 12
All-Round Machinist, 9
Alternative Fuels Vehicle Technician, 6
Aluminum and Copper Industry, 9
Ambulance Driver, 7
Amusement and Recreation
    Attendant, 8
Anatomist, 6
Anesthesiologist, 7
Animal Caretaker, 8
Announcer, 2
Anthropologist, 6
Apparel Industry, 9
Appliance Service Worker, 5
Appraiser, 5
Archaeologist, 6
Architect, 4
Architectural Drafter, 4
Architectural Model Maker, 4
Armed Services Career, 11
Art Director, 2
Art and Music Therapist, 7
Artificial Intelligence Specialist, 6
Artist, 2

Assembler, 9
Astronomer, 6
Athletic Coach, 8
Athletic Trainer, 8
Auctioneer, 10
Auditor, 3
Auto Body Repairer, 12
Auto Parts Counter Worker, 10
Auto Sales Worker, 10
Automated Manufacturing Manager, 9
Automobile Driving Instructor, 12
Automotive Exhaust Emissions
    Technician, 12
Automotive Industry, 9
Automotive Mechanic, 12
Avionics Technician, 12

Bank Clerk, 3
Bank Officer, 3
Bank Teller, 3
Barber and Hairstylist, 5
Bartender, 8
Bicycle Mechanic, 12
Biochemist, 6
Biological Technician, 6
Biologist, 6
Biomedical Engineer, 6
Biomedical Equipment Technician, 7
Blacksmith and Forge Shop Worker, 9
Blood Bank Technologist, 7
Boat Motor Mechanic, 12
Boiler Tender, 9
Boilermaking Worker, 9
Bookbinder, 2
Bookkeeper, 3
Border Patrol Agent, 11
Botanist, 6
Bricklayer, 4
Broadcast Technician, 2
Brokerage Clerk, 3
Building Custodian, 11
Building Inspector, 4
Business Family and Consumer
    Scientist, 5
Business Machine Operator, 3

Cable Television Engineer, 2
Cable Television Technician, 2
CAD Specialist, 6
Cafeteria Attendant, 8
CAM Operator, 9
Camera Operator, 2
Candy, Soft Drink, and Ice Cream
    Manufacturing Worker, 1
Car Rental Agent, 12
Car Wash Worker, 12
Cardiac-Monitor Technician/
    Perfusionist, 7

Cardiology Technologist, 7
Carpenter, 4
Cartographer, 1
Cartoonist, 2
Cashier, 10
Casino Worker, 8
Caterer, 8
Cement Mason, 4
Ceramic Engineer, 6
Ceramics Industry, 9
Chauffeur, 5
Cheese Industry Worker, 1
Chemical Engineer, 6
Chemical Technician, 6
Chemist, 6
Child Care Worker, Private, 5
Chiropractor, 7
Choreographer, 2
City Manager, 11
Civil Engineer, 4
Civil Engineering Technician, 4
Claim Adjuster, 3
Claim Examiner, 3
College Student Personnel Worker, 11
College/University Administrator, 3
Commercial Artist, 2
Companion, 5
Comparison Shopper, 10
Compensation Specialist, 3
Composer, 2
Composite Technician, 9
Computer Artist, 2
Computer Consultant, 3
Computer Database Manager, 3
Computer Network Technician, 3
Computer Operator, 3
Computer Programmer, 3
Computer Security Engineer, 3
Computer Servicer, 3
Computer Software Documentation
    Writer, 3
Construction Electrician, 4
Construction Equipment Dealer, 4
Construction Equipment Mechanic, 4
Construction Laborer, 4
Construction Millwright, 4
Construction Supervisor, 4
Consumer Advocate, 5
Consumer Credit Counselor, 5
Controller, 3
Convention Specialist, 8
Cook and Chef, 8
Cooperative Extension Service Worker, 1
Corrections Officer, 11
Correspondence Clerk, 3
Cosmetologist, 5
Court Clerk, 11
Craftsperson, 2

Looking Into — Public and Community Services

Public and community services date back to the colonial era, when settlements often took responsibility for the welfare of poor people in their midst. In New England, towns established public schools to ensure that all children would be able to read the Bible and financed these facilities by collecting taxes from residents. Yet despite their support of public services such as these, colonial citizens resisted government intervention in their lives. One of the major issues leading to the Declaration of Independence was the colonists' objection to paying taxes to Great Britain without being represented in Parliament, which decided how tax revenues would be spent. Once the citizens of the 13 colonies had won their independence, they had no desire to give it up to another distant government.

This ambivalence in the relationship between American citizens and their governments—federal, state, and local—has continued into the present day. In general, Americans count on public institutions and agencies to assist citizens who are vulnerable, to perform routine functions such as mail delivery and road maintenance, to educate their children, and to handle a wide range of crises, from quelling riots to cleaning up tornado-ravaged communities. Yet people tend to regard government at all levels with some degree of caution or even skepticism. Concern about the actions of government has led many citizens to guard against excessive limits on their freedom, to watch for signs of inappropriate or unnecessary taxing and spending practices and, increasingly, to comparison shop for alternatives to public sector services.

Public and community service jobs often have parallels in private business, but there are important differences. One distinction is in the way they judge success. Private organizations usually gauge success by the profits earned, whereas public ones are more apt to measure it according to the results achieved. For example, if a student learns to read or use a computer,

Americans count on public institutions and agencies to provide a wide range of services from educating their children and delivering their mail to maintaining roads and protecting their property.

the teacher has succeeded. Another difference is that public services are more likely than private ventures to be created in response to specific conditions or needs, such as transportation systems for the elderly or immunization programs during flu epidemics.

A third difference is in accountability, a worker's obligation to answer to others about job performance or problems within the organization. Private sector workers are accountable to their managers who, in turn, answer to a company's owner. Managers and owners of larger firms often must justify decreased revenues or other concerns to a board of directors and to stockholders. In the public sector, employees answer to agency administrators, who account to the elected officials overseeing the agency. Those officials must account to taxpayers for the way in which the operation is run because taxpayers are bearing the cost. Citizens who are dissatisfied are likely to show it at the polls.

THE GOVERNMENT AND PUBLIC SERVICES

To protect against a powerful central government, the representatives of the new nation formed a central body that would govern the nation under laws set down in the U.S. Constitution. Many agreed with Thomas Jefferson that "that government governs best which governs least." Central government powers were kept in check by dividing the federal government into three branches—executive, legislative, and judicial—and then limiting the powers of each by a series of constitutional checks and balances.

Another means of limiting the powers of the federal government (and, by extension, the number of government workers) was the idea of delegated and reserved powers. As listed in the Constitution, the delegated, or assigned, powers of the federal government include the powers "to lay and collect taxes . . . to borrow money . . . to coin money . . . to regulate commerce with foreign nations, and among several states . . . to raise and support armies . . . to provide and maintain a navy." The signers of the Constitution clearly intended the federal government to exercise authority only over matters of common concern to the people of all states. The states reserved control over any matters not expressly delegated to the federal government or excluded from state authority. Among the powers placed under state control were transportation within the state, matters of marriage and divorce, and public education. In addition, the Constitution divided the power to tax between state and federal governments.

These constitutional provisions discouraged growth of the central government, and this fact was reflected in the small number of government workers during most of the nation's early history. Local governments provided schools and law enforcement. Counties and states established court systems and built and maintained roads. The federal government took care of defense, diplomacy, and other matters of national concern. Private groups, religious organizations, or individual families took care of welfare and public assistance functions.

After the Civil War there were significant changes, including the end of rural, agricultural America. In the years after the war, cities grew rapidly as Americans moved away from farms and waves of immigrants poured into the country. Problems that were once handled privately were magnified in concentrated urban populations. When crime, poverty, and disease became more visible, responsibility for addressing them was gradually assumed by local governments.

As many of these problems outgrew local resources, the federal government became involved. Its ability to help, however, was limited by difficulty in raising the money necessary to hire and pay federal employees. It was not until 1913, when passage of the 16th Amendment to the Constitution instituted a federal income tax, that the federal government was able to generate enough revenues to expand its services and its workforce.

The Establishment of the Civil Service System

Once the federal government had the money to hire people, it was able to fill jobs with qualified individuals under a civil service system started in the 1880s. This initiative was designed to correct long-standing abuses in apportioning federal jobs, which previously had been filled according to the spoils system. Under this system newly elected officials gave jobs to their friends and political allies after dismissing the previous officeholders' appointees. This system failed to recognize the need for qualified, trained government employees and resulted in an entirely new staff every time a different party took office.

The abuses of the spoils system eventually became serious enough to attract congressional attention. In 1883 Congress established a civil service commission to prepare and administer competitive examinations to job applicants. Several states also passed civil service laws and began to fill jobs through similar examinations. These laws underscored the idea that merit and suitability are the criteria for public employment.

An Explosion of Civil Service Employees

No single event changed the civil service system more than the Great Depression of the 1930s. In this period of record unemployment and devastating poverty, the federal government began to hire people to provide jobs as well as services. Federal employees in public works programs built and maintained roads and post offices and worked on soil conservation projects. They painted murals on public buildings and wrote travel guides. Because federal revenues fell during the Great Depression, the government had to resort to deficit spending; that is, it had to borrow money to pay its employees and to meet its financial obligations. The government had been in debt in the past, usually during wartime, but it had never made borrowing money a tool to offset economic recession. The idea was that deficit spending would help fuel the economy and that repaying the debt would be less burdensome when the economy improved.

Deficit spending, a radical departure in the 1930s, became an enduring feature of economic policy. As the government grew, so did the national debt. In the 1980s and early 1990s a soaring budget deficit contributed to discussions about the role of government in providing community services and the need for employee cutbacks. The Clinton administration and the legislature launched initiatives to eradicate the deficit and cut the national debt. Among the president's cost-saving measures was elimination of 160,000 jobs in the first half of the 1990s, with a promise to cut about as many in the second half.

In recent years political leaders have called for religious and community groups, families, and volunteers to take more responsibility for community services such as care of the poor, elderly, and disabled. They also debate which type of government is better equipped to manage community services: federal government or state and local governments. Some leaders favor returning tax money to the states in the form of block grants, believing that state officials understand the needs of their residents better than do the politicians in faraway Washington, DC. Other leaders fear that without federal control, states will spend money in an indiscriminate and wasteful fashion.

Much has been discussed about "reinventing" and "reengineering" government to make it more cost-efficient and responsive to citizens. This includes "downsizing," especially at the federal level, and "decentralizing," or moving the center of government away from Washington, DC. These discussions, and the initiatives already emerging from them, will affect not only the types and number of jobs available on the federal level but also those on the state and local levels. These trends should also have an increasing impact on the private sector employment picture, especially if the practice of "privatizing" public services continues to take hold.

CAREERS IN THE PUBLIC SECTOR

As noted previously, the public sector employs people in a wide range of occupations that are also found in the private sector. These occupations include engineers, health practitioners, computer technicians, secretaries, accountants, mechanics, and construction trade workers. Some occupations, such as legislators, revenue agents, city planners, and drill sergeants, are unique to the public sector.

Federal Government

According to the U.S. Bureau of Labor Statistics, the federal government employed nearly 2.9 million civilian workers in 1995. Although employees work in the legislative, judicial, and executive branches, 99 percent work in the executive branch, which includes 14 cabinet departments and more than 90 agencies. Two out of three federal workers have white-collar jobs. Among those, systems analysts and computer scientists form the largest occupational group. Although most federal departments and agencies are headquartered in Washington, DC, only 14 percent of federal employees work in or near the nation's capital. About 90 percent of federal government employees fall under the jurisdiction of civil service, or competitive service, laws. The remaining 10 percent, or excepted service employees, are mostly top-level appointees.

Individuals seeking employment with the federal government generally must take a written, oral, or performance examination related to their occupational field. If they pass the examination, their names are placed on a waiting list according to their scores. When a vacancy occurs within an agency, the hiring agent may select any of the three highest-rated people on the list. For many jobs, however, the hiring agent simply evaluates applicants on the basis of their education, training, and experience in the occupation.

The civil service system has a number of pay plans for various types of work. For example, the General Pay Schedule covers most white-collar employees, whereas the Federal Wage System covers most blue-collar employees. Each plan consists of a series of pay grades, or levels, and a range of salary steps within each grade. Workers enter the civil service system at the starting grade for their occupation. Their work is regularly evaluated, and if it is satisfactory, they advance to the next salary step.

Armed Services

The military had nearly 1.8 million people on its payroll in 1996. Defending the nation in times of conflict and deterring aggression are the missions of the armed services, which include the U.S. Army (landbased), the U.S. Air Force (air and space), the U.S. Navy (sea), the U.S. Marine Corps (a branch of the navy that defends against land invasions), and the U.S. Coast Guard (which enforces federal maritime laws, recovers distressed vessels and aircraft, and prevents smuggling). The Coast Guard, normally under the Department of Transportation, becomes part of the U.S. Navy in wartime.

Job opportunities in the armed services are varied. Their personnel perform a wide range of functions, including some not usually associated with the military, such as operating hospitals and offices, programming computers, and maintaining equipment. There are approximately 3,000 basic and advanced military occupations for enlisted personnel and about 1,600 for officers. Although approximately 30 percent of these occupational specialties are specific to the military, the remainder have civilian counterparts. Job training is perhaps the most attractive benefit for those who enter the armed services.

State and Local Government

More than 4 million people work in state government, and nearly 12 million others are employed at local levels of government such as township, city, and county. State governments hire more workers in managerial, administrative support, and professional occupations than do local governments. Local governments, however, employ more workers in service occupations, such as firefighters, police officers, and sanitation workers.

Working for state and local governments is much like working for the federal government. The majority of state and local employees work under a merit system and advance according to set procedures and schedules if they work competently. Unlike federal employees, however, most state and local employees

Top-Dollar Jobs in Public and Community Services

These are high-paying jobs described in this volume. The figures represent typical salaries or earnings for experienced workers.

| $100,000–$1,000,000 | Judge |
| | Lawyer |

$65,000–$100,000	City Manager
	Fund-Raiser
	Political Consultant

$45,000–$65,000	Criminologist
	FBI Special Agent
	School Administrator
	Teacher, College
	Urban and Regional Planner

| $30,000–$45,000 | Police Officer |
| | Social Worker |

Job openings should be plentiful for all branches of the armed services through the year 2006 since the number of people in the prime age group for recruiting has decreased.

have the right to negotiate their wages through collective bargaining.

Challenges Facing State and Local Governments

State and local governments face many challenges that call for creative leadership and management of new and ongoing issues. As a result of federal cutbacks, many programs are being turned over to the states to operate. States must often pick up much of the expense. Because many states also have financial difficulty, it remains to be seen which of these programs will remain intact, which will be scaled down to fit various state budgets, and which will simply be eliminated.

Another challenge confronting local and state governments is urban sprawl and the decline of inner cities. As people and industry have moved farther away from city centers, local governments have been burdened with the cost of building new roads and highways, providing water and sewer systems, and supplying police and fire protection for new neighborhoods. At the same time, dwindling tax bases in cities make it difficult to fund programs needed to combat ongoing urban problems such as crime, poverty, and homelessness.

Education

Approximately 5.6 million jobs existed for teachers in the United States as of 1996, at all levels of education from kindergarten to colleges and universities, as well as special education. Other jobs in education include clerical and administrative workers, school librarians, social workers, health-related specialists, and counselors.

Elementary and Secondary Education Nearly 3.1 million teachers are currently employed at the elementary and secondary levels. More than 9 out of 10 jobs are in the public school systems.

Dissatisfaction with the overall performance of public school students in America on standardized achievement tests has led to many recommendations for improving the quality of education. One idea that has gained considerable popularity during the 1990s is to introduce competition among schools. This concept has prompted a number of intensive studies along with various types of experimental programs, including educational voucher systems and charter schools.

Voucher programs enable parents to apply their child's "share" of a district's funding to the school of their choice. A school may be selected because of its overall academic reputation, or other factors may take precedence. For example, parents may seek a school in a safer neighborhood; one that is strong in a particular subject area, such as music or the sciences; or one with especially attractive facilities, such as new computers or a swimming pool. The school of choice also may offer religious education, a point of strong contention.

Although the definitions of charter schools vary among states, the term generally refers to autonomous public schools that receive the same per-pupil funding as traditional schools but operate independently of school district and labor union regulations. In return for this autonomy, charter schools are expected to achieve better results. The premise behind the charter school movement is that bureaucracy burdens schools and teachers and prevents them from being creative and effective. Since 1991, 28 states, as well as Puerto Rico and the District of Columbia, have enacted laws permitting charter schools, and at least 5 more had similar laws in the works as of early 1998.

Under a competitive system, parents are able to choose the school they think is best for their children. The schools selected less frequently are assumed to provide a poorer educational environment. Proponents of this approach believe that choice forces teachers and administrators to improve programs or allows them to use more innovative teaching strategies. Some opponents claim these alternatives divert money from an already underfunded system and weaken it further.

Concern over the quality of public education has also put a premium on teacher experience and training. In the past, school districts tended to hire recent graduates because they were cheaper to employ. Realizing the value of classroom experience, many school administrators now strive to retain or hire veteran teaching staff. School authorities also encourage teachers to keep their own learning as current and comprehensive as possible by continuing to build on their skills and knowledge. In addition to sponsoring in-service and professional development classes, many districts fund and offer pay increases for completion of graduate courses. School districts also recognize the merits of experience in the private sector and welcome former businesspeople into the classroom.

Postsecondary Education There are approximately 910,000 faculty members teaching at colleges and universities across the United States, with the majority at public institutions. College and university faculty teach more than 14 million full-time and part-time students and conduct a significant part of the nation's research. Although for many years "typical" college students were in their late teens or early 20s, that is no longer the case. Nearly one-third of the students on college campuses today are over the age of 30. Many adults are returning to college for new careers or for retraining.

Vocational and Adult Education There are about 300,000 teachers in vocational education and many more in community-based adult education programs. Students in vocational schools train for a variety of occupations that do not require a college degree, such as those of welder, machinist, mechanic, cosmetologist, and word processor. Adult education programs, which are usually run by local school districts, offer courses as diverse as reading, writing, mathematics, cooking, aerobics, investing, and dog training.

Social Work

About 745,000 jobs exist in the broad field of social work, nearly 40 percent of them in the public sector. A career in social work, or human services, involves helping people cope with a wide range of problems. Social workers help people through direct counseling or by referring them to other specialists or placing them in specialized assistance programs. They work in child welfare and family services programs, mental health facilities, schools, hospitals, community organizations, and corporations.

Traditionally, social workers help the poor, disabled, and disadvantaged obtain food, shelter, and clothing. In addition, they may work in the mental health field, where they provide such services as crisis intervention, social rehabilitation, and life skills training. Medical social workers help patients and their families cope with catastrophic illness. School social workers counsel troubled children and help integrate children with disabilities into the general school population.

In line with the trend toward serving these populations within the community, people formerly housed in large institutions now live with their families or in community living programs. At the same time, many social work jobs have shifted from institutions to community facilities such as group homes for people with physical disabilities and vocational programs for people with mental illnesses.

The corporate sector also hires social workers. Many businesses employ them to ensure compliance with regulations such as accessible facilities for workers or customers who have disabilities. Social workers often manage employee assistance programs, performing such tasks as counseling workers whose job performance is affected by emotional problems or substance abuse.

Law

A lawyer is both an adviser and an advocate. As an adviser, a lawyer counsels clients regarding their legal rights and obligations. As an advocate, a lawyer presents arguments to support his or her client in court. Of the more than 800,000 lawyers in the United States today, about 20 percent are in government positions. A majority of these are at the local level. In the federal government, most jobs for lawyers are in the departments of Justice, Treasury, and Defense. There are some administrative and managerial jobs in law for which legal training is an asset but not a requirement.

The legal profession, both public and private, faces increasing demands to handle litigation more quickly and inexpensively and to discourage frivolous product-liability and personal-damage lawsuits. A result of this movement is that large law firms are lowering the salaries of their lawyers and hiring fewer lawyers. At the same time, there has been a huge increase in the number of paralegals and legal assistants. Paralegals, currently numbering 307,000 and growing, help law firms lower their expenses by doing research, preparing documents, and performing other legal work previously done by high-priced lawyers.

Protective Services

Workers in the field of protective services seek to safeguard people and property in a community. These workers include approximately 960,000 police officers, detectives, and special agents; more than 200,000 firefighters; and about 270,000 corrections officers. Whereas most police officers and firefighters are employed by local governments, the majority of corrections officers are employed at state correctional institutions: prisons, prison camps, and reformatories. In the past the job of corrections officer consisted of enforcing the rules of the institution.

Local governments are the biggest employer of police officers. Since most police departments fall under civil service regulations, interested applicants must pass a test for the job.

More and more, however, corrections officers are assisting with inmates' rehabilitation by serving as informal counselors and by reinforcing remedial training.

TRENDS IN THE PUBLIC SECTOR

At a time when the need for public services is increasing, the resources to provide these services are decreasing. Committed public servants at all levels of government are searching for ways to provide services economically and efficiently. Teamwork is becoming more common as personnel from different agencies and different levels or branches of public service collaborate on problem solving.

Privatization and Competition

Privatization is one way in which governments attempt to save taxpayers money and deliver quality services. In the United States privatization means contracting with for-profit businesses to deliver publicly funded services. A city sanitation department, for example, might replace its refuse collectors with a private company that guarantees more economical and efficient trash removal.

Governments have always used privatization to obtain services or goods that they were unable to supply. For instance, the federal government hires private contractors to make weapons and build highways. Local school boards contract out cafeteria and busing services. During the 1980s and 1990s, however, governments began privatizing services traditionally managed by public sector employees. Among these have been services relating to wastewater treatment plants, motor vehicle inspection stations, correctional facilities, and vocational training programs and employment workshops for people with mental and physical disabilities. Privatization has even extended to public schools. School boards in Maryland and Massachusetts, for example, have turned poorly performing public schools over to private education companies.

As might be expected, public sector employees object to privatization that leads to job loss. Unions representing these workers generally fight efforts to privatize public employees' functions. Even those outside the workforce fear that this trend will revive the spoils system if it is misused to reassign civil service jobs to entrepreneurs who are political allies of and campaign contributors to government officeholders.

The premise behind privatization is that business is more efficient than government. However, private companies that have a monopoly on a service or that operate without adequate government supervision can also be inefficient. Consequently, government policy is now shifting from privatization to managed competition. Under this system more than one company must be available for bidding on a public-service contract. This managed competition also allows public sector workers to bid against private companies for contracts. Competition provides public employees added incentive to perform their jobs well. For example, when the city of Indianapolis put the job of filling potholes up for bidding, employees of the public works department figured out how they could do the job more economically than private companies.

Electronic Technology

The public sector lags behind the private sector in adopting Information Age technology. Even so, government at all levels now uses new electronic media for better delivery of public services.

Electronic Pathways to Government Federal, state, and local governments are using computer bulletin boards to provide quick, convenient access to information and to facilitate communication. From the comfort of their homes, citizens with a computer and modem can obtain the latest U.S. census statistics, read summaries of bills in the state legislature, send electronic mail (e-mail) to the mayor, access the card catalog at the local library, or find out the cost of a driver's license.

In some parts of the country, governments have installed interactive kiosks in shopping malls, grocery stores, and other central locations. The kiosks, which resemble ATM banking machines, inform users about where to go and whom to contact about city services. They also list employment opportunities and explain unemployment benefits. Some kiosks dispense marriage licenses and other government forms.

Saving Time and Money The public sector is taking advantage of new technology to cut expenses and speed up services. For example, many local government departments now use electronic-pen scanners to read information on monthly bills. The speed and accuracy of this technology allow clerks to spend more time on other tasks.

At the federal level, the Social Security Administration now issues Social Security cards in 5 days (instead of 6 weeks), using automated equipment. In addition, its banking is being converted to a computerized direct deposit system to eliminate costly paper checks. The U.S. Postal Service handles more than 50 percent of all mail at least partly by automation, resulting in enormous cost savings. Automated mail sorting, for example, is reported to cost only one-fourth as much as sorting mail by hand. It is predicted that increased automation will eliminate more than 40,000 postal jobs by the year 2006.

Customer Service

A growing trend in the public sector is to regard recipients of community services as customers. A customer service attitude emphasizes courtesy, efficiency, and know-how. Many public agencies and institutions now provide mandatory training in customer service to promote more effective service and a more consumer-friendly attitude among workers.

One-Stop Shopping The customer service approach is making the biggest impression in the delivery of human services, especially services to the poor, the elderly, and the disabled. Many people qualify for more than one type of aid, and the human services system is fragmented and confusing. For instance, an elderly blind woman with medical problems may find that the resources she needs lie within four or five different agencies or departments. Clients must shuttle from office to office—often in different towns or even different counties—and submit to repetitive questions. After all that, they may still receive only incomplete assistance. Responding to clients' frustration, government officials in many areas have installed "one-stop shopping." Services such as Medicaid, employment counseling, and welfare benefits may be grouped together in an accessible location, or clients may be assigned one social worker to negotiate various branches of the system.

Plastic for Paper Electronic benefit systems are another means by which government is improving delivery of human services. With this innovation, social service agencies issue welfare recipients a plastic

Industry Snapshots

GOVERNMENT

The government employs 19.5 million workers—that's more than any business in the United States. Between the present time and 2006, government employment can be expected to grow at the state and local levels but decline at the federal level as program responsibilities shift away from the national government. Population growth in the nation's cities and suburbs is also predicted to contribute to more jobs in state and local government.

MILITARY

The decreased threat from Eastern European countries and the former Soviet Union has led all U.S. military forces, except the Coast Guard, to undergo planned reductions. Nevertheless, job openings should be plentiful for all branches of the armed services through 2006. The reason is that the number of people in the prime age group for recruiting has decreased. As military jobs become more technical and complex, standards for new recruits will continue to rise.

EDUCATION

Education employment is expected to rise from 10.2 million workers in 1996 to 12.5 million workers in 2006. This increase will result from population growth among children in kindergarten, elementary school, and high school, as well as growth in the number of older, foreign, and part-time students at the postsecondary level. Demand for special education teachers

will be high because of legislation focusing on the needs of individuals with disabilities.

SOCIAL WORK

The medical and social needs of an aging population and growing numbers of individuals and families in crisis will require more social services. In particular, more school social workers will be needed to respond to the adjustment problems of immigrants, children from backgrounds of poverty and abuse, and children with mental and physical disabilities. More medical social workers will be needed to facilitate the trend toward early discharge from hospitals.

CORRECTIONS

The number of corrections officers has grown by 80 percent since 1985. Thousands of job openings are generated each year. A surge in drug-related crime and a shift toward mandatory sentencing have boosted the nation's prison population and led to an overwhelming demand for corrections officers.

LAW

Demand for lawyers will continue as the population grows and as middle-income groups increase their use of legal services. Jobs in the public sector are expected to increase because the government now provides more legal and related services to the poor and elderly. Despite the number of job openings, competition for employment will be intense because of the large number of law students graduating each year.

card, similar to a bank debit card, to pay for food or to obtain cash. The plastic cards are safer, more convenient, and more efficient than paper checks and food stamp coupons.

Government Marketing

Governments collect income taxes, property taxes, sales taxes, and many other fees and surcharges to raise money to fund public services. In addition, many localities are now turning to so-called government marketing to help pay the bills.

Government marketing takes several forms. A government unit might operate a store or a mail-order catalog that sells merchandise to the public. The Los Angeles County Coroner's Office, for example, grossed about $20,000 a month in the mid-1990s through sales of key chains, coffee mugs, towels, and other merchandise.

Another form of government marketing is selling advertising space on public property such as trash barrels and bicycle racks at city parks. Whereas public transit departments have long sold advertising space on buses, they now offer advertisers the entire vehicle—from headlights to taillights and from roof to road—for their "body-wrap" ads. Advertisers also donate uniforms, automobiles and vans, and other equipment—all of which bear the company's name and logo—to local governments.

Some government units sell their services for profit. For example, some fire departments hire out their firefighters as ambulance drivers. The U.S. Department of Energy signed a contract with factories along the Mexican border to consult on pollution control.

OTHER AVENUES TO PUBLIC AND COMMUNITY SERVICES

In addition to government entities, nonprofit agencies employ workers who serve the public. Corporations also hire people to serve as liaisons with the community. Volunteer opportunities in community service abound.

Nonprofit Organizations

Nearly 23,000 private, nonprofit service organizations exist at the national level, and many more exist at state, county, and community levels. Such organizations operate prenatal clinics, food banks, shelters for battered women and the homeless, hospices for people with AIDS, vocational training and sheltered workshops for workers with disabilities, counseling centers for troubled youth, and many other programs. Federal, state, and local governments contract extensively with nonprofit agencies to provide key social services. Religious and fraternal organizations also sponsor many social service organizations.

Corporations

Many large corporations have community service or public affairs divisions that direct corporate philanthropy. Their initiatives include donations of funds or goods such as surplus merchandise or used office equipment to events and projects in the surrounding community. In some cases they also donate the services of executives to run civic or charitable projects or give other employees time off to participate in these activities. Community service

Federal, state, and local governments contract extensively with nonprofit agencies to provide key social services. Nonprofit organizations employ many workers who serve specific groups in the community, including the elderly, the homeless, youths, and battered women.

divisions, especially in banks and other financial institutions, may also look for ways to invest money and other corporate resources in the community. These efforts are driven by a desire to build good public relations and the realization that a healthy community is good for business.

A growing trend is for corporations to work with public and private community organizations to revive neighborhoods, improve schools, and curb violence. A good example is the Atlanta Project, launched by former president Jimmy Carter, which divided the city of Atlanta into 20 clusters and assigned a corporation to each. Residents of each cluster and corporate employees work together to try to solve problems related to housing, public safety, health, and education.

Summer Jobs in Public and Community Services

GOVERNMENT

Summer jobs and internships are available at all levels of government. Workers needed include clerical, administrative, and technical staff. The federal government employs summer staff in positions such as congressional aide and legislative assistant. At the state level, jobs are available in state capitals as well as regional offices. Summer jobs in local government include positions in county courthouses and in town parks, pools, and other recreational programs and facilities. Contact:
• local government offices
• governor's office and state agencies
• members of Congress and federal agencies

Sources of Information
Government Job Finder
Planning/Communications
7215 Oak Avenue
River Forest, IL 60305-1935

Washington Information Directory
Congressional Quarterly, Inc.
1414 Twenty-second Street, NW
Washington, DC 20037

SOCIAL SERVICES

Summer workers are needed in day care centers and senior centers. Institutions for dependent children and children and adults with disabilities need care workers, as do hospitals, long-term care facilities, and specialized camps. Youth organizations need day camp counselors, recreation helpers, and aides to run summer programs. Contact:
• state department of education
• child care institutions
• public and private day care centers
• social service agencies

Sources of Information
National Association for the Education of Young Children
1509 Sixteenth Street, NW
Washington, DC 20036

National Association of Social Workers/NASW Press
750 First Street, NE, Suite 700
Washington, DC 20002

PUBLIC SERVICES

Summer positions are available for aides in public and university libraries. Aides and fund-raisers are needed for public-interest groups. Municipal projects may require summer help, such as highway maintenance workers. Refuse workers and firefighters are needed to replace vacationing staff. Contact:
• local libraries
• local government agencies
• private maintenance, construction, and sanitation contractors
• public-interest groups

See individual job profiles for Sources of Information.

LAW

Law firms often hire summer office workers, including receptionists, typists, word processors, and researchers. Law students can work as summer associates or possibly participate in summer training programs. For details, contact:
• law firms
• legal aid associations
• company legal departments

Sources of Information
American Bar Association
750 North Lake Shore Drive
Chicago, IL 60611

Martindale Hubbell Law Directory
Martindale Hubbell, Inc.
121 Chanlon Road
New Providence, NJ 07974

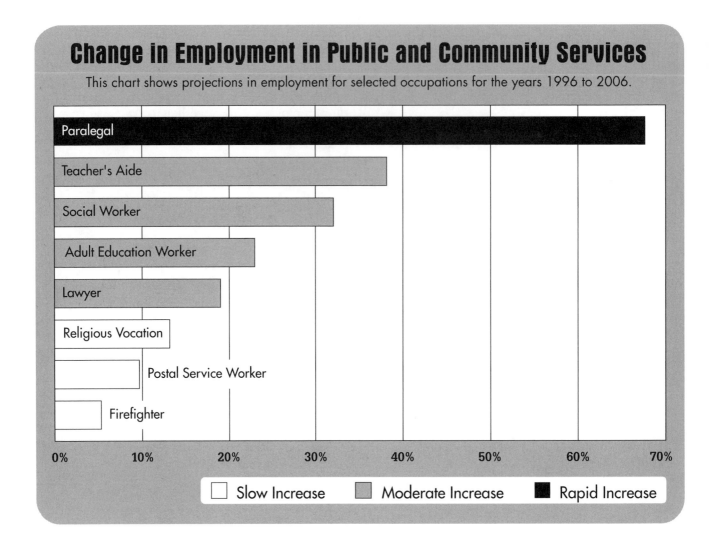

Change in Employment in Public and Community Services

This chart shows projections in employment for selected occupations for the years 1996 to 2006.

| | Slow Increase | Moderate Increase | Rapid Increase |

Paralegal
Teacher's Aide
Social Worker
Adult Education Worker
Lawyer
Religious Vocation
Postal Service Worker
Firefighter

0% 10% 20% 30% 40% 50% 60% 70%

Volunteer Organizations

Nonprofit agencies, religious groups, and other community organizations offer opportunities for volunteers to get involved in public service. For example, volunteers are needed to construct low-income housing, clean up polluted areas, patrol neighborhoods, serve as companions to neighbors who are elderly or disabled, be mentors for disadvantaged youths, and deliver meals to the homebound. Although volunteers usually receive no pay for their work, they learn skills that may be useful in future careers.

Government programs such as Volunteers in Service to America (VISTA) and Job Corps also offer volunteer opportunities. Some government programs provide financial assistance, health care, or other benefits. AmeriCorps, a national service program established in 1993, repays community service with grants for college tuition.

PUBLIC AND COMMUNITY SERVICES—AND YOU

Many changes are occurring in public and community services. Although job security, benefits, and the overall employment outlook in the public sector have become more variable in recent years, what will not change is the main reason people seek careers in this area. Such careers present opportunities to individuals who want to make a difference in the quality of people's lives. Public and community service jobs offer a chance to be part of a network of people performing tasks that provide their community with the services it requires.

ood jobs rarely, if ever, just fall out of the sky. As anybody who has ever been in the job market knows, getting the right job takes planning, perseverance, and patience. There are, however, a number of ways to make the process easier and more rewarding. This is true whether you are looking for your first job, reentering the job market, trying to get a new job, or planning a mid-career change.

This essay is designed to serve as your guide to the process of finding a job in the field of public and community services. It starts off with the basics—helping you define your career objectives. Then it takes you through a number of steps you can use to work out a strategy to achieve these goals.

EVALUATING YOURSELF

Most people enjoy doing a job well. Apart from any praise from employers or fellow workers, there is an inner satisfaction in knowing that you've taken on a challenge and then succeeded in accomplishing something worthwhile. If you are unhappy or dissatisfied in your job and are just trying to do enough to get by, you may not be in the right job or the right field.

Making a Self-Inventory Chart

Before you make any career decisions, think about areas that interest you and things you do well. One way to go about this is to compile a self-inventory chart. Such a chart will be helpful when you decide what jobs you want to consider. It will also save time when you write cover letters and resumes, fill in applications, and prepare for job interviews.

Begin your self-inventory chart by listing all the jobs you have ever had, including summer employment, part-time jobs, volunteer work, and any freelance or short-term assignments you have done. Include the dates of employment, the names and addresses of supervisors, and the amount of money you earned. Then add a similar list of your hobbies and other activities, including any special experiences you have had, such as travel. Next, do the same for your education, listing your schools, major courses of study, grades, special honors or awards, courses you particularly enjoyed, and extracurricular activities.

In determining what you do well and what you enjoy doing, you may find a career pattern beginning to develop. If the picture still lacks detail or focus, try making a list of aptitudes, and then rate yourself *above average, average,* or *below average* for each one. Some of the qualities you might include in your list are administrative, analytic, athletic, clerical, language, leadership, managerial, manual, mathematical, mechanical, sales, and verbal abilities. You might also rate your willingness to accept responsibility and your ability to get along with people.

Compiling a Work Characteristics Checklist

Another way to choose a career path is to compile a checklist. Go through the questions in the "Work Characteristics Checklist" and then make a list of the work characteristics that are most important to you.

Do not expect a job to meet all your requirements. You have to consider which job characteristics are most important to you. If the characteristics of a job match most of your preferences, you might want to give the position serious consideration.

Work Characteristics Checklist

Do you want a job in which you can

- work outdoors?
- be physically active?
- work with your hands?
- be challenged mentally?
- work with machines?
- work independently?
- work on a team?
- follow clear instructions?
- earn a lot of money?
- have a chance for quick promotion?
- have good benefits?
- travel in your work?
- work close to home?
- work regular hours?
- have a flexible schedule?
- have a variety of tasks?
- have supervisory power?
- express your own ideas?
- be a decision maker?

13

Evaluating Your Career Options

It's important to evaluate yourself and your career options realistically. If you need help doing this, you can consult an experienced career counselor or take on-line aptitude tests.

Most guidance and counseling departments of high schools, vocational schools, and colleges provide vocational testing and counseling. Some local offices of the state employment services affiliated with the federal employment service offer free counseling. Career centers also offer these services.

Although vocational interest and aptitude testing can be done with paper and pencil, a variety of on-line programs can be used to test your interests and aptitudes. The results are measured against job skills and your personal profile is matched with potential jobs to show the training that is necessary. Some of these programs are self-administered on a personal computer whereas others must be administered and interpreted by a counselor.

Most major cities have professional career consultants and career counseling firms. You should, however, check their reputations before paying for their services. A list of counseling services in your area is available from the American Counseling Association, 5999 Stevenson Avenue, Alexandria, VA 22304 (www.counseling.org). (If you write, send a stamped, self-addressed envelope.)

You can also use the World Wide Web for services that career counselors would provide. Some sites have on-line counselors who can help you with a variety of tasks, such as obtaining information on jobs, careers, and training. They may be able to provide information on available services, including housing assistance, day care facilities, and transportation.

EVALUATING SPECIFIC JOBS

After you have taken a good look at what you do well and what you enjoy doing, you need to see how different jobs measure up to your abilities and interests. First, make a note of all the jobs in this volume that interest you. Then examine the education and training required for these jobs. Decide whether you qualify and, if not, whether you have the resources available to gain the qualifications. If possible, talk with someone who has such a job. Firsthand information can be invaluable. Also look through the appropriate trade and professional journals listed at the end of this essay and check the sections in this volume called "Resources" for books, audiovisual materials, and web sites that contain more detailed information about the job. In addition, counselors usually have helpful information on careers in public and community services. For more detailed information, you can write to any of the trade and professional associations listed at the end of each occupational profile.

Once you have found out all you can about a particular job, compare the features of the job with your work characteristics checklist. See how many characteristics of the job match your work preferences. By completing these steps for all the jobs that appeal to you, you should be able to come up with a list of jobs that match your interests and abilities.

WAYS TO FIND JOB OPENINGS

Once you've decided what kind of job suits you, the next step is to look for available positions. Obviously, the more openings you can find, the better your chance of landing a job. People usually apply for a number of job openings before they are finally accepted.

There are many ways to find out about job openings. A number of job-hunting techniques are explained on the pages that follow and information is given on how you can follow up on job leads.

Applying in Person

For some jobs, especially entry-level positions, your best method may be to apply directly to the company or companies for which you would like to work. If you are looking for a position as a meter reader or refuse worker, for example, you might make an appointment to see the person responsible for hiring. This is a good method to use when jobs are plentiful or when a company is expanding. However, applicants for professional or supervisory positions generally need to send a cover letter and resume to the company first.

Applying in person will sharpen your interviewing techniques and give you a look at different places of employment. However, in most fields, it is not the method to use unless you are directed to do so.

Phone and Letter Campaigns

To conduct a phone campaign, use the Yellow Pages of your telephone directory to build a list of companies for which you might like to work. Call their personnel departments and find out whether they have any openings. This technique is not useful in all situations, however. If you're calling from out of town, a phone campaign can be very expensive. You may not be able to make a strong impression by phone. You also will not have a written record of your contacts.

Letter-writing campaigns can be very effective if the letters are well thought-out and carefully prepared. Your letters should always be typed. Handwritten letters and photocopied letters convey a lack of interest or motivation.

You may be able to get good lists of company addresses in your field of interest by reading the trade and professional publications listed at the end of this essay. Many of the periodicals publish directories or directory issues. Other sources you can use to compile lists of companies are the trade unions and professional organizations listed at the end of each job profile in this volume. The reference librarian at your local library can also help you find appropriate directories.

You can e-mail letters to human resource departments of companies with web sites, too. Be sure, however, that you follow all the same guidelines as you would for a letter you mail.

Your letters should be addressed to the personnel or human resources department of the organization. If possible, send it to a specific person. If you don't know who the correct person is, try to find the name of the personnel director through the directories in the library. You can also call on the phone and say, "I'm writing to ask about employment at your company. To whom should I address my letter?" If you can't find a name, use a standard salutation. It's a good idea to enclose a resume (described later in this essay) with the letter to give the employer a brief description of your education and work experience.

Keep a list of all the people you write to, along with the date each letter was mailed, or keep a photocopy of each letter. Then you can follow up by writing a brief note or calling people who do not reply within about 3 weeks.

Job Databases on the Web

The latest tool to use in looking for a job is the World Wide Web. The Internet currently has thousands of career-related sites to use to find job openings and to post your resume. Some sites, such as The Monster Board (www.monsterboard.com), help you build a resume and post it on-line as well as allow you to search through a massive database of help-wanted listings. Others, including E.span (www.espan.com), employ a search engine to find jobs that match your background, then post your resume on-line for employers. Another site called CareerBuilder (www.careerbuilder. com) has an interactive personal search agent that lets you key in job criteria such as location, title, and salary, and then it e-mails you when a matching position is posted in the database.

If you find a job that interests you in an ad on the web, you can respond by sending your resume and cover letter directly to the employer. Many companies even post job openings of their own in their company's human resource web pages. This allows you to target specific firms. Job hunters in many fields can also use professional associations to find jobs.

Some states, such as New Jersey, even have a home page (www.wnjpin.state.nj.us) designed to meet the needs of four groups: job seekers, students looking to make career choices, career counselors, and employers looking for workers. This one-stop career center has direct links to a variety of job listing sites on the web. You can post your resume, get information on training and education required for various jobs, read about occupations in demand, and even find out about job fairs.

Job Finder's Checklist

The following list of job-hunting tips may seem obvious, but getting all the bits and pieces in order beforehand helps when you're looking for a job.

Resume. Find out whether you will need a resume. If so, bring your resume up to date or prepare a new one. Assemble a supply of neatly typed copies or have a resume ready to e-mail to prospective employers.

References. Line up your references. Ask permission of the people whose names you would like to use. Write down their addresses, phone numbers, and job titles.

Contacts. Put the word out to everyone you know that you are looking for a job.

Job market. Find out where the jobs are. Make a list of possible employers in your field of interest.

Research. Do a little homework ahead of time—it can make a big difference in the long run. Find out as much as you can about a job—the field, the company—before you apply for it. A well-informed job applicant makes a good impression.

Organization. Keep a file on your job-hunting campaign with names and dates of employers contacted, ads answered, results, and follow-up.

Appearance. Make sure that the clothes you plan to wear to an interview are neat and clean. You may need to dress more formally than you would on the job, particularly if you are visiting a personnel office or meeting with a manager. Keep in mind that people may form an opinion of you based on their first impressions.

Help-Wanted Ads

Many people find out about job openings by reading the help-wanted sections of newspapers, trade journals, and professional magazines. Many employers and employment agencies use help-wanted classifieds to advertise available jobs.

Classified ads have their own telegraphic language. You will find some common abbreviations in the chart in this essay entitled "Reading the Classifieds." You can usually decode the abbreviations by using common sense, but if one puzzles you, call the newspaper and ask for a translation. Classified ads explain how to contact the employer, and they usually list the qualifications that are required.

As you find openings that interest you, follow up on each ad by using the method requested. You may be asked to call a specific person or send a resume. Record the date of your follow-up, and if you don't hear from the employer within 2 to 3 weeks, place another call or send a polite note asking whether the job is still open. Don't forget to include your phone number and address.

Some help-wanted ads are "blind ads." These ads give a box number but no name, phone number, or address. Employers and employment agencies may place these ads to avoid having to reply to all of the job applicants. In other words, you may not receive a response after answering a blind ad.

Situation-Wanted Ads

Another way to get the attention of potential employers is with a situation-wanted ad. You can place one of these in the classified section of your local newspaper or of a trade journal in your field of interest. Many personnel offices and employment agencies scan these columns when they're looking for new employees. The situation-wanted ad is usually most effective for people who have advanced education, training, or experience, or who are in fields that are in great demand.

A situation-wanted ad should be brief, clear, and to the point. Its main purpose is to interest the employer enough so you are contacted for an interview. It should tell exactly what kind of job you want, why you qualify, and whether you are available for full-time or part-time work. Use abbreviations that are appropriate.

If you are already employed and do not want it known that you are looking for a new position, you can run a blind ad. A blind ad protects your privacy by listing a box number at the publication to which all replies can be sent. They are then forwarded to you.

Reading the Classifieds

HELP WANTED

ACADEMIC AIDE—Local college needs a person to handle a variety of student services incl. academic & social counseling. Good oppty. Degree, similar exp. pfd. Call 000-0000 weekdays 10–4, Sat. 10–12.

CHILD CARE　　　　　　　　**RESIDENT DIRECTOR**
Suburban child care agency needs capable person to assume direction of residential program. Must have MSW & min. 3 yrs. admin. and supervisory bkgd. Salary commensurate w/experience. Good fringe benefits. M4711 Chronicle. An Equal Oppty. Employer

CORRECTIONS OFFICER
HALFWAY HOUSE
Immediate opening for mature, reliable person to supervise and counsel residents at County Pre-Release Center in City, State. Revolving shift work will require evening and weekend hours. Apply in person.

CUSTODIAN f/p $0/hr. Mon–Fri. 2–8:30, Sun. 8–9:30. Protestant Church. Carlson Agency, Main Street

LEGAL SECY. with top qualifications to work with partner in attractive offices. Good skills essential incl. WP. Salary commensurate with ability. 000-0000.

LIBRARIAN
School year. Small private h.s. Metropolitan area. Bachelor of Library Science req. Knowledge of computerized databases helpful. Write Journal Box T 7431.

SECURITY GUARDS
Immediate openings. Full and part time. Uniform supplied. Must be U.S. resident, have no criminal convictions, have car and phone. 000-0000.

SOCIAL WORKER—Child welfare agency seeks MSW to supervise foster care program. Competitive salary, excel. benefits. Call/send resume and sal. req. to:
S. Allen
Broadfield Child Care
24 Lincoln Ave.
City, State 00000

CLASSIFIED ABBREVIATIONS

addl.	additional
admin.	administrative, administration
avail. immed.	available immediately
avg.	average
bkgd.	background
excel.	excellent
exp.	experience
fee neg.	fee negotiable (fee can be worked out with employer)
figs.	figures
f/p., f/pd.	fee paid (agency fee paid by employer)
f/t	full time
gd. bnfts.	good benefits
incl.	including
mgr.	manager
natl.	national
pfd.	preferred
p/t	part time
refs.	references
req.	required
sal.	salary
sec., secy.	secretary
temp.	temporary
trnee.	trainee
typ.	typist, typing
w/	with
WP	word processing

SITUATION WANTED

DAY CARE WORKER
seeks p/t work, 3 days/wk. Experienced, good refs. 000-0000.

PRIVATE
DETECTIVE
Available by hour, day, week, job. Confidential background, missing person, matrimonial investigations. Experienced, reasonable. 000-0000.

ELEMENTARY TEACHER
wishes to tutor child/children for summer. Any subject.Call 000-0000.

FUND RAISER
4 yrs. exp. direct mail and local campaign planning for natl. organization. Willing to travel, work odd hrs.　　　　　　　　M3136 Times.

LEGAL SECRETARY—top skills, 3 yrs. exp. with patent attorney. Computer literate. Avail. August. Box 823, Chronicle.

LIBRARIAN
MLS & 3 yrs. technical & reference exp. seeks p/t library job metropolitan area. 000-0000.

MINISTER
DUTCH REFORMED
CHURCH
Wishes to relocate to Midwest. 8 yrs. exp., heavy youth work. Box Z47 Gazette.

SCHOOL CUSTODIAN. Avail. immed., West County area. 6 yrs. school exp. Alex Rudman, 000-0000.

YOUTH WORK
Sociology student wants f/t summer job with youth organization. Urban location preferred. Camp counselor exp. Call Chuck, 000-0000 after 6 p.m.

TEACHER—Exp. in H.S. art and computer graphics desires job in any related field. 000-0000.

You do not need to give your name, address, or phone number in the ad.

Networking

A very important source of information about job openings is networking. This means talking with friends and acquaintances about jobs in your area of interest. If you would like to work in law, get in touch with all the people you know who work as lawyers, judges, or paralegal aides. Speak with people you know who have friends or relatives in the field. It makes sense to use all the contacts you have.

There's nothing wrong with telling everyone who will listen that you are looking for a job—family, friends, counselors, and former employers. This will multiply your sources of information many times over.

You can use the web to make contacts, too. You can meet people with similar interests in news groups, which are organized by topic. Then you can write to them by e-mailing back and forth. Many fields have professional organizations that maintain web sites. You might use them to keep current on news affecting your field.

Sometimes a contact knows about a job vacancy before it is advertised. You can have an advantage, then, when you get in touch with the employer. Don't, however, use the contact's name without permission. Don't assume that a contact will go out on a limb by recommending you, either. Once you have received the inside information, rely on your own ability to get the job.

Placement Services

Most vocational schools, high schools, and colleges have a placement or career service that maintains a list of job openings and schedules visits from companies. If you are a student or recent graduate, you should check there for job leads. Many employers look first in technical or trade schools and colleges for qualified applicants for certain jobs. Recruiters often visit colleges to look for people to fill technical and scientific positions. These recruiters usually represent large companies. Visit your placement office regularly to check the job listings, and watch for scheduled visits by company recruiters.

State Employment Services

Another source of information about job openings is the local office of the state employment service. Many employers automatically list job openings at the local office. Whether you're looking for a job in private industry or with the state, these offices, which

are affiliated with the federal employment service, are worth visiting.

State employment service offices are public agencies that do not charge for their services. They can direct you to special programs run by the government in conjunction with private industry. These programs, such as the Work Incentive Program for families on welfare, are designed to meet special needs. Some, but not all, of these offices offer vocational aptitude and interest tests and can refer interested people to vocational training centers. The state employment service can be a valuable first stop in your search for work, especially if there are special circumstances in your background. For example, if you did not finish high school, if you have had any difficulties with the law, or if you are living in a difficult home environment, your state employment service office is equipped to help you.

Private Employment Agencies

State employment services, though free, are usually very busy. If you are looking for more personal service and want a qualified employment counselor to help you find a job, you might want to approach a private employment agency.

Private employment agencies will help you get a job if they think they can place you. Most of them get paid only if they're successful in finding you a job, so you need to show them that you are a good prospect. These agencies will help you prepare a resume if you need one, and they will contact employers they think might be interested in you.

Private employment agencies are in the business of bringing together people who are looking for jobs and companies that are looking for workers. For some positions, usually middle- and higher-level jobs, the employment agency's fee is often paid by the employer. In such cases, the job seeker pays no fee. In other cases, you may be required to pay the fee, which is usually a percentage of your annual salary. Paying a fee is a worthwhile investment if it leads to a rewarding career. In addition, the fee may be tax deductible.

Some agencies may also ask for a small registration fee whether or not you get a job through them. Some agencies may demand that you pay even if you find one of the jobs they are trying to fill through your other contacts. Just be sure to read and understand the fine print of any contract you're about to sign, and ask for a copy to take home. Since the quality of these agencies varies, check to see if an agency is a certified member of a state or national association.

Some employment agencies, called staffing services, operate in a different way. They are usually paid by employers to screen and refer good candidates for job openings. They earn money when they refer a candidate who is hired by the employer. The employee pays no fee. Staffing firms, however, only spend time on candidates they think they may be able to place.

Private employment agencies are usually helping many people at one time. They may not have the time to contact you every time they find a job opening. Therefore, you may need to phone them at reasonable intervals after you have registered.

Computer Placement Services

Computer placement services are basically data banks (computerized information files) to which you send your resume or employment profile. When a company that subscribes to the service has a job to fill, it can call up on its computer a certain combination of qualifications and quickly receive information on qualified candidates.

Computer placement is very limited in scope and in the number of users. It seems to be most useful for people looking for technical or scientific jobs.

Civil Service

In your search for work, don't forget that the civil service—federal, state, and local—may have many public and community services jobs. You may contact the state employment office or apply directly to the appropriate state or federal agency. The armed services are a major employer of many civilians in public and community services. Don't neglect these avenues for finding jobs.

Civil service positions in this field include border patrol agents, firefighters, police officers, and customs workers. Books are available to help you prepare for civil service exams, and your local civil service office can give you information, too.

Unions

In certain jobs in public and community services, such as highway maintenance work, power plant work, and teaching, unions can be useful sources of information. If you are a member of a union in your field of interest, you may be able to find out about jobs in the union periodical or through people at the union local. If you do not belong to a union, you may contact a union in the field you are interested in for information about available employment services. You will find addresses for some unions in the job profiles in this book.

Temporary Employment

A good way to get a feel for the job market—what's available and what certain jobs are like—is to work in a temporary job. There are many agencies that specialize in placing people in short-term jobs in public and community services. Legal work, child care, and security guard work are among the types of work most in demand.

Temporary employment can increase your job skills, your knowledge of a particular field, and your chances of hearing of permanent positions. In today's tight labor market, many companies are using the services of temporary workers in increasing numbers. In fact, temporary agencies may sign multimillion-dollar contracts to provide businesses with a range of temporary workers. In some cases, temporary workers are in such demand that they may receive benefits, bonuses, and the same hourly wages as equivalent full-time workers. Some temporary agencies are even joining with companies to create long-term career paths for their temporary workers.

PRESENTING YOURSELF ON PAPER

An employer's first impression of you is likely to be based on the way you present yourself on paper. Whether it is in an application form or on a resume, you will want to make a good impression so that employers will be interested in giving you a personal interview. A potential employer is likely to equate a well-written presentation that is neat with good work habits and a sloppy, poorly written one with bad work habits.

Writing an Effective Resume

When you write to follow up a lead or to ask about job openings, you should also send information about yourself. The accepted way of doing this is to send a resume with a cover letter.

The work *resume* is derived from the French word *résumer*, meaning "to summarize." A resume does just that—it briefly outlines your education, work experience, and special abilities and skills. A resume may also be called a curriculum vitae, a personal profile, or a personal data sheet. This summary can act as your introduction by mail or e-mail, as your calling card if you apply in person, and as a convenient reference for you to use when filling out an application form or when being interviewed.

A resume is a useful tool in applying for almost any job in the field of public and community services. It is valuable, even if you use it only to keep a record of where you have worked, for whom, and the dates of employment. A resume is usually required if you are being considered for professional or executive positions. Prepare it carefully. It's well worth the effort.

The goal of a resume is to capture the interest of potential employers so they will call you for a personal interview. Since employers are busy people, the resume should be as brief and as neat as possible. You should, however, include as much relevant information about yourself as you can. This is usually presented under at least two headings: "Education" and "Experience." The latter is sometimes called "Employment History." Many people add a third section titled "Related Skills," "Professional Qualifications," or "Related Qualifications."

If you prepare a self-inventory such as the one described earlier, it will be a useful tool in preparing a resume. Go through your inventory, and select the items that show your ability to do the job or jobs in which you are interested. Plan to highlight these items on your resume. Select only those facts that point out your relevant skills and experience.

Once you have chosen the special points to include, prepare the resume. At the top, put your name, address, and phone number. After that, decide which items will be most relevant to the employer you plan to contact.

State Your Objective Some employment counselors advise that you state a job objective or describe briefly the type of position for which you are applying. The job objective usually follows your name and address. Don't be too specific if you plan to use the same resume a number of times. It's better to give a general career goal. Then, in a cover letter, you can be more specific about the position in which you are interested.

Describe What You've Done Every interested employer will check your educational background and employment history carefully. It is best to present these sections in order of importance. For instance, if you've held many relevant jobs, you should list your work experience first, followed by your educational background. On the other hand, if you are just out of school with little or no work experience, it's probably best to list your educational background first and then, under employment history, to mention any part-time and summer jobs or volunteer work you've done.

Under educational background, list the schools you have attended in reverse chronological order, starting with your most recent training and ending with the least recent. Employers want to know at a glance your highest qualifications. For each educational experience, include years attended, name and location of the school, and degree or certificate earned, if any. If you have advanced degrees (college and beyond), it isn't necessary to include high school and elementary school education. Don't forget to highlight any special courses you took or awards you won, if they are relevant to the kind of job you are seeking.

Chronological and Functional Resume Information about your employment history can be presented in two basic ways. The most common format is the chronological resume. In a chronological resume, you summarize your work experience year by year. Begin with your current or most recent employment and then work backward. For each job, list the name and location of the company for which you worked, the years you were employed, and the position or positions you held. The order in which you present these facts will depend on what you are trying to emphasize. If you want to call attention to the type or level of job you held, for example, you should put the job title first. Regardless of the order you choose, be consistent. Summer employment or part-time work should be identified as such. If you held a job for less than a year, specify months in the dates of employment.

It is important to include a brief description of the responsibilities you had in each job. This often reveals more about your abilities than the job title. Remember, too, that you do not have to mention the names of former supervisors or how much you earned. You can discuss these points during the interview or explain them on an application form.

The functional resume, on the other hand, emphasizes *what you can do* rather than *what you have done*. It is useful for people who have large gaps in their work history or who have relevant skills that would not be properly highlighted in a chronological listing of jobs. The functional resume concentrates on qualifications—such as teaching experience, organizational skills, or managerial experience. Specific jobs may be mentioned, but they are not the primary focus of this particular type of resume.

Explain Special Skills You may wish to include a third section called "Related Skills," "Professional Qualifications," or "Related Qualifications." This is useful if there are points you want to highlight that

DO YOU KNOW YOUR RIGHTS?

JOB DISCRIMINATION—WHAT IT IS

Federal and State Law

An employer cannot discriminate against you for any reason other than your ability to do the job. By federal law, an employer cannot discriminate against you because of your race, color, religion, sex, or national origin. The law applies to decisions about hiring, promotion, working conditions, and firing. The law specifically protects workers who are over the age of 40 from discrimination on the basis of age.

The law also protects workers with disabilities. Employers must make their workplaces accessible to individuals with disabilities—for example, by making them accessible to wheelchairs or by hiring readers or interpreters for blind or deaf employees.

Federal law offers additional protection to employees who work for the federal government or for employers who contract with the federal government. State law often provides protection also, for instance, by prohibiting discrimination on the basis of marital status, arrest record, political affiliations, or sexual orientation.

Affirmative Action

Affirmative action programs are set up by businesses that want to make a special effort to hire women and members of minority groups. Federal employers and many businesses that have contracts with the federal government are required by law to set up affirmative action programs. Employers with a history of discriminatory practices may also be required to establish affirmative action programs.

Discrimination Against Job Applicants

A job application form or interviewer may ask for information that can be used to discriminate against you illegally. The law prohibits such questions. If you are asked such questions and are turned down for the job, you may be a victim of discrimination. However, under federal law, employers must require you to prove that you are an American citizen or that you have a valid work permit.

Discrimination on the Job

Discrimination on the job is illegal. Being denied a promotion for which you are qualified or being paid less than coworkers are paid for the same job may be forms of illegal discrimination.

Sexual, racial, and religious harassment are forms of discrimination and are prohibited in the workplace. On-the-job harassment includes sexual, racial, or religious jokes or comments. Sexual harassment includes not only requests or demands for sexual favors but also verbal or physical conduct of a sexual nature.

JOB DISCRIMINATION— WHAT YOU CAN DO

Contact Federal or State Commissions

If you believe that your employer practices unfair discrimination, you can complain to the state civil rights commission or the federal Equal Employment Opportunity Commission (EEOC). If, after investigating your complaint, the commission finds that there has been unfair discrimination, it will take action against the employer. You may be entitled to the job or promotion you were denied or to reinstatement if you were fired. You may also receive back pay or other financial compensation.

Contact a Private Organization

There are many private organizations that can help you fight job discrimination. For example, the American Civil Liberties Union (ACLU) works to protect all people from infringement on their civil rights. The National Association for the Advancement of Colored People (NAACP), National Organization for Women (NOW), and Native American Rights Fund may negotiate with your employer, sue on your behalf,

do not apply directly to educational background or work experience. Be sure these points are relevant to the kind of work you are seeking. This section is most effective if you can mention any special recognition, awards, or other evidence of excellence. It is also useful to mention if you are willing to relocate or can work unusual hours.

Have References Available Employers may also want to know whom they can contact to find out more about you. At the start of your job search, you should ask three or four people if you may use them as references. If you haven't seen these people for a while, you may want to send them a copy of your resume and let them know what kind of position you're seeking. Your references should be the kind of people your potential employer will respect, and they should be able to comment favorably on your abilities, personality, and work habits. You should indicate whether these people are personal references or former work supervisors. Avoid using any relatives. You can list the names and addresses of

or start a class action suit—a lawsuit brought on behalf of all individuals in your situation.

WHAT TO DO IF YOU LOSE YOUR JOB

Being Fired and Being Laid Off

An employer usually has the right to fire an employee at any time. In many cases, however, an employer can fire you only if there is good cause, such as your inability to do the job, violation of safety rules, dishonesty, or chronic absenteeism.

Firing an employee because of that employee's race, color, religion, sex, national origin, or age (if the employee is over 40) is illegal. Firing an employee for joining a union or for reporting an employer's violation (called whistle-blowing) is also prohibited. If you believe you have been wrongfully discharged, you should contact the EEOC or the state civil rights commission.

At times, employers may need to let a number of employees go to reduce costs. This reduction in staff is called a layoff. Laying off an employee has nothing to do with the employee's job performance. Federal law requires employers who lay off large numbers of employees to give these employees at least two months' notice of the cutback.

Unemployment Compensation

Unemployment insurance is a state-run fund that provides payments to people who lose their jobs through no fault of their own. Not everyone is entitled to unemployment compensation. Those who quit their jobs or who worked only a few months before losing their jobs may not be eligible.

The amount of money you receive depends on the amount you earned at your last job. You may receive unemployment payments for only a limited period of time and only so long as you can prove that you are actively looking for a new position.

Each claim for unemployment compensation is investigated before the state makes any payments. If the state unemployment agency decides to deny you compensation, you may ask the agency for instructions on how to appeal that decision.

OTHER PROTECTIONS FOR EMPLOYEES

Honesty and Drug Testing

Many employers ask job applicants or employees to submit to lie-detector tests or drug tests. Lie-detector tests are permitted in the case of high-security positions, such as police officers. Some states prohibit or restrict the testing of applicants or employees for drug use. Aptitude and personality tests are generally permitted.

Other Federal Laws

The Fair Labor Standards Act prescribes certain minimum wages and rules about working hours and overtime payments. Workers' compensation laws provide payment for injuries that occur in the workplace and wages lost as a result of those injuries.

The Occupational Safety and Health Act sets minimum requirements for workplace safety. Any employee who discovers a workplace hazard should report it to the Occupational Safety and Health Administration (OSHA). The administration will investigate the claim and may require the employer to correct the problem or pay a fine.

Rights Guaranteed by Contract

Not every employee has a written contract. If you do, however, that contract may grant you additional rights, such as the right to severance pay in the event you are laid off. In addition, employees who are members of a union may have certain rights guaranteed through their union contract.

Before you sign any contract, make sure you understand every part of it. Read it thoroughly and ask the employer questions. Checking the details of a contract before signing it may prevent misunderstanding later on.

RYAN RADVIK

391 Macarthy Drive
Malvern, PA 12345
(555) 123-5678
Rradvik@email.com

EXPERIENCE

Summer, 1999 — *Assembly Worker*, Olsen Manufacturing Company, Inc., Malvern, PA.

Responsible for assembly of metal casing for lighting equipment. Served as member of inspection team on a rotating basis.

Part-time 1995 to 1998 — *Coach*, YMCA, West Chester, PA.

Supervised training and competition matches of boys' soccer team. Planned practice sessions for beginners and experienced players. Organized competition schedule with other teams. Responsible for team safety and security of equipment.

1995 — *Groundskeeper*, Twin Meadows Country Club, Ridgewood, NJ.

Responsible for care of golf course. Duties included fertilizing, mowing, trimming lawns, and collecting litter. Operated club vehicles and power equipment. Planted and tended ornamental flowers and shrubs.

EDUCATION

1995 — *Diploma*, Windsor High School, Ridgewood, NJ.

General business program.

Captain, soccer and track teams.

REFERENCES

Available upon request.

- State your name, address, and telephone number first.
- State job objective or general career goal in a few words.
- List education and work experience in reverse chronological order, with most recent item first.

DOROTHY LEHMAN

Apartment 8
989 Cameron Boulevard
Arlington, VA 12345
(555) 123-4567
dlehman@email.com

OBJECTIVE: *Position as reference librarian in public or university library.*

EXPERIENCE:

1990 to 1998 — **School Librarian**, Manchester School District, Arlington, VA.

Responsible for administration and program planning for library of midsize elementary school. Handled all acquisitions, cataloging, and maintenance of library materials. Worked with superintendent on annual library budget proposal. Organized video, film, and pamphlet collections. Supervised library study groups. Provided reference services for students and faculty.

1989 to 1990 — **Cataloger**, Hamilton University Library, Richmond, VA.

Responsible for identification, cataloging, and cross-referencing of new acquisitions. Recataloged older holdings to conform to new system. Entered all data in university computer system as well as main library card file. Prepared cases and bindings for nonstandard material. Coordinated work with catalog staff in special collection libraries.

EDUCATION:

1990 — **Master of Library Science**, Hamilton University, Graduate School of Library Science, Richmond, VA.

1987 — **Bachelor of Arts**, University of Virginia, Charlottesville, VA. Major in Modern Languages.

RELATED SKILLS AND QUALIFICATIONS: Reading and speaking knowledge of Spanish and German.

Member, American Library Association.

REFERENCES: *Available upon request.*

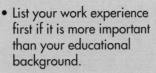

- List your work experience first if it is more important than your educational background.
- Keep descriptions of your education and work experience brief.
- List special skills and qualifications if they are relevant to the job.

---

your references at the end of your resume or in a cover letter. Or, you can simply write, "References available upon request." Just be sure you have their names, addresses, and phone numbers ready if you are asked.

Present Yourself Concisely Tips for making your resume concise include using phrases instead of sentences and omitting unnecessary words. When appropriate, start a sentence with a verb, such as _maintained_ or _coordinated_. There is no need to say "I"—that is obvious and repetitive.

Present Yourself Well Employment counselors often recommend that resumes be no longer than one page because employers won't take the time to read a second page. If you've held many positions related to your occupation, go on to the second page, but don't include beginning or irrelevant jobs. If you have a lot of work experience, limit the education section to just the essentials.

You should also concentrate on the appearance of your resume. It should be typed on a good grade of 8½" × 11" white bond paper. If you can't type, a professional typist can do it for you for a small charge. Be sure that it is neatly typed with adequate margins. The data should be spaced and indented so that each item stands out. This enables a busy executive or personnel director to see at a glance the facts of greatest interest.

You will probably need many copies of your resume during your job search. Each copy should be as neat and as clear as your original. If possible, input your resume on a computer and print copies on a good-quality printer. You may want to have your resume reproduced professionally. A photo-offset printer can make several hundred excellent copies for a moderate fee. A photocopying machine may be more economical for smaller quantities.

These suggestions for writing a resume are not hard-and-fast rules. Resumes may be adapted to special situations. For example, people with a variety of work experience often prepare several versions of their resume and use the experience that's most relevant when applying for a particular job.

If this is your first resume, show it to someone else, perhaps a guidance counselor, for constructive advice. No matter what, be truthful while emphasizing your assets. You can do that by showing the abilities, skills, and specific interests that qualify you for a particular job. Don't mention any weaknesses or deficiencies in your training. Do mention job-related aptitudes that showed up in previous employment or in school. Don't make up things about yourself; everything that's in your resume can, and sometimes will, be checked.

Writing Cover Letters

When you send your resume through the mail or the Internet, you should send a cover letter with it. This is the same whether you are writing to apply for a specific job or just to find out if there are any openings.

A good cover letter should be neat, brief, and well written with no more than three or four short paragraphs. Since you may use your resume for a variety of job openings, your cover letter should be very specific. Try to get the person who reads it to think that you are an ideal candidate for a particular job. If at all possible, send the letter to a specific person, either to the personnel director or to the person for whom you would be working. If necessary, call the company and ask to whom you should write.

Start your letter by explaining why you are writing. Say that you are inquiring about possible job openings at the company, that you are responding to an advertisement in a particular publication, or that someone recommended that you should write. (Use the person's name if you have received permission to do so.)

Let your letter lead into your resume. Use it to call attention to your qualifications. Add information that shows why you are well suited for that specific job. For example, the librarian in the sample letter pointed out that she has worked with automated library equipment and on-line reference systems. She also mentioned that she is familiar with community events run at the library in question. In the second sample letter, the applicant for a letter carrier position mentioned his experience working outdoors and stressed that he has a good driving record.

Completing the Application Form

Many employers ask job applicants to fill out an application form. This form usually duplicates much of the information on your resume, but it may ask some additional questions. Give complete answers to all questions except those that are discriminatory. If a question doesn't apply to you, put a dash next to it.

You may be given the application form when you arrive for an interview, or it may be sent to your home. When filling it out, print neatly in ink. Follow the instructions carefully. For instance, if the form asks you to put down your last name first, do so.

The most important sections of an application form are the education and work histories. As in your resume, many applications request that you write these in reverse chronological order, with the most recent experience first. Unlike your resume, however, the application form may request information about your earnings on previous jobs. It may also ask what rate of pay you are seeking on this job.

RYAN RADVIK

391 Macarthy Drive
Malvern, PA 12345
(555) 123-5678
Rradvik@email.com391

November 5, 1999

Ms. Amy Liebowitz
Postmaster
Malvern Central Post Office
Malvern, PA 12345

Dear Ms. Liebowitz:

As I mentioned during our telephone conversation this morning, I am interested in employment as a letter carrier with the Malvern Central Post Office.

I am accustomed to outdoor work because two of my previous positions have involved this type of work. I have a valid driver's license and a good driving record. I am available to work any shift.

I enclose my resume as requested. I would be grateful if you would send me the application form you mentioned. I have arranged to take the postal service employee's exam this month.

Thank you for explaining the application process to me. I look forward to receiving the material.

Sincerely yours,

Ryan Radvik

Ryan Radvik

Enclosure

DOROTHY LEHMAN

Apartment 8
989 Cameron Boulevard
Arlington, VA 12345
(555) 123-4567
dlehman@email.com

January 12, 1999

Mr. Joseph Delgado
Director of Library Services
Middlesex Township
62 Marlboro Avenue
Richmond, VA 12347

Dear Mr. Delgado:

Rita Spalding, reference librarian at Middlesex Public Library, mentioned that she will be retiring in February. I am interested in applying for her position.

I have experience in school and university libraries and am familiar with the major classification systems. I have worked extensively with automated catalog equipment and on-line reference systems. I am familiar with the county interlibrary loan system and with the community programs run at Middlesex and other local libraries.

I enclose my resume. Since Ms. Spalding has just announced her retirement, perhaps you would let me know how you will be conducting the search for her successor. I am available at any time for an interview and can be reached at my home.

Sincerely yours,

Dorothy Lehman

Dorothy Lehman

Enclosure

Be prepared to answer these and other topics not addressed on your resume. Look at the sample application form, and make note of the kinds of questions that you are likely to be asked—for example, your Social Security number, the names of previous supervisors, your salary, and your reason for leaving. If necessary, carry notes on such topics with you to an interview. You have a responsibility to tell prospective employers what they need to know to make an informed decision.

Neatness Counts Think before you write on an application form so you avoid crossing things out. An employer's opinion of you may be influenced just by the general appearance of your application form. A neat, clearly detailed form may indicate an orderly mind and the ability to think clearly, follow instructions, and organize information.

Know Your Rights Under federal and some state laws, an employer cannot demand that you answer any questions about race, color, creed, national origin, ancestry, sex, marital status, age (with certain exceptions), number of dependents, property, car ownership (unless needed for the job), or arrest record. Refer to the information on job discrimination in this essay for more information about your rights.

PRESENTING YOURSELF IN AN INTERVIEW

An interview is the climax of your job-hunting efforts. On the basis of this meeting, the prospective employer will decide whether or not to hire you, and you will decide whether or not you want the job.

Prepare in Advance

Before an interview, there are a number of things you can do to prepare. Begin by giving some more thought to why you want the job and what you have to offer. Then review your resume and any lists you made when you were evaluating yourself so that you can keep your qualifications firmly in mind.

Learn as much as you can about the organization. Check with friends who work there, read company brochures, search the Internet, or devise other information-gathering strategies. Showing that you know something about the company and what it does will indicate your interest.

Try to anticipate some of the questions the interviewer may ask and think of how you would answer. For example, you may be asked: Will you work overtime when necessary? Are you ready to go to night school to improve some of your skills? Preparing answers in advance will make the process easier for you. It is also wise to prepare any questions you may

have about the company or the position for which you are applying. The more information you have, the better you can evaluate both the company and the job.

Employers may want you to demonstrate specific skills for some jobs. An applicant for a job as a legal secretary, for example, might be given tests to determine clerical skills.

On the appointed day, dress neatly and in a style appropriate for the job you're seeking. When in doubt, it's safer to dress on the conservative side, wearing a tie rather than a turtleneck or wearing a dress or blouse and skirt rather than pants and a T-shirt.

Be on time. Find out in advance exactly where the company is located and how to get there. Allow extra time in case you get lost, get caught in a traffic jam, can't find a parking spot, or encounter another type of delay.

Maintain a Balance

When your appointment begins, remember that a good interview is largely a matter of balance. Don't undersell yourself by sitting back silently. Don't oversell yourself by talking nonstop about how wonderful you are. Answer all questions directly and simply, and let the interviewer take the lead.

Instead of saying, "I'm reliable and hardworking," give the interviewer an example. Allow the interviewer to draw conclusions from your example.

It's natural to be nervous before and during a job interview. However, you need to try to relax and be yourself. You may even enjoy the conversation. Your chances of being hired and being happy if you get the job are better if the employer likes you as you are.

Avoid discussing money until the employer brings it up or until you are offered the job. Employers usually know in advance what they are willing to pay. If you are the one to begin a discussion about the salary you want, you may set an amount that's either too low or too high.

Be prepared to ask questions, but don't force them on your interviewer. Part of the purpose of the interview is for you to evaluate the company while you are being evaluated. For instance, you might want to ask about the company's training programs and its policy on promotions.

Don't stay too long. Most business people have busy schedules. It is likely that the interviewer will let you know when it's time for the interview to end.

Don't expect a definite answer at the first interview. Employers usually thank you for coming and say that you will be notified shortly. Most employers want to interview all the applicants before they make a hiring decision. If the position is offered at

1 Always print neatly in blue or black ink. When completing an application at home, type it, if possible.

2 Read the application carefully *before* you start to fill it out. Follow instructions precisely. Use standard abbreviations.

3 If you aren't applying for a specific job, indicate the kind of work you're willing to do.

4 You don't have to commit to a specific rate of pay. Write "open" or "negotiable" if you are uncertain.

5 Traffic violations and so on do not belong here. Nor do offenses for which you were charged but not convicted.

6 If a question doesn't apply to you, write "NA" (for not applicable) or put a dash through the space.

7 Take notes along to remind you of school names, addresses, and dates.

8 If you're short on "real" employment, mention jobs such as babysitting, lawn mowing, or any occasional work.

9 Your references should be people who can be objective about you, such as former employers, teachers, and community leaders.

10 Under the heading "Reason for Leaving," a simple answer will do. Avoid saying "better pay"—even if it's so.

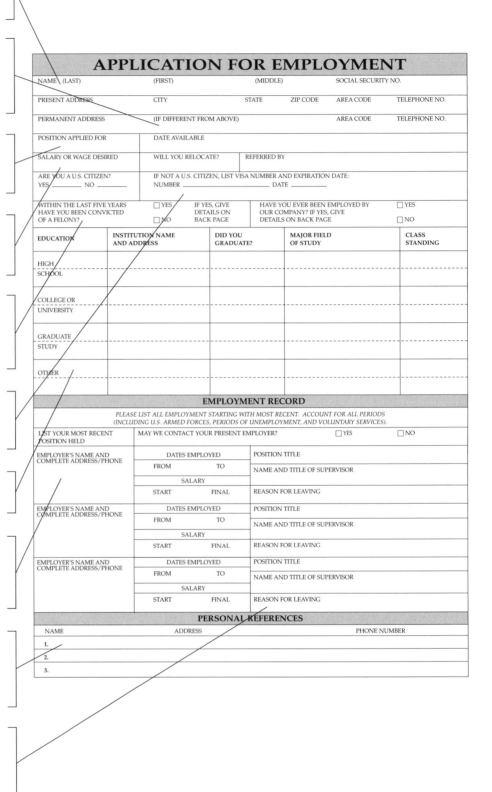

the time of the interview, you can ask for a little time to think about it. If the interviewer tells you that you are not suitable for the job, try to be polite. Say, "I'm sorry, but thank you for taking the time to meet with me." After all, the company may have the right job for you next week.

Follow Up After the Interview

If the job sounds interesting and you would like to be considered for it, say so as you leave. Follow up after the interview by writing a brief thank-you note to the employer. Express your continued interest in the position and thank the interviewer for taking the time to meet with you.

It's a good idea to make some notes and evaluations of the interview while it is still fresh in your mind. Write down the important facts about the job—the duties, salary, promotion prospects, and so on. Also evaluate your own performance in the interview. List the things you wish you had said and things you wish you had not said. These notes will help you make a decision later. They will also help you prepare for future interviews.

Finally, don't hesitate to contact your interviewer if you haven't heard from the company after a week or two (unless you were told it would be longer). Write a brief note or make a phone call in which you ask when a decision might be reached. Making such an effort will show the employer that you are genuinely interested in the job. Your call will remind the interviewer about you and could work to your advantage.

TAKE CHARGE

The field of public and community services offers many job opportunities. Job hunting is primarily a matter of organizing a well-thought-out campaign. Scan the classified ads, search through online job banks, watch for trends in local industry that might be reported in the news, and check with people you know in the field. Take the initiative. Send out well-crafted resumes and cover letters. Respond to help-wanted advertisements. Finally, in an interview, state your qualifications and experience in a straightforward and confident manner.

TRADE AND PROFESSIONAL JOURNALS

The following is a list of some of the major journals in the field of public and community services. These journals can keep you up-to-date with what's happening in your field of interest. These publications can also lead you to jobs through their own specialized classified advertising sections.

TRADE AND PROFESSIONAL JOURNALS

The following is a list of some of the major journals in public and community services. These journals can keep you up to date with what's happening in all branches of your field of interest. These publications can also lead you to jobs through their own specialized classified advertising sections.

Armed Services

Armed Forces Journal International, 2000 L Street, NW, Suite 520, Washington, DC 20036. *www.afji.com*

Legal Work

ABA Journal, 750 North Lake Shore Drive, Chicago, IL 60611.
Trial, Association of Trial Lawyers of America, 1050 Thirty-first Street, NW, Washington, DC 20007-4499.

Public, Civil, and Social Services

Academe, American Association of University Professors, 1012 Fourteenth Street, NW, Suite 500, Washington, DC 20005.
Administration in Social Work, 10 Alice Street, Binghamton, NY 13904-1580.
American City and County, 6151 Powers Ferry Road, NW, Atlanta, GA 30339-2941.
American Libraries, 50 East Huron Street, Chicago, IL 60611.
American School Board Journal, 1680 Duke Street, Alexandria, VA 22314.
American Sociological Review, 1722 N Street, NW, Washington, DC 20036.
APA Monitor, American Psychological Association, 750 First Street, NE, Washington, DC 20002-4242. *www.apa.org/monitor*
Association Management, 1575 I Street, NW, Washington, DC 20005-1168. *www.asanet.org*
Child Welfare, Transaction Periodicals Consortium, Department 3092, Rutgers University, New Brunswick, NJ 08903. *www.transactionpub.com*
Christian Century, 407 South Dearborn Street, Chicago, IL 60605.
Chronicle of Higher Education, 1255 Twenty-third Street, NW, Suite 700, Washington, DC 20037.

Community College Journal, 1 Dupont Circle, NW, Suite 410, Washington, DC 20036.

Corrections Today, American Correctional Association, 4380 Forbes Boulevard, Lanham, MD 20706-4322.
www.corrections.com/aca/pubs.html

Environmental Science and Technology, 1155 Sixteenth Street, NW, Washington, DC 20036.
pubs.acs.org/hotartcl/est/est.html

Journal of Career Planning and Employment, 62 Highland Avenue, Bethlehem, PA 18017-9085.

Law Library Journal, 53 West Jackson Boulevard, Suite 940, Chicago, IL 60604.

Library Journal, 249 West 17th Street, New York, NY 10011.
www.ljdigital.com

Public Administration Review, American Society for Public Administration, 1120 G Street, NW, Washington, DC 20005-3885.

Science and Children, National Science Teachers Association, 1840 Wilson Boulevard, Arlington, VA 22201.
www.nsta.org

Social Service Review, University of Chicago Press, Journals Division, P.O. Box 37005, Chicago, IL 60637.
www.journals.uchicago.edu

Armed Services Career

Definition and Nature of the Work

The armed services offer jobs in the United States and abroad that are comparable to hundreds of civilian jobs. The U.S. Army, Navy, Air Force, Marine Corps, and Coast Guard train people for jobs such as postal clerk, helicopter repairer, court reporter, and dental hygienist in addition to the strictly military jobs, such as those in weapons crews or in the infantry. Some people spend their entire career in the armed services. Others enlist in the military for 3 to 6 years, become well trained in their field, and return to civilian life with valuable experience and military training. Still others stay in the armed services for 20 years, retire from the military with a pension, and obtain a civilian job.

In the field of administration, enlisted personnel assist in office duties. They type correspondence, compose letters, process orders, work on budgets, and so on. Experienced enlisted personnel and officers have more complex and more responsible duties, such as supervising other personnel.

Those who choose a field such as Maneuver Combat Arms learn to operate and maintain weapons, vehicles, and other equipment. Beginners may first be trained for jobs such as rifleman or ammunition handler. With experience and ability, enlisted personnel may be assigned more difficult positions, such as armor reconnaissance specialist.

In the field of medicine beginning military personnel help care for patients, serve meals, treat minor cuts and wounds, and transport patients within a medical center. Those who had training prior to enlistment, such as registered nurses, are assigned similar jobs in the military. Those who have no previous training may learn jobs such as X-ray technician and physical therapy specialist.

There are many more fields of opportunity, but they are too numerous to mention here. In every field, however, enlistees receive classroom and field training throughout their military careers and are encouraged to advance to the limit of their capabilities.

Education and Training Requirements

Military service is now entirely voluntary, although in an emergency Congress can reactivate the draft. You must be at least 17 years of age to enlist in any branch of the military. Enlistment requirements vary from branch to branch of the service. U.S. Air Force personnel must enter active duty before their 28th birthday, but in general, you must be no older than age 35 to enlist. Some jobs are open only to

Education and Training
Varies—see profile

Salary Range
Average—$28,000

Employment Outlook
Very good

Although certain fields in the armed services may be nearly filled, the armed services offers a wide variety of careers for anyone who wants to enter military service.

those who have completed high school. You will be given aptitude tests before you enlist. You may enter any field for which you qualify and for which the service has need. If you are interested only in a specific training program, you can enlist for that program and occupation. If you do not qualify for that job, you are free to change your mind about enlisting.

You can enlist for 3 or more years of active duty. If you wish to enlist instead for 6 years of reserve duty, at least 4 months of that time must be spent on active duty. You also may be qualified to apply for Officer Candidate School (OCS) training. College students can join the Reserve Officers Training Corps (ROTC) and begin training while in school. Under this program you receive a monthly allowance while in school. After you graduate and are commissioned, you must serve on active duty for 2 years. Full-tuition scholarships are also available.

Another way to join the military is to enter one of the service academies, such as the Air Force Academy in Colorado Springs, CO, the Coast Guard Academy in New London, CT, the army's Military Academy in West Point, NY, or the Naval Academy in Annapolis, MD. Your tuition and expenses are paid, and you receive an allowance while you attend these schools. You must serve on active duty for 5 years after you graduate.

Armed services enlistees are given classroom training as well as on-the-job training. You may participate in off-duty programs ranging from correspondence courses to courses taken at military bases or local civilian schools. You also may be eligible to participate in a transition program offered to personnel 6 months before they resign from the armed services. This program provides counseling, placement, training, and education services to service personnel who have no civilian skills, have been disabled in combat, or have not earned their high school diploma.

Getting the Job

Each branch of the military service has its own recruiting operation. For information about the branch in which you are interested, you should see the local recruiter. Recruiters have many publications that describe career opportunities and military life. Your school placement office and state employment office may also have some of these brochures.

Advancement Possibilities and Employment Outlook

There are many possibilities for advancement in the armed services. Those who work hard and show leadership abilities are given additional training to prepare them for advanced positions. Almost all who enlist are rapidly promoted to higher pay grades.

About 1.8 million people are employed in the armed services. Although certain fields may be nearly filled, there are many opportunities for anyone who wants to enter military service. The armed services offer a wider variety of careers than any other employer. They have developed attractive training and education programs. As a result, a growing number of people are deciding that they want a career in the military.

Working Conditions

People who are considering a career in the armed services should remember that the primary goal of the military is to train professional soldiers. Enlisted personnel and officers should have a strong desire to serve their country in peace and war. They must be willing to accept the discipline that is necessary to maintain a strong military force. Military personnel must be able to work well with others and obey orders from superiors without question.

Armed services personnel who have noncombat jobs work under conditions similar to people who hold comparable civilian jobs. They generally work a 40-hour week and often have weekends off. Those in combat zones may have jobs that require great courage and physical stamina. When in direct combat, they may work around the clock with very little sleep and no time off. Living quarters for military personnel vary from barracks at training camps and trenches in war zones to comfortable apartments at military bases.

Earnings and Benefits

Salaries for armed services personnel vary according to length of service, type of job, and level of performance. The average annual salary, including allowances, for all armed services personnel is $28,000.

Although military salaries are somewhat lower than those received by civilians doing similar jobs, armed services personnel receive many other benefits that make their total compensation equal to that received by civilians. They receive free meals and living quarters when they live on the military base. If they do not live on the base, they receive an allowance for food and lodging. They receive special pay for hazardous duty, a uniform allowance, free medical and dental care, and 30 days of vacation each year. Other benefits include reduced prices for entertainment and travel and for items purchased at military institutions. Military personnel are eligible for low-cost life insurance, retirement pensions of half pay after 20 years and three-fourths pay after 30 years, and many educational and career training benefits.

Where to Go for More Information
Look in the Federal Government blue pages of your local telephone directory for the nearest armed services recruiting offices.

Border Patrol Agent

Definition and Nature of the Work

Border patrol agents work at ports of entry and at border crossings. They are federal law enforcement workers who make sure that laws are observed when people or goods cross the U.S. border. One of their tasks is to check the identification papers of people entering the United States. Agents try to prevent smuggling and the entrance of illegal aliens into this country. To carry out their job properly, they must know all the laws concerning entry into the United States.

Border patrol agents conduct investigations when necessary and speak for the federal government at hearings. They are also responsible for arresting aliens who live in this country illegally. They make suggestions to the courts about immigration matters, including applications for citizenship.

Education and Training Requirements

Border patrol agents should have a high school diploma and must be in good physical condition. Participation in high school sports and physical education classes is helpful. Agents must pass written and oral civil service tests for the job. Furthermore, they must be fluent in Spanish. Those who do not know the language are given a year to learn it. Agents undergo a 14-week training program to learn the duties of the job.

Education and Training
High school

Salary Range
Starting—$19,400
to $24,000
Average—$35,000

Employment Outlook
Fair

Border patrol agents work at border crossings to check the identification papers of people entering the United States from a foreign country.

Getting the Job

Contact your local Federal Information Center to learn about job openings.

Advancement Possibilities and Employment Outlook

New agents may be promoted after a 1-year probationary period. They may be promoted again at the end of their third year of service. Other promotions are possible, including those to supervisory positions. Some agents are eventually transferred to other jobs dealing with immigration and naturalization.

Each year between 100 and 200 openings occur. The number of openings depends largely on government funding for the patrol. Because the number of people entering the country illegally is increasing, the need for Border patrol agents is expected to remain constant.

Working Conditions

Border patrol agents often work outside along international borders. Their job involves working with people. Like all law enforcement personnel, agents must be responsible and able to act quickly. The work can be dangerous. Agents work 40 hours a week and have occasional overtime work. Because borders and ports of entry are open at all times, Border patrol agents usually work in shifts.

Earnings and Benefits

Earnings depend on the agents' years of service. Border patrol agents start at about $19,400 to $24,000 a year. Experienced agents earn an average of about $35,000 a year. Agents receive paid vacations, health and life insurance, pensions, and other benefits given to federal employees.

Where to Go for More Information

Immigration and Naturalization Service
425 I Street, NW
Washington, DC 20536
(202) 514-2000

National Immigration Law Center
1102 South Crenshaw Boulevard,
   Suite 101
Los Angeles, CA 90019
(213) 487-2531

United States Government Federal
   Information Center
Phone number in local directory.

Building Custodian

Definition and Nature of the Work

Building custodians, or janitors, clean and maintain a variety of buildings ranging from schools to factories. They make minor repairs, such as replacing lightbulbs and fixing leaky faucets. Custodians also wash and wax floors, dust, sweep, vacuum carpets, clean bathrooms, and wash windows. They generally do not do work that requires special skills.

In some buildings custodians are responsible for tending furnaces. They kill insects and rodents, if necessary, and collect and discard trash. In northern climates building custodians clear snow from sidewalks. Some custodians mow lawns and do general yard work. A few collect rent and enforce building management rules.

Most companies, hospitals, and schools employ building custodians. Many custodians work during the day, when buildings are occupied, making repairs, such as unclogging drains in public bathrooms, that cannot wait until after the building is empty. Some custodians work only at night, when the building is empty, because it is easier to clean without disturbing anyone. Many building custodians work for janitorial service firms and clean a number of different buildings.

Custodians use tools such as floor-waxing machines, carpet sweepers, pliers, and screwdrivers. They often use chemicals to wash floors and clean carpets and bathrooms. Custodians work in every state, although the majority work in cities where there are many large buildings.

Education and Training Requirements

No special educational requirements exist. However, high school courses in wood and metal shop that teach how to make simple repairs are very useful in this field. Custodians must be able to do simple arithmetic. Many employers also require good character references. Building custodians generally learn under the supervision of an experienced custodian. They start by doing cleaning and other basic tasks. As they gain experience, they learn to make repairs and are given more complex duties.

Getting the Job

You can apply directly to schools, apartment buildings, manufacturing plants, and large office buildings. You can also check with janitorial service firms. Another way to find a job is to answer want ads listed in local newspapers. You may be able to find a job through your state employment office. If you would like to work for the state or federal government, you should apply at your local civil service office.

Advancement Possibilities and Employment Outlook

For those who work in a building in which there is only one custodian, there is not much chance for advancement. However, experienced building

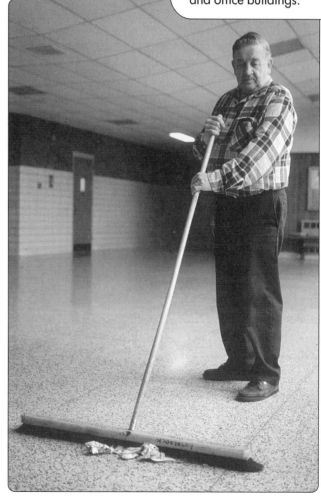

Building custodians, or janitors, clean and maintain buildings such as schools, hospitals, and office buildings.

custodians who work in large buildings can advance to the position of building custodian supervisor. Custodians with administrative ability sometimes start their own cleaning and maintenance services.

The employment outlook for building custodians is good. Almost 2.9 million people are currently employed as building custodians. New buildings are being constructed every day, and more custodians will be needed to maintain these buildings. Employment growth in this field may be slightly set back by improvements in cleaning equipment and chemical compounds, which will make cleaning easier and faster and thus require fewer workers to do the job.

Working Conditions

Building custodians work during the day or at night, depending on the individual job. They generally work between 40 and 48 hours a week. Most of the work is done indoors, although some work, such as snow removal and ground maintenance, is done outdoors.

Most building custodians have a variety of duties. In addition, they are under relatively little pressure during their workday. However, the work is sometimes tiring because custodians have to move furniture and lift heavy objects. Custodians sometimes work around noisy boilers. At times they work with dirty and greasy machinery. They may get minor cuts, bruises, and burns while operating machinery or handling chemicals.

Custodians must be able to get along well with others and be courteous to other employees and occupants of the building. They must be honest and trustworthy.

Where to Go for More Information

Service Employees International Union
1313 L Street, NW
Washington, DC 20005
(202) 898-3200

Earnings and Benefits

Many building custodians are members of unions, which set wages by contract. Building custodians earn between $12,500 and $20,000 a year The average salary is about $15,600 a year. Building custodians generally receive benefits such as paid sick leave and vacations, life and health insurance, and retirement plans. Custodians who work for apartment buildings are often provided with housing at no charge.

Day Care Worker

Education and Training
High school

Salary Range
Average—$210
to $320 a week

Employment Outlook
Very good

Definition and Nature of the Work

Workers in day care centers help preschool children up to 5 years of age in their educational and personal growth. Under a director's supervision, day care workers provide infants with all the necessary primary care. For toddlers and older children, they provide both independent and group activities designed to develop the children's self-esteem, encourage curiosity, and offer security and comfort. Workers use a variety of games and exercises to aid in the growth of children's imaginations, physical skills, and speech. Day care workers are also concerned with the children's health and nutrition. They may encourage the children to participate in the preparation of breakfast and lunch.

Some day care centers are nonprofit organizations that are operated or subsidized by community or government agencies. Other day care centers are privately owned operations. There are also companies that run day care centers for the children of their employees. In some day care centers the children's parents are trained to assist staff members.

Education and Training Requirements

The minimum requirement for day care workers is a high school education. Some centers require some form of on-the-job training. Many workers find it useful to enroll in formal education programs that include courses in education, nutrition, home economics, psychology, English, history, biology, and speech. Many 2-year colleges have programs that lead to an associate degree in preschool or early childhood education.

Workers interested in going on to an administrative position in day care need a bachelor's degree. Some centers require teaching certification for higher-level positions.

Getting the Job

The best way to find a job in the field is to apply directly to day care centers. Your state department of education can tell you where state-run centers are located. Job openings are often listed in the newspaper and on the Internet. If you have taken college courses or have a bachelor's degree, your school's placement office can help you.

Advancement Possibilities and Employment Outlook

Day care workers usually start as staff assistants. After a period of training, they may be given the responsibility of caring for their own group of children. After extensive experience working in day care centers, it is possible to move up to a position of supervisor. Workers with college degrees in early childhood development or in related fields may start at positions of more responsibility.

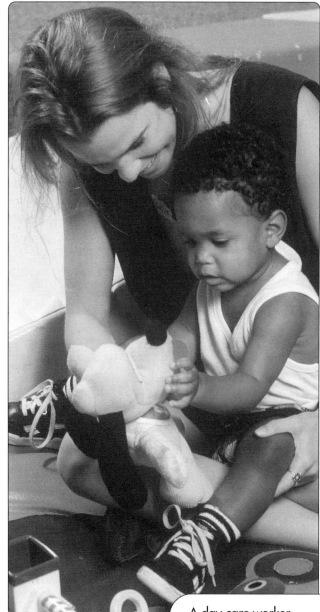

A day care worker cares for the needs of preschool children at a day care center. Day care workers must enjoy being with children and must know how to make them feel secure.

The job outlook for day care workers is expected to be very good through the year 2006. More parents are now working outside the home, and women are returning to work sooner after childbirth. In addition, many employers are increasing day care benefits to their employees in the form of vouchers or subsidies and on-site day care facilities. There is also very high turnover in this field. All of these factors will create numerous openings for day care workers.

Working Conditions

Many day care centers are open 12 hours each day. Their staff members generally work 8-hour shifts. Usually a worker is in charge of a group of from 6 to 12 children. Some centers are in modern buildings specially designed for day care. Others are in remodeled homes or older buildings. Some are on the premises of the factories or businesses that provide care for the children of their employees.

Day care workers must enjoy being with children and must know how to make them feel secure. Day care workers must be able to share ideas and develop programs with other workers on the staff.

Earnings and Benefits

The earnings and benefits of day care workers vary according to education, experience, and the type of day care center. Generally, the salaries are lower at nonprofit centers. The earnings of day care workers average about $210 to $320 a week.

Electric Power Service Worker

Education and Training
None

Salary Range
Varies—see profile

Employment Outlook
Fair

Definition and Nature of the Work

Service workers for electric companies handle matters that relate to customer use. Service workers arrange to have electricity turned on; handle customer complaints; discuss and collect bills; and install, test, and repair electric meters.

The most familiar service worker is the service representative. *Service representatives* work in the offices of the electric company. Some handle customers' questions and complaints on the telephone. Some speak with customers who come into the office. In either case their responsibilities are the same. Suppose someone just purchased a home. To have electricity supplied, the customer must contact the electric company's service representative. The representative sees that the power is turned on, gets the customer's address for proper billing, and also informs the customer of the different kinds of service available. Service representatives also discuss customers' bills with them to explain how rates are calculated and the reasons for increases.

Electric meter installers and repairers are a skilled group of service workers. They install, test, and repair the meters at the customers' homes, businesses, and factories. Different kinds of meters are used for different kinds of electricity demands. The meters used in factories are different from the ones used in private homes. The service workers must know which kind of meter to use for each kind of customer.

In regions that are not heavily populated, the electric power company may appoint one person to perform all customer service jobs. This person is called a *district representative*. This representative answers questions about service; collects money for bills; installs, tests, and repairs meters; and reads the meters at the proper time. If a major repair is necessary, the district representative may contact the central office so that a skilled meter repairer can be sent to the customer.

Education and Training Requirements

Employers generally prefer to hire high school graduates. Although it is not necessary, some service representatives have some college education. Electric meter installers and repairers need a basic knowledge of how electricity works. High school or vocational school courses in electricity and shop are useful.

All training for electric power service workers is done on the job. Meter installers and repairers are trained by experienced workers. The training period can take up to 4 years. Service representatives and district representatives are also taught by more experienced workers. The amount of time the training takes varies according to the size and location of the power company. Because some electric power companies are owned by municipalities, workers may be required to pass a civil service exam.

Getting the Job

Contact the local electric power company to see whether there are any openings. Sometimes openings are listed in newspaper want ads. Check with the placement office of your high school or technical school. For jobs with municipally owned power companies, contact your municipal civil service commission.

Advancement Possibilities and Employment Outlook

Experienced and diligent service workers have good advancement possibilities with electric power companies. Meter installers and repairers, for example, may advance to working with special, complicated equipment used only by large companies. Service representatives may advance to the position of supervisor.

Most workers advance by demonstrating superior skills on the job. Sometimes advancement is based on seniority alone. Workers with civil service jobs can expect regular advances after a certain period of time. Sometimes an exam must be taken for each step up.

There should be little change in the number of jobs for service workers through the year 2006. Although more power is being used than ever before, increased automation is cutting down on the number of workers needed. Most openings will result when experienced workers retire or leave their jobs for other reasons. Because electric power is always in demand, electric power service workers have very secure jobs.

Working Conditions

Conditions vary with the type and location of the job. Service representatives work in offices, usually with other representatives. Meter installers and repairers do most of their work at the homes and businesses of the customers. They must drive a company car or truck. District representatives have to do a great deal of driving because they must cover an area by themselves. All service representatives deal directly with the public. They must be tactful and courteous. Almost all electric power service workers work a 40-hour week.

Earnings and Benefits

Earnings vary with the type of job and the company's location. Because they have the most diverse jobs, district representatives generally earn more than other service workers. They average about $25,000 to $35,000 a year. The wages of meter installers and repairers vary according to the workers' experience. They average about $18,000 to $22,000 a year. Benefits generally include paid holidays and vacations and health insurance.

Where to Go for More Information

Edison Electric Institute
701 Pennsylvania Avenue, NW
Washington, DC 20004-2696
(202) 508-5000
www.eei.org

International Brotherhood of Electrical
    Workers
1125 Fifteenth Street, NW
Washington, DC 20005
(202) 833-7000

Utility Workers Union of America
815 Sixteenth Street, NW, Suite 605
Washington, DC 20006
(202) 347-8105
www.aflcio.org/uwua

Electric Power Transmission and Distribution Worker

Definition and Nature of the Work

Electricity is generated in power plants. Once electricity is generated, electric power transmission and distribution workers see that it gets to homes, offices, and factories. One group of workers controls the flow of energy from the generating plant to the customers. Another group of workers takes care of installing and maintaining transmission and distribution equipment such as power lines.

The person in command of electricity flow is the *load dispatcher*. A dispatcher works in the control room of the generating plant, usually with several assistants. The dispatcher makes sure that the amount of electricity produced matches the amount that customers need at any given time. The dispatcher learns how much electricity is required by watching gauges in the control room. When an adjustment in electricity flow is necessary, the dispatcher tells the power plant workers to start or shut down generators. The dispatcher throws switches to route the current to specific areas where there is demand for electricity.

Substation operators work in smaller, regional relay stations. They receive orders from the load dispatcher, who works at the generating plant. Substation operators control the flow of electricity for a specific area. Electric power is not generated at substations. Substation operators may have other responsibilities, however. For example, in small substations there may be only a single worker, who is in charge of maintaining the equipment as well as directing the energy flow.

Line installers and repairers install cables to service new electric customers and repair broken or unsafe electrical lines.

The lines that send electric power from generating stations to customers are installed and maintained by *line installers and repairers*. For example, when a new housing development is built, installers place cables under the ground or on poles to service the new customers. They also set up the connections between the community power lines and individual customers. The job of repairing broken or unsafe lines is done by the same work crews. Some crews are specialized; that is, certain workers may do only installation, while others may specialize in repairing cables.

Line installers and repairers are assisted by ground helpers and cable splicers. *Ground helpers,* or laborers, dig holes in which the poles are placed. They may hold wires and tools for the installers. *Cable splicers* are responsible for making sure that the connections between two different cables are safe. Poor insulation can result in a serious fire. Cable splicers spend much of their time repairing old connections. They must know the proper way to wire connections and the most efficient way of using cable. Some splicers also inspect cables to make sure that they are in good condition.

Troubleshooters are line installers and repairers who have special training. They are in charge of answering emergency calls, and they must be able to choose the safest course of action when a crisis arises. They repair and replace equipment in order to restore service.

Education and Training Requirements

Electric power companies train most of their employees after they are hired. Much of the training is done on the job. Substation operators and load dispatchers train their assistants in the duties of electric power control. Power companies may provide classroom instruction for new workers and for workers seeking advancement. These classes teach the fundamental laws of electricity, safety rules, and how to read blueprints.

A good way to prepare for these jobs is to enroll in a vocational or technical school. You should also take technical courses in high school: mechanical drawing, shop, and any courses related to electricity. Most utility companies prefer to hire high school graduates.

Getting the Job

Job openings are often listed in local newspapers. Check with your school placement office. Contact your local power company to see if it has any openings. Because some power companies are owned by municipalities, you may have to take a civil service test.

Advancement Possibilities and Employment Outlook

Advancement possibilities are good for experienced workers who have shown that they are reliable. Ground helpers may, with experience, move up to become cable splicers or line installers and repairers. It usually takes about 4 years of experience to become a skilled line worker. Assistants at substations may move on to become substation operators. This takes, on the average, from 3 to 7 years. Substation operators with between 7 and 10 years of experience may become load dispatchers.

Only a small increase in the number of job openings is expected through the year 2006. The increasing need for electrical energy will create jobs, but the demand for workers will be offset somewhat by increased mechanization. It is anticipated that only a few thousand new positions will open each year for transmission and distribution workers.

Working Conditions

Working conditions vary greatly, depending on the type of job. Load dispatchers and substation operators work inside in comfortable surroundings. They generally work 8 hours a day, 40 hours a week. Weekend and evening work may be required. Because electricity is needed around the clock, a rotation of shifts is normal.

The workers who maintain lines and equipment may have to work in all kinds of weather and during emergencies. Installation workers, however, ordinarily work only during the day. They work 40 hours a week. Troubleshooters and maintenance workers may rotate shifts.

Earnings and Benefits

Electric power transmission and distribution workers' wages vary according to their particular job and the location of the power company. Load dispatchers and other power plant workers earn an average of $837 a week. Extra pay is given for overtime. Line installers and cable splicers earn an average of $620 a week. Experienced troubleshooters earn $40,000 or more a year. Benefits generally include medical and accident insurance, life insurance, and paid holidays and vacations. Union workers often receive pension plans.

Firefighter

Education and Training
Varies—see profile

Salary Range
Average—$26,700 to $43,300

Employment Outlook
Fair

Definition and Nature of the Work

Firefighters protect life and property from fires. They save lives by rescuing people from fires. They prevent property damage by inspecting buildings for fire hazards and by putting out fires.

Firefighters are organized in companies under commanding officers. Each person in the fire company has a special task. *Drivers* drive the fire trucks. *Tillers* guide the vehicle attached to the fire truck that carries long ladders. *Hose operators* connect the hoses to fire hydrants. *Pump operators* pump water to make a strong stream of water run through the hoses to put out the blaze. Firefighters use axes to break down walls or windows so they can enter burning buildings. All firefighters are trained to give first aid to people who are hurt in fires. Between alarms, firefighters perform maintenance duties so that their equipment is in working order for the next blaze. Most firefighters work for the government of their city or community. Some work for private companies. Some firefighters have another full-time job and fight fires as volunteers.

In large cities firefighters may work on rescue squads. They go to the scenes of fires in vans that have first-aid equipment. They help the injured until ambulances arrive. In addition, rescue squads may be called for injuries and accidents not caused by fire. For example, firefighters are trained to help citizens who have heart attacks.

Fire inspectors and fire science specialists work to prevent fires. *Fire inspectors* usually work for fire departments. They inspect buildings to make sure that safety laws are obeyed. For example, they tour buildings to see that fire escapes are in good condition. They also check automatic fire alarms and sprinkler systems to see that they are working properly.

Fire science specialists work in a number of jobs. Some work for large public buildings owned by the government and private industry. They inspect buildings to see that they are safe from fire. They help plan ways to prevent fires and suggest equipment for fighting fires. Some fire science specialists work for insurance companies. They inspect buildings to set insurance rates. They investigate arson. They work with insurance adjusters to decide the amounts that should be paid to people who suffer injury or loss of property due to fire.

Education and Training Requirements

You may need to pass a civil service exam to get a job as a firefighter. You can improve your chances of passing the test by completing high school. In addition, you generally must pass a comprehensive physical exam. Working as a firefighter in a volunteer fire department or in the armed services is useful experience. Newly hired firefighters receive several weeks of formal training. Some fire departments offer apprenticeship programs that last 3 to 4 years. Experienced firefighters continue to go on practice drills to maintain their skills at a high level.

Each firefighter in a fire company has a special task. These firefighters are hose operators who connect the fire hoses to fire hydrants.

Many 2-year colleges and some 4-year colleges offer programs in fire science and fire engineering. Experienced firefighters sometimes take these courses to prepare for promotion. These courses are also useful for those preparing for jobs as fire science specialists.

Getting the Job

To get a job as a firefighter, you should apply to take the civil service test in your community. You must be at least 18 years old to apply.

Advancement Possibilities and Employment Outlook

Firefighters are promoted within the department. They advance to higher ranks by passing civil service tests. Supervisors' recommendations are considered when a promotion is made. Advanced ranks include captain, battalion chief, and fire chief. The fire chief has complete responsibility for the entire city or community fire department.

There are currently about 305,000 firefighters. Some growth should occur in this field as fire departments enlarge or new departments are formed. The outlook is fair, and competition will be keen for jobs in most large cities. Most openings occur when experienced workers retire or leave their jobs for other reasons.

Working Conditions

Firefighters work under extremely dangerous conditions. Their job requires great physical strength as well as stamina and courage. They are often required to enter burning buildings. They may risk their own lives to save others. Despite the dangers, firefighters take satisfaction from knowing that they provide a very important public service.

Because fire protection is provided around the clock, firefighters work in shifts. Hours are irregular. The length of a shift varies from one community to the next. Some firefighters work an 8-hour day shift or a 14-hour night shift. Others work for 24 hours and then receive equal time off. Firefighters may be required to live in the fire station for days at a time. They must be able to work as part of a team and follow orders. Many firefighters belong to labor unions.

Earnings and Benefits

Salaries vary, depending on location and years of experience. The average salary for firefighters is between $26,700 and $43,300 a year. Fire lieutenants and captains earn more.

Firefighters generally receive paid sick days and vacations and health insurance. They are usually permitted to retire at half pay when they are 50 years old and have served for 25 years. Firefighters who are unable to work because of injury on the job may retire at any age.

Where to Go for More Information

International Association of Fire Fighters
1750 New York Avenue, NW, Third Floor
Washington, DC 20006-5395
(202) 737-8484

National Fire Protection Association
1 Batterymarch Park
P.O. Box 9101
Quincy, MA 02269-9101
(617) 770-3000
www.nfpa.org

Geriatric Aide

Education and Training
None

Salary Range
Average—$12,100
to $19,300

Employment Outlook
Excellent

Definition and Nature of the Work

Geriatric aides offer personal care and assistance to elderly people who no longer have the health, strength, or resources to remain completely self-sufficient. These aides offer a wide range of services in nursing homes, adult day care centers, specialized recreation programs, health care facilities, and private homes.

Some geriatric aides assist medical personnel in caring for patients who are ill, disabled, or medically fragile. Aides' duties may include feeding, dressing, and bathing these individuals as well as monitoring their overall conditions. Other aides are assigned to work in physical therapy, occupational therapy, speech, nutrition, or recreation programs for the elderly. The older adults they serve may range from critically ill patients who need constant medical attention to relatively healthy individuals who require only social activities, transportation, or companionship.

Education and Training Requirements

Many geriatric aide positions have no educational requirements, although a high school diploma is often preferred. Many colleges now offer 2- or 4-year degrees in gerontology for those who plan to work with the elderly. On-the-job training is often provided, but individuals who wish to prepare ahead of time might take first-aid and cardiopulmonary resuscitation (CPR) training, as well as classes in biology, psychology, health care, and sociology.

Getting the Job

College students or graduates might check with the school placement office. Job listings may also appear in newsletters or other publications in the geriatric

Geriatric aides assist elderly people in a variety of settings, including nursing homes, adult day care centers, specialized recreation programs, health care facilities, and private homes.

field. However, you may be able to break into the field by applying directly to nursing homes or public agencies serving the elderly in your area.

Advancement Possibilities and Employment Outlook

Aides who pursue higher education may advance to professional positions in the field, becoming geriatric nurses, therapists, or counselors. Others may obtain additional training and become medical assistants. The employment outlook is excellent. The older adult population is increasing dramatically, and many people in this age group will require assistance.

Working Conditions

At facilities that offer around-the-clock care, aides are needed at all hours, so night and weekend work is usually required. In addition, aides may be on call for emergencies. The job may be somewhat strenuous if the person being cared for must be lifted or carried. It also may be highly stressful. Because many older individuals are failing mentally or physically, crises may occur frequently. Patience, sensitivity, and good judgment are essential.

Earnings and Benefits

On average, salaries range from about $12,100 to $19,300, depending on experience and geographic location. Experienced workers can earn up to $26,000 a year. Most of these jobs offer benefit packages that include health insurance, pension plans, and holiday and vacation pay. Opportunities for overtime pay are available frequently.

Where to Go for More Information

National Council on the Aging
409 Third Street, SW
Washington, DC 20024
(202) 479-1200
www.ncoa.org

Highway Maintenance Worker

Definition and Nature of the Work

Highway maintenance workers keep highways and roads in safe condition. They work on state, county, and local highways. They work in large cities, small towns, and rural areas. Their specific tasks vary with the location of the roads they maintain.

Highway maintenance workers repair guardrails and snow fences that are placed along roadsides. They erect and repair highway markers such as stop signs and signs that direct travelers to major routes. They paint dividing lines between traffic lanes. When the road surface has potholes caused by snow, rain, or heavy traffic, the maintenance crew travels by truck to the place that needs attention. A pneumatic drill, or jackhammer, is used to prepare the eroded spot for repair. Asphalt is then dumped from the truck into the hole. Crew members spread and smooth the asphalt. When it snows, maintenance workers drive trucks and tractors with snowplows and blowers to clear the roads. During the fall and spring they use trucks that collect leaves that have cluttered street gutters and surface drains. They remove trees that have been damaged in a storm and have fallen across the road. They sometimes cut down and clear away overhanging branches that block drivers' views of stoplights and other road directions.

Highway maintenance workers work as part of a crew to repair and repave a major highway.

Education and Training Requirements

Workers with a high school education are preferred for the job. They may need a doctor's certificate of health to get the job. Workers who drive maintenance trucks must have a driver's license. Those who work in large cities or on state highways must take a civil service examination. This examination tests workers' ability to read, write, and speak to make sure that they can follow and give directions. Many small towns and cities do not give a written test for the job. Beginners work with more experienced people who train them on the job.

Some highway maintenance workers take courses to acquire special skills. Some communities pay the tuition for these courses. For instance, workers who cut and clear away trees may take a course in tree climbing and cutting.

Getting the Job

The best way to get a job as a highway maintenance worker is to apply to the administrator of the borough, town, or county where you wish to work. If you want to work on state turnpikes or highways, you should apply through your state highway commission. If a civil service test is given for the job, apply to take the test. Job openings may also be listed with the state employment office.

Advancement Possibilities and Employment Outlook

Highway maintenance workers can advance from the first grade of laborer to senior maintenance worker to other supervisory positions. Some workers go on to become highway inspectors. These levels of job advancement are common to most departments, whether the department is under civil service or not.

The employment outlook for highway maintenance workers is very good. An increase in the number of new roads built throughout the country is expected to create many jobs for highway maintenance workers. Whenever the amount of traffic increases in states, counties, cities, or towns, more highway maintenance workers are needed. Job openings will also occur when workers retire or change fields.

Working Conditions

Highway maintenance workers need to have good health and physical stamina. They work outdoors in snow, sleet, rain, and summer heat. They use heavy equipment and often must lift fallen trees. Heavy snowfalls and rains often require them to work at night to clear the roads for early morning commuters. They work as part of a team and can enjoy the companionship of other workers.

Earnings and Benefits

Highway maintenance workers are paid through tax monies. Their earnings depend on the size and wealth of the community, county, or state in which they work. Highway maintenance workers often earn about $18,000 to $23,000 a year. Some highway inspectors earn $30,000 a year. In large cities and for certain specialized types of work, the rate of pay is higher.

All highway maintenance workers receive good health benefits, workers' compensation, and paid vacations and holidays. Many highway maintenance workers belong to unions.

Where to Go for More Information

American Federation of State, County and
  Municipal Employees
1625 L Street, NW
Washington, DC 20036
(202) 452-4800

International Brotherhood of Teamsters,
  AFL-CIO
25 Louisiana Avenue, NW
Washington, DC 20001-2198
(202) 624-6800

Institutional Housekeeper

Education and Training
None

Salary Range
Average—$240
to $420 a week

Employment Outlook
Good

Definition and Nature of the Work

Institutional housekeepers clean the interiors of public residential and service areas such as hotels, hospitals, school dormitories, and government residences. The size of the institution determines the number of workers on the housekeeping staff and the range of duties that an individual housekeeper performs. Members of a hotel's housekeeping staff may be required only to clean and straighten up guest rooms. Housekeepers employed at a government residence such as an embassy may do everything from serving at a banquet to walking dogs.

Institutional housekeepers clean floors, windows, and furniture. They make beds and change linens, wash dishes, and take care of indoor plants. Head housekeepers coordinate cleaners, maintenance staff, kitchen workers, and doorkeepers. They may also order linen and cleaning supplies and act as the liaison between management and housekeeping staff.

Education and Training Requirements

While some employers prefer housekeepers to have a high school education, experience and a sense of responsibility are more important than formal qualifications. Institutional housekeepers may supervise a large housekeeping staff, many of whom may not speak English, so foreign language skills and the ability to deal with people will prove useful.

Some vocational schools and community colleges offer training programs in housekeeping. These courses may help in promotion to head housekeeper positions.

Getting the Job

In large cities employment agencies specialize in finding jobs for domestic and institutional housekeepers. You can register with one of these agencies or apply directly to hotels and hospitals in your area. Also check newspaper ads for these positions.

Advancement Possibilities and Employment Outlook

Housekeepers usually advance by receiving higher wages. They can also take jobs in institutions that offer better working conditions. Housekeepers can become head housekeepers who supervise other workers. Some housekeepers start their own firms that provide domestic and institutional housekeeping services.

The employment outlook is good through the year 2006. Housekeeping has always been an occupation with high turnover, and more firms are reducing costs by hiring independent contractors.

Working Conditions

The work of housekeepers is often physically demanding. They may have to lift and carry heavy objects

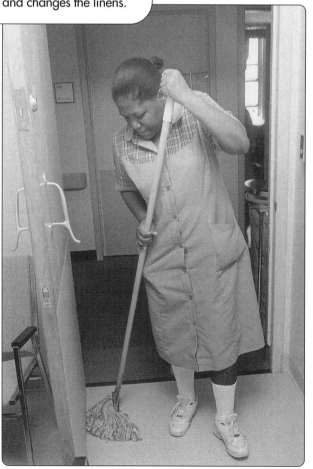

Before a new patient arrives, an institutional housekeeper cleans the hospital room and bathroom, makes the bed, and changes the linens.

during cleaning. They may spend long hours standing. Working hours vary. Institutional housekeepers often begin working before breakfast and finish after the rooms and halls are clean and tidy. Others work later shifts and may even have accommodations provided.

Earnings and Benefits

Housekeepers earn $240 to $420 a week. Cleaning supervisors earn between $300 and $570 a week. Most institutional housekeepers receive limited health insurance, retirement plans, and vacation benefits.

Where to Go for More Information

Service Employees International Union
1313 L Street, NW
Washington, DC 20005
(202) 898-3200

Postal Service Worker

Definition and Nature of the Work

Postal workers direct the mail to the right destination. Their work involves sorting, distributing, and delivering mail; knowing postal rates and regulations; and helping the public with information.

There are more than 578,000 postal workers and many types of jobs. Most jobs fall into one of two categories. *Postal clerks* work indoors and handle the bulk of the mail. *Letter carriers* work most of the time outdoors and deliver mail to the correct address.

In large cities postal clerks may have specialized tasks. *Distribution clerks* unload the mail from trucks and do rough sorting into parcel post, magazines, letters, and foreign mail. They have to memorize distribution "schemes" according to geographic areas. *Window clerks* weigh mail, sell stamps and money orders, and answer questions and complaints. In small towns postal clerks attend to all of the above duties.

Letter carriers may have residential, business, parcel post, or rural routes. They arrive at the post office early in the morning to sort the mail for their routes. They know the names of people and companies on their routes. They handle insurance receipts and registered and COD mail, and they keep records for the post office. They may deliver the mail on foot with a shoulder bag or small cart, or they may use a small truck. Rural letter carriers cover their routes by car.

Overseeing the work of letter carriers is a supervisor. Another supervisor directs the postal clerks. These supervisors are usually employed at large post offices where there is a large staff. *Postmasters* manage post offices and have complete responsibility for them.

Education and Training Requirements

All postal workers must be citizens of the United States, have a high school education or its equivalent, and be at least 18 years of age. They are required to take an examination that tests their reading accuracy and speed and their ability to follow instructions. Letter carriers and postal clerks must also be able to carry a 35-pound shoulder bag and lift 70-pound mailbags. Many jobs require a driver's license and passing a road test.

On-the-job training is given to all postal workers. Postal clerks and letter carriers usually train as substitutes until vacancies occur in their office or department.

Education and Training
High school

Salary Range
Starting—$21,700
to $22,900
Average—$34,000
to $36,000

Employment Outlook
Poor

Beginning clerks learn many postal regulations and practice sorting for speed and accuracy. In large towns they are taught how to run a sorting machine. Letter carriers work inside the post office for a while to understand postal procedures.

Getting the Job

You can ask your local post office for a job application blank and the times and places of the examinations. After you take the test, your name is put on a list. The appointment is made from the three highest scores. The remaining names of applicants are kept for future selection.

Advancement Possibilities and Employment Outlook

Job advancement in the postal service varies with the size of the post office. There are more opportunities in large offices that employ supervisors. Postal workers with seniority may receive a preferred assignment, such as working the day shift. Whenever there is an opening, a request for a preferred assignment is made by a written bid. The job is then given to the qualified bidder with the longest service.

The usual path for advancement for postal clerks is from top-level clerk to supervisor to postmaster. Postal clerks and letter carriers are first graded as substitutes. The time they serve at this level depends on the size of the community, although efforts are being made to reduce the waiting period for everyone. Supervisors' and postmasters' jobs require experience, education, and passing an examination.

The employment outlook is poor. Although there are thousands of openings each year to replace workers who retire or transfer, there are many applicants for each position. Also, automation is eliminating many jobs. For this reason employment in the postal service will decline somewhat through the year 2006.

Most jobs in the postal service fall into one of two categories. Postal clerks work indoors handling the mail. Letter carriers work outdoors delivering the mail.

Working Conditions

There are many modern post office buildings, and a major effort is being made to replace or modernize older buildings. Most jobs require strenuous lifting and moving of mail. Letter carriers need good health and physical stamina to work outside in all kinds of weather. Postal clerks sometimes have periods of pressure when large mail loads need to be dispatched quickly. They often work in groups or teams and enjoy the friendship and cooperation of their fellow clerks. Everyone in the postal service enjoys steady work because the ups and downs of business cycles do not affect their jobs. Many postal workers belong to labor unions.

Earnings and Benefits

Salaries and benefits vary with the worker's experience and the location of the post office. Entry-level pay for full-time mail-handling clerks is currently between $21,700 and $22,900 a year. Window clerks and clerks who run scanning and sorting machines begin at a higher rate. The average pay for all experienced postal workers, including mail carriers, is between $34,000 and $36,000 a year. Postal workers receive time and a half for overtime and premium pay on holidays. Benefits include pension plans and health and life insurance. Paid vacations range from 13 days the first 3 years to 26 days after 15 years of service. Paid sick leave can be accumulated over several years.

Where to Go for More Information

American Postal Workers Union
1300 L Street, NW
Washington, DC 20005
(202) 842-4200

National Association of Letter Carriers
100 Indiana Avenue, NW
Washington, DC 20001
(202) 393-4695

National Rural Letter Carriers Association
1630 Duke Street, Fourth Floor
Alexandria, VA 22314-3465
(703) 684-5545

Power Plant Worker

Definition and Nature of the Work

Education and Training
None

Salary Range
Average—$43,500

Employment Outlook
Fair

Power plants produce electricity by drawing energy from various natural resources. Some plants burn oil or coal to create steam. Others make use of the power of falling water to turn turbines and generate power. Still others draw on radioactive ores such as uranium to produce nuclear power. Power plant workers' jobs vary somewhat from plant to plant, depending on the type of fuel used and the age of the equipment. Nuclear power plants have their own specialized technology and require several specialized workers. However, some jobs in nuclear power plants are very much like jobs in conventional plants. For instance, nuclear reactor operators do a job similar to that of boiler operators.

Some jobs that are central to the operation of most power plants are boiler operator, turbine operator, and switchboard operator. *Boiler operators* run the boilers that burn coal or oil to heat water until it becomes steam. The pressure of the steam turns the turbines that generate electricity. Boiler operators see that the right mixture of fuel and air gets into the boiler. The pressure must be high enough to turn the turbines but not so high that the boiler will explode. Boiler operators read gauges, meters, and thermometers to get the information they need to regulate the boiler. In large power plants workers sometimes operate more than one boiler.

Turbine operators also watch pressure gauges and thermometers. Their equipment tells them how fast the turbines are spinning and at what temperature they are operating. Turbine operators record readings from the gauges and thermometers and check to see that the turbines are working properly as they spin to turn the electrical

Power plant workers are employed by plants that produce electricity by burning oil or coal, by using falling water, or by drawing on radioactive ores.

generators. Turbine operators shut down the turbines when less electricity is needed and start them again when the need increases. Turbine operators often have helpers and junior operators working with them.

Switchboard operators regulate the amount of electricity that flows out of the power plant onto the power lines. They also control the voltage of the electricity and check to see that it is maintained at the proper level. The switchboard operator usually sits at a desk facing a wall filled with meters and dials. These show how much electricity is being produced and where it is going. Operators use remote control switches to run generators and distribute electricity. They take orders over the telephone from load dispatchers who monitor the needs of customers in the system. The switchboard operators in turn tell turbine operators when to start up or shut down the turbines.

In some modern plants *control room operators* do the work of boiler, turbine, and switchboard operators. All the necessary meters, dials, and gauges are centralized so that one operator can run the generator and distribute electricity using remote control switches. Control room operators work with several assistants. Whether a plant is new or old, the operators are supervised by the *watch engineer,* who sees that each worker does what is necessary to keep the electricity flowing. The watch engineer reports to the *plant superintendent,* who takes final responsibility for all work done in the plant and is the chief supervisor of all the workers.

Power plants are located throughout the country. Most plants are in population centers where energy needs are highest.

Education and Training Requirements

Many employers prefer applicants with a high school education. You can prepare for power plant jobs by taking algebra, science, and shop courses in high school. Most operators learn their skills by working in power plants as cleanup workers, helpers, and then junior or assistant operators.

Many workers spend a long time as assistant operators before being promoted to operators. It usually takes 4 to 8 years of on-the-job training before a worker is considered fully qualified as a boiler, turbine, or switchboard operator. Some states require operators of power plant machinery to be licensed.

Getting the Job

Apply directly to power plants. These jobs are rarely advertised in newspapers because there are usually more applicants than there are jobs. You would therefore be wise to apply to several plants.

Advancement Possibilities and Employment Outlook

A boiler operator or turbine operator may be promoted to assistant switchboard operator and then to switchboard operator. Switchboard operators usually must have 5 to 10 years of experience before becoming watch engineers.

Little change in the employment of power plant workers is expected through the year 2006. Although production of electricity is expected to increase, the larger and more automated equipment that is used in power plants generally will require fewer operators.

Working Conditions

During a typical day power plant workers come in contact with other workers. There is usually plenty of light and fresh air in power plants, but the equipment is often noisy. Most power plants are clean and safe. However, there is much controversy over whether workers in nuclear power plants are endangered by radiation leaks.

Boiler and turbine operators spend most of their time on their feet. Switchboard operators can usually sit down as they work. All operators can expect to work on some holidays and weekends. Because there is a demand for electricity 24 hours a day, operators must take turns working night shifts. When they work weekends and evenings, plant operators usually receive extra pay. Standard are 8-hour days and 40-hour weeks. Operators may be required to work overtime in an emergency. Many operators belong to labor unions.

Earnings and Benefits

Salaries for operators depend on where they work and what jobs they do. The average earnings of all experienced power plant workers is about $43,500 a year, depending on the position and level of seniority. Workers usually receive higher wages for night shifts. Nuclear power plant workers receive slightly higher wages. Benefits generally include paid vacations and holidays, health insurance, and pension plans.

Where to Go for More Information

Edison Electric Institute
701 Pennsylvania Avenue, NW
Washington, DC 20004-2696
(202) 508-5000
www.eei.org

International Brotherhood of Electrical
  Workers
1125 Fifteenth Street, NW
Washington, DC 20005
(202) 833-7000

National Association of Power Engineers
1 Springfield Street
Chicopee, MA 01013
(413) 592-6273

Refuse Worker

Definition and Nature of the Work

Refuse workers clear cities and towns of waste materials. They remove refuse from industrial plants, institutions, businesses, and private homes, and they oversee the final disposal of waste material.

Generally, refuse workers are employed in either of two categories. *Refuse collectors* collect garbage and other waste material and deliver it by truck to a disposal area. Crews of refuse collectors dump waste material from trash containers into the truck. The truck driver starts a device that raises the refuse bin attached to the rear of the truck. This refuse bin dumps the waste material into an opening in the truck body. The driver then takes the refuse to the disposal area.

Refuse workers who work at the disposal area are called incinerator operators and landfill operators. *Incinerator operators* control the equipment that burns the refuse and garbage. They direct other workers who feed the refuse into a furnace.

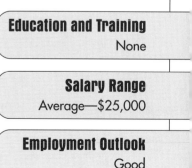

Education and Training
None

Salary Range
Average—$25,000

Employment Outlook
Good

A refuse collector dumps garbage and other waste material into a truck before it is transported to a disposal area.

Incinerator operators turn a valve to admit liquid or gaseous fuel, or they signal workers to shovel coal into the furnace. They light the fire and see that the furnace is kept at the right temperature to burn the refuse. They supervise the ash removal from grates. They may turn a valve or water line to sprinkle and settle ashes. They also may supervise the maintenance of equipment. *Landfill operators* use equipment that dumps refuse into landfills, where the waste material is pressed down and covered with earth.

Refuse workers may work directly for cities or towns. However, many cities and towns contract for this work with a privately owned disposal service. Private disposal services may have many trucks and crews that operate in a number of different municipalities. Incinerator and landfill operators may work for a single municipality or for a centrally located waste disposal area that provides service to several cities and towns.

Education and Training Requirements

Those who have a high school or vocational school education are preferred. You may qualify for the job by passing a civil service examination or other oral or written test. Because refuse workers must be strong, a doctor's certificate of health is required. Truck drivers must have a driver's license. Beginners are trained on the job. They work with more experienced workers who teach them the necessary skills.

Getting the Job

The best way to apply for work as a refuse worker is through your city or town administrator located at your town or city hall. Or you can apply directly to a private disposal service. You can also apply to take a civil service test, or you can contact the state public utility commission.

Advancement Possibilities and Employment Outlook

Refuse collectors usually start as laborers. Later they may become truck drivers or supervisors, usually after passing a written test or civil service examination. Most incinerator and landfill operators are under civil service and must take a civil service examination for advancement. Laborers in incinerator plants may be promoted to truck drivers, heavy equipment operators, or incinerator operators by taking civil service examinations for each advancement.

The employment outlook for refuse workers is good. Jobs become available when workers retire or leave the job for other reasons. Whenever the population of a town or city increases, there are more job openings. The increasing emphasis on recycling refuse may create new jobs for refuse workers.

Working Conditions

Refuse workers should enjoy physical labor and working outdoors. They lift heavy containers, drive trucks, and operate heavy equipment. They work a 40-hour week, but sometimes overtime work is required. They work as part of a team and enjoy the companionship of their fellow workers. Refuse workers enjoy steady employment and security in their jobs.

Earnings and Benefits

The earnings of refuse workers vary greatly, depending on geographic location, the specific task that is performed, and union status. Refuse workers earn an average salary of $25,000 a year. Refuse truck drivers earn more. In general, wages for refuse workers tend to be higher in large cities than in small municipalities. Most refuse workers are members of labor unions. Differences in union scales also greatly affect earning levels of refuse workers.

The benefits that are available to most refuse workers include paid holidays and vacations, medical and hospital insurance, workers' compensation, and pension plans.

Where to Go for More Information

American Federation of State, County and
 Municipal Employees
1625 L Street, NW
Washington, DC 20036
(202) 452-4800

International Brotherhood of Teamsters,
 AFL-CIO
25 Louisiana Avenue, NW
Washington, DC 20001-2198
(202) 624-6800

Security Guard

Definition and Nature of the Work

Security guards protect people and property. They keep buildings and their contents safe from robberies, fires, and other damage. Sometimes they give directions or information to visitors who enter the building. Guards work in public buildings such as banks, museums, and government offices. Many work in retail establishments. Others work in factories and offices. They are employed by the companies they protect, by building management, and by private security agencies that provide protective services for clients.

The duties of security guards vary according to the size of the building they guard, the number of guards who share the work, and the kind of security system used. In large security systems guards generally work under security directors. In small establishments guards may work alone. Most security guards patrol buildings and grounds on foot. Those who cover a large area may use a car or motor

Education and Training
None

Salary Range
Varies—see profile

Employment Outlook
Excellent

A security guard at a central station communicates with other guards in the building to ensure that all areas are properly secured.

scooter. They may work with trained dogs who alert them to intruders. Guards check windows, lights, and doors for clues to suspicious activities. They make sure that fire extinguishers, sprinkler systems, and alarm systems are in working order. In some security systems guards report to a central station at regular intervals on their rounds of duty. If a guard fails to report, the central office sends investigators to find out if there is a disturbance. Guards summon police officers and firefighters when necessary. Guards who work in buildings in which there are many robberies may carry guns.

Some security guards work at loading platforms in warehouses, factories, railroads, and ports. They prevent thieves from stealing material or equipment that is being prepared for shipment. Security guards also protect people carrying jewels or large sums of money. Some guards work with up-to-date electronic alarm systems. They monitor panels of dials and closed-circuit television screens in a central station. If any unusual activities show up on the panel, they send a runner to investigate.

Guards may have other duties as well. They may answer the telephone at night or run the elevator. Some guards ask people who enter and leave the building to sign in and out in a register. They stop people they do not know and question them about their reasons for entering the building. They also check the packages of those entering and leaving to prevent theft.

Education and Training Requirements

Employers generally prefer high school graduates. Previous training in police or military police work is useful. Many employers train guards on the job. Others provide several weeks of formal classroom training in alarm systems operations and first-aid and emergency procedures.

Getting the Job

You can apply directly to businesses and protective agencies for which you wish to work. If you apply for a job in a government agency, you must pass a civil service test. Jobs are sometimes listed with private employment agencies, in newspaper want ads, and at state employment offices. Large department stores require extra guards during holiday rush periods. Part-time or temporary work can help you get a permanent guard job.

Most employers require that guards be bonded, or insured. Bonding companies investigate the background and character of security guards. Bonding companies protect employers against dishonest and unreliable workers.

Advancement Possibilities and Employment Outlook

With experience, guards can advance to supervisory positions. Security guards who work in government agencies have the best opportunities for advancement. These guards are promoted by civil service tests. In small companies advancement may be limited.

The employment outlook is generally expected to be excellent. Jobs will be created as industrial plants and stores expand. Openings will also occur as experienced guards retire or change jobs. Some jobs may be eliminated by automation, however.

Working Conditions

Security guards are on their feet most of the time as they patrol their places of work. Most guard work is done at night. In small companies guards may be needed only for an 8-hour shift during the night. In large institutions and companies guards may be needed to cover a full 24-hour day, 7 days a week. Guards generally rotate shifts. The work may be dangerous. Many guards wear uniforms. Some employers provide uniforms or a uniform allowance. Many guards belong to labor unions.

Earnings and Benefits

Earnings vary, depending on experience, location, and duties. Wages of guards in private industry range from about $14,600 to $25,000 a year. Federally employed guards earn an average salary of $22,900 a year. Benefits generally include paid vacations and holidays, health insurance, and pension plans. Government guards receive the same benefits as do other workers in government service.

Where to Go for More Information

American Federation of State, County and
    Municipal Employees
1625 L Street, NW
Washington, DC 20036
(202) 452-4800

International Union of Security Officers
2404 Merced Street
San Leandro, CA 94577
(510) 895-9905

Corrections Officer

Education and Training
High school plus training

Salary Range
Average—$26,100

Employment Outlook
Excellent

Definition and Nature of the Work

Corrections officers, or prison guards, are in charge of the daily activities of prisoners. They guard inmates inside and outside the prison. They counsel individuals and groups on prison rules and listen to their complaints and needs.

Corrections officers inside the prison escort inmates from their cells to the dining room, classroom, hospital, chapel, and work areas. They stand guard over recreational activities. Some corrections officers patrol areas in the building or on the grounds. They check locks, windows, bars, and gates to see that they cannot be used by prisoners to escape. They count the prisoners at set times and report absentees to the central office. They watch for possible disturbances and attempted escapes. Corrections officers also check prisoners for any forbidden articles they may have in their possession.

Some corrections officers work as sentries. They are posted on the grounds or inside the prison in order to watch for suspicious actions. They look for anyone who breaks the prison rules. Anything they judge to be dangerous to the security of the prison is reported to their supervisors.

Other corrections officers escort inmates outside the prison boundaries. They guard prisoners who have jobs in the community as they go to and from their work. Sometimes they escort inmates on court-ordered trips. They bring back

Corrections officers guard inmates inside and outside the prison, counsel them on prison rules, and listen to their complaints and needs.

escapees and those who have violated parole. Corrections officers may watch over people who have been arrested and those who are waiting to go to trial.

Corrections officers are trained in the use of guns, handcuffs, and other restraint equipment. Most of the officers work in state and county correctional institutions. Some work in federal prisons.

Education and Training Requirements

A high school education is required or preferred for jobs in state and county institutions. Most states require a written examination that tests reading and the ability to follow directions. Other states give a civil service examination. A few states request a psychological examination as well. All corrections officer applicants must undergo a rigorous physical examination.

Corrections officers must be U.S. citizens. Age requirements vary from state to state, although most states require that applicants be at least 18 to 21 years old.

High school courses in government and communications will help you enter the field. Many 2-year colleges now offer an associate degree in correctional science. Courses offered in such programs include crime and delinquency, administration of justice, the court system, psychology, and sociology.

All newly appointed officers go through a training period that lasts from 1 to 6 months, depending on the size of the prison. This training may be given in the state department of correction or in the prison itself. Trainees take courses in the principles, practices, terminology, and rules of modern correctional methods. Personal defense, physical restraint of prisoners, and the use of guns are also studied. Many prisons require that officers practice their riflery skills at regular intervals.

Getting the Job

You can apply to any of the state or county correctional institutions in which you wish to work. Your state employment service may list job openings for corrections officers. In some areas you can apply through your local and state civil service commissions. There are more jobs in state prisons than in federal prisons. If you would like a federal job, apply to take the necessary civil service test.

Advancement Possibilities and Employment Outlook

Promotional opportunities for most corrections officers are good. With additional experience, education, and training, qualified officers may advance to a higher rank and salary. Advancement in larger prisons is from corrections officer to sergeant to lieutenant to corrections captain to deputy keeper. The titles for each rank may be different in each institution.

The employment outlook for corrections officers is excellent through the year 2006. Additional officers will be hired for closer supervision of prisoners in existing correctional institutions. New job opportunities will also result from expansion and the construction of new prison facilities. In addition, there will be jobs to replace officers who retire or change fields.

Working Conditions

Corrections officers usually work an 8-hour day, 5 days a week. They may take turns working the day and night shifts. They are on call for emergencies and may work weekends and holidays. All officers wear uniforms. In large prisons they must stand inspection before their daily work begins.

When officers are in emergency situations, they need to keep calm and act quickly. At times there may be trouble between prisoners. Officers may find themselves in personal danger. Corrections officers need to understand the emotional and other needs of the prisoners in their charge. They must respect the rights of prisoners.

Earnings and Benefits

Pay scales vary from one branch of government to another and from state to state. The average annual salary for federal and state corrections officers is about $26,100. Salaries for county and municipal corrections officers are comparable to state salaries. There are fewer supervisory positions available in county facilities than in state or federal prisons.

Often housing is provided for corrections officers. In most prisons officers receive life and health insurance, pension plans, sick leave, and paid holidays and vacations.

Court Clerk

Education and Training
Varies—see profile

Salary Range
Varies—see profile

Employment Outlook
Fair

Definition and Nature of the Work

Court clerks are responsible for the nonjudicial work of the city, county, state, and federal court systems. Their work is clerical or administrative, and they may perform a variety of duties depending on the courts they serve.

Court clerks maintain the records of court cases, prepare the docket of scheduled cases, obtain information for judges, administer the oath to jurors and witnesses, and take jury verdicts. They also record and transcribe the minutes of court proceedings, direct the courtroom staff, and carry out court orders. They may collect court fees or fines and issue certified copies of records. Some clerks have special duties, such as processing passports or swearing in new citizens. Court clerks in the larger courts direct a staff or department and are more involved in reviewing legal papers and conferring with lawyers and judges on court matters.

Assistant court clerks, or *deputy clerks,* assist the clerk of the court. They prepare reports and court forms, such as petitions and warrants, and process court decisions for publication. They may impanel jurors and provide information on court procedure.

Education and Training Requirements

A high school diploma or its equivalent is the minimum educational requirement, although 2 years of college or business school study is often required. A bachelor's degree is preferred, and many federal court clerks have a master's degree or a law degree. In addition to having legal knowledge, candidates should be skilled in word processing, bookkeeping, business and personnel management, accounting, and budgeting.

Court clerks are responsible for clerical and administrative duties relating to the city, county, state, and federal court systems. They maintain the records of court cases, obtain information for judges, and take jury verdicts.

An excellent command of the English language is essential, and knowledge of a foreign language may be helpful in some areas of the United States. Discretion, good judgment, and integrity are crucial.

Getting the Job

College graduates should contact their college placement office for information on job openings. Local court offices can also provide information on jobs in county or city courts. For positions in the federal court system, you can inquire at the office of the nearest district court.

Advancement Possibilities and Employment Outlook

Advancement depends on experience, skill in handling responsibilities, additional education, and test performance. Assistant or deputy court clerks can become chief deputy clerks or court clerks. Clerks can also advance by moving from city to district or federal courts. Some court clerks become legal aides, parole or probation officers, or lawyers.

The job outlook for court clerks is fair through the year 2006. Because the judicial system is becoming more complex, court clerks are needed to keep the courts running smoothly and efficiently.

Working Conditions

Court clerks work in offices and courtrooms. Their work is often stressful because of the exacting nature of their duties and the strict time limits in which they must accomplish them. They may use computers, stenotype and copy machines, microfilm, and card indexes.

Earnings and Benefits

Salaries for court clerks vary according to the type and size of the court, the responsibilities involved, and the experience and level of education attained. Salaries can range from $18,700 to $35,300 a year for clerks with 2 years of experience and some college credits. Deputy clerks with several years of management experience and a bachelor's degree can earn $63,600 to $82,000 annually. Most clerks receive benefits such as health insurance, paid holidays and vacations, and a pension plan.

Crime Laboratory Technician

Education and Training
2-year or 4-year college

Salary Range
Average—$20,000
to $29,000

Employment Outlook
Fair

Definition and Nature of the Work

Crime laboratory technicians, also called police science technicians, help solve crimes. They use scientific laboratory methods to analyze evidence found at the scene of a crime or an accident. Their findings often determine the guilt of criminals or the innocence of those falsely accused.

Crime lab technicians specialize in many different areas of analysis within the crime laboratory. *Ballistics technicians* examine bullets found in the body of a victim or at the scene of a crime. They match the bullets to the gun believed to have been used in the crime. *Chemical and physical analysis technicians* may examine a chip of paint from an automobile or a piece of glass found in a victim's clothes to determine facts about a crime or accident. They also examine hair, earth, blood, narcotics, biological tissues and fluids, and poisons. *Documents technicians* analyze handwriting on various pieces of evidence, including checks suspected of being forged, blackmail notes, and anonymous letters. They also examine the paper and other materials on which the handwriting exists for possible leads. *Instruments technicians* match marks found on the victims to the tools thought to have been used by the suspects, such as crowbars or rocks. *Fingerprint technicians* analyze fingerprints, footprints, and tire treads to help identify criminals. *Photography technicians* go to the scene of the crime to take pictures of the victim and the surrounding area where the crime has occurred. *Polygraph technicians* give lie detector tests to suspects and interpret the results.

Crime lab technicians work closely with agents of the Federal Bureau of Investigation (FBI) and with state and local police officers. Sometimes the evidence from the scene of the crime is collected by detectives, crime investigators, or other police officers, who deliver the evidence to the crime laboratory. However, at other times police science technicians themselves go to the place where the crime or accident has occurred.

The technician uses many kinds of equipment in the crime lab. A microscope may be used to examine a strand of hair or a piece of glass or to match a suspect's shoe to a shoe print. Infrared photography or ultraviolet light may be used to analyze documents and handwriting or stains of blood on clothes. X-ray machines can reveal the contents of packages without opening them, or they can be used to photograph dental work to help identify a victim. Spectrographs enlarge tiny fragments of evidence ranging from metal to a speck of earth.

The work of crime lab technicians is supervised by crime scientists or professional criminologists. Police science technicians may work in local police departments or in state, regional, or federal agencies that have crime laboratories. They are civilians with scientific training who aid in law enforcement.

Education and Training Requirements

A strong background in science is very important for the work of crime lab technicians. High school courses that help prepare a person for this kind of work include mathematics, biology, chemistry, and physics. Many crime laboratories now require an associate degree in crime technology from a 2-year college. The program of study includes courses in scientific crime detection. More advanced criminology courses can be taken either in 2-year colleges or in 4-year colleges and universities. These courses include investigative photography, fingerprint science, criminal investigation and evidence, criminal law, and court procedures.

Getting the Job

If you want to become a crime lab technician, you can apply directly to any police department that has a crime laboratory. College placement offices are helpful, and state employment offices may list job openings. Many employers prefer those who have taken civil service tests. In addition, you may be required to interview with the crime scientist who will be your supervisor.

A crime laboratory technician uses a scientific laboratory method to dust for fingerprints at the scene of a crime. This evidence may be used by FBI agents or police officers to solve the crime.

Advancement Possibilities and Employment Outlook

There are several ranks for crime lab technicians, which are set by the civil service. To advance from one rank to another, crime lab technicians may need to take a civil service examination. This examination requires advanced knowledge in a technical specialty. For this reason crime lab technicians should study the newest techniques in their field. They can advance through several ranks to a supervisory position.

The employment outlook for crime lab technicians is fair. An increasing population often results in higher crime rates in some areas, so this occupation should experience some employment growth in the next decade.

Working Conditions

Precision and accuracy are absolutely necessary for scientific investigation. There is satisfaction in preparing scientific evidence for court cases. Sometimes crime lab technicians present evidence in court themselves. They also take satisfaction in knowing that their scientific work brings criminals to justice.

Earnings and Benefits

Salaries of crime lab technicians vary with the employer. Most earn from about $20,000 to $29,000 a year. Salaries increase when technicians advance from one rank to another. Excellent health and life insurance and paid vacations, holidays, and sick leave are provided by all law enforcement agencies that employ crime lab technicians.

Where to Go for More Information

International Association of Chiefs of Police
515 North Washington Street
Alexandria, VA 22314-2340
(703) 836-6767

Customs Worker

Education and Training
High school plus training

Salary Range
Average—$37,000
to $42,000

Employment Outlook
Fair

Definition and Nature of the Work

Customs workers enforce the laws governing the import and export of goods. Most of these laws are designed to protect citizens' health and to raise revenues for the federal government. Some tariff laws protect selected businesses from foreign competition. Occasionally, under congressional order, customs workers enforce boycotts of certain nations' goods for political reasons. Overall, the task of customs workers is to protect the interests of the American people.

There are many categories of customs workers. *Customs inspectors* look for banned or taxable items in tourists' belongings and in the cargo of ships and planes. For example, it is against the law to bring narcotics into the country. Inspectors check to see whether anyone is trying to smuggle in such illegal items. Inspectors have other duties as well. Tourists must pay taxes, or duties, if they bring back goods whose value exceeds a certain limit. Inspectors make sure that the tourists declare the true value of goods they are bringing into the country. Then the inspectors collect the tax. If items are being brought into the country illegally, it is the job of customs inspectors to confiscate them.

Customs agents investigate violations of the law. They are highly trained in the field of investigation. In some cases agents and inspectors cooperate in an investigation by combining their powers of observation and action. *Import specialists* perform the paperwork necessary for the processing and issuing of customs documents. They also classify goods. They decide how much duty is owed by interpreting the

At an airport a customs inspector goes through tourists' bags to check for banned or taxable items.

relevant customs regulations. Because a wide variety of merchandise passes through U.S. borders and ports of entry, import specialists often become expert in one or two fields of goods, such as antiques or machinery.

Education and Training Requirements

Most customs workers must be at least 21 years old. They must be U.S. citizens. High school course work in foreign languages, English, and history may be useful. College-level courses in foreign languages and business are also helpful. Because a majority of customs work involves interpreting and enforcing the law, some knowledge of legal affairs is valuable. All customs workers must have a high school diploma and some further education or experience. Customs inspectors and import specialists generally need either a bachelor's degree or 3 years of experience relating to customs control. They may also be required to pass a civil service examination. Customs agents usually have at least a bachelor's degree or prior law enforcement experience, including several years of experience in criminal investigation.

Getting the Job

Contact your local Federal Information Center for information about customs workers' jobs. State employment offices may have the civil service information on applications and on job openings. Newspapers published near an international border or a port of entry may list openings. Also check the placement office of your school.

Advancement Possibilities and Employment Outlook

Government employees have many opportunities for advancement. Supervisory or management jobs are available to workers who qualify. Years of experience usually qualify workers for high-level office jobs. Many high-level customs officers work their way up through the ranks.

The employment outlook is moderately favorable. The great volume of goods being imported and exported, as well as increased efforts against smuggling, will probably result in a slight increase in the number of job openings through the year 2006.

Working Conditions

Customs personnel usually work in rotating shifts because ports and borders operate 24 hours a day. Most customs workers have a 40-hour workweek and receive extra pay for overtime. They often work outside in all kinds of weather. Sometimes the job calls for quick thinking and action. Agents should be accurate judges of character and be both alert and observant. Their work may be dangerous. Most jobs are located along U.S. borders, in airports, and near large cities.

Earnings and Benefits

Customs workers have civil service ratings, so their salaries vary according to their grade and rank. Most import specialists, inspectors, and customs agents earn average salaries of about $37,000 to $42,000 a year. Salaries can increase as responsibilities increase. Workers can expect excellent benefits, including paid vacations, sick leave, and health insurance.

Where to Go for More Information

National Customs Brokers and Forwarders
  Association of America
1200 Eighteenth Street, NW, Suite 901
Washington, DC 20036
(202) 466-0222
www.ncbfaa.org/ncbfaa

National Treasury Employees Union
901 E Street, NW, Suite 600
Washington, DC 20004-1475
(202) 783-4444

United States Government Federal
  Information Center
Phone number in local directory.

Detective

Definition and Nature of the Work

Detectives investigate, prevent, and solve crimes against people and property. Many work for police departments, and others are employed by business and industry. Detectives use modern techniques and tools, including computers and elaborate communications systems, to prevent and solve crimes ranging from shoplifting to mass murder.

Police detectives investigate criminals' actions, gather facts for cases, observe suspects, and assist in the arrest of criminals. They develop sources of information to help them solve murders, robberies, narcotics crimes, and other illegal actions. Many police detectives are dressed in civilian clothes while on duty. They work undercover and are called *plainclothes detectives*. They often go to places that a suspect is known to frequent, familiarizing themselves with the suspect's habits and actions. For example, a detective assigned to a gambling case might spend a great deal of time at the suspect's favorite bar, posing as another gambler and trying to learn as much as possible about the case. The detective might also have an informer in the neighborhood who provides information on the suspect. Having gathered enough information against the suspect, the detective can make the arrest with the help of police reinforcements.

Some detectives work for private detective agencies or individual clients. These private detectives are often former police officers, although some are trained by the private agencies themselves. Because they are not part of the police force, they have no power to make arrests. *Private investigators* gather information from police sources, interview witnesses, and observe suspects. Lawyers and other companies hire investigators to gather information for court trials and to investigate fraud, the passing of bad checks, and other matters. Many insurance companies hire private detectives to investigate insurance claims. Parents may hire them to locate missing children.

Some private detectives work as *bodyguards* for people who are in personal danger. Detectives are also employed by private companies as security guards, house detectives, store detectives, and bouncers. *Store detectives* guard against customer shoplifting and employee theft and make sure that no disturbances are created. *Bouncers* work in restaurants, nightclubs, bowling centers, and other places of entertainment to ensure that order is maintained and bills are paid. *House detectives,* or hotel detectives, protect hotel guests from disturbances and evict troublemakers.

Education and Training Requirements

A high school education is required for both police and private detectives. While in high school you should take college preparatory subjects such as English, science, math, and social science. It is also helpful to take a foreign language, journalism, and typing. In addition, you should take physical education courses to keep physically fit. If possible, continue your education at a college where you can major in police science and take courses in criminology and law.

If you want to work on a police force, you will begin as a police officer. Applicants for positions as police officers usually must be at least 21 years old, meet certain height and weight requirements, and be in good physical condition. After you have demonstrated that you have the skills necessary for detective work, you may be assigned to detective duty on a probationary basis. Some police departments require that you pass an exam.

Most police detectives are trained for 6 weeks to several months, depending on the program. If you successfully complete the training program, you will probably be assigned to detective work permanently. During your career you may be required to take refresher courses periodically to update your skills and techniques.

Because many private detectives are former police detectives, their education and training requirements are similar to those of police detectives. Private detectives also learn skills on the job from experienced private detectives. Private agencies may or may not have formal training programs. Private detectives may have to meet licensing requirements before they are eligible to be employed in some states.

Getting the Job

You can apply directly to police departments and private detective agencies in your area. For a job as a private detective, apply to hotels, restaurants, manufacturing firms, and department stores. Law firms also use the services of private detectives.

Advancement Possibilities and Employment Outlook

Skilled and experienced police detectives can advance to chief of detectives or chief of police. Private detectives can advance to senior positions in detective agencies or become supervisors of security or detective staffs in private companies. Good detectives can start their own detective agencies.

The employment outlook for detectives is good. Those who want to work on police forces should keep in mind that they first may have to work as uniformed police officers for several years. Some openings will occur because of growth of police forces, but most openings appear as police detectives retire or change fields. Companies, hotels, and restaurants increasingly use private detectives to protect their own and their customers' property.

Many detectives work for police departments, investigating criminals' actions, gathering facts for cases, observing suspects, and assisting in the arrest of criminals.

Working Conditions

A detective's job may be exciting and dangerous or routine and safe, depending on the types of assignments. A police detective working on a narcotics smuggling case may be exposed to the threat of physical violence or death. On the other hand, a private detective working as a security guard may only check employee identification cards and handle routine complaints. The work of most detectives falls between these two extremes.

Detectives often work irregular hours, including nights and weekends. Although they may have to work more than 40 hours a week on certain cases, they are generally given time off to compensate for their overtime.

Detectives usually find their work interesting because of the variety of cases on which they work. Although they are exposed to danger at times, they are trained in self-defense. At times they may find the work discouraging if they cannot solve cases or if they spend a great deal of time pursuing false leads.

Earnings and Benefits

Salaries for detectives vary widely and depend on the location and responsibilities of the job and the detective's experience. Police detectives earn between $25,700 and $45,300 a year. Detectives in supervisory positions may earn $55,000 or more a year. Generally, private detectives make considerably less than police detectives with comparable experience. However, talented private detectives who run their own agencies may earn considerably more.

Detectives may receive benefits such as paid sick leave and vacations, life and health insurance, and retirement pensions. Detectives who have their own agencies must provide their own benefits.

Federal Government Worker

Education and Training
Varies—see profile

Salary Range
Varies—see profile

Employment Outlook
Fair

Definition and Nature of the Work

The federal government employs about 3.2 million civilians in the United States and abroad. Almost all of these workers hold jobs that fall under the direction of the Office of Personnel Management. This operating unit oversees the testing procedures for applicants, wage scales for workers, and methods of promoting and firing employees.

Many federal employees hold jobs similar to those existing in private industry. For example, the federal government employs secretaries, lawyers, physicians, biologists, truck drivers, and painters. Other jobs such as postal service worker, government page, internal revenue agent, legislative clerk, and Border patrol agent are unlike jobs available in private industry.

The Central Intelligence Agency (CIA) employs specialists from many different fields. The CIA gathers information that is used in making foreign policy. Among the agency's personnel are engineers, chemists, and geologists. In addition, there are accountants, linguists, economists, and others. Furthermore, the agency employs clerical and administrative workers.

Federal government workers are employed by all branches of the federal government. Most work for the agencies of the executive branch. For example, they deliver the mail, print money, care for disabled veterans, forecast weather, and catalog and store documents. A smaller number are employed by the legislative and judicial branches of government and work as pages, court stenographers, legislative clerks, and in other jobs.

Opportunities for laborers and skilled workers exist in every branch of the government. The government employs mechanics, maintenance workers, chauffeurs, food service workers, plumbers, truck drivers, and countless other workers of various skills.

About one out of every eight federal government employees works in Washington, DC. The rest work in all 50 states and in foreign countries.

Federal government workers are employed by all branches of the federal government. Some work in Washington, DC, whereas others work in individual states or in foreign countries.

Education and Training Requirements

Educational requirements vary according to the individual job. High school education is sufficient for some jobs. Others require a bachelor's, master's, or doctoral degree. To apply for jobs in the United States, the minimum age is 16; for overseas jobs the minimum age is 20.

Most federal government jobs are filled by applicants who have taken competitive exams administered by the Office of Personnel Management. The examinations vary, depending on the requirements of the job. Some tests measure the applicants' ability to learn to do the job. Other tests measure the applicants' ability to do the job for which they apply.

Some government agencies use their own testing procedures and merit systems. These include the Federal Bureau of Investigation (FBI), the Foreign Service of the Department of State, the Department of Medicine and Surgery of the Veterans Administration, the Atomic Energy Commission, the Central Intelligence Agency, and the Tennessee Valley Authority.

Various training programs are available to federal government employees. Many federal employees receive some form of on-the-job training. They may receive additional job-related training in their own agencies, in other government agencies, or in facilities outside government. Apprenticeship programs exist for certain kinds of trade workers. A few work-study programs and summer programs are available for college students.

Getting the Job

All native-born and naturalized U.S. citizens may take the civil service examinations. Announcements for the exams and job openings and application forms may be obtained from your local branch of the Federal Information Center.

Once you have taken an exam you will be notified whether you are eligible for certain government jobs. The names of those who are eligible are placed on a list in descending order of test scores. If an opening occurs in a federal agency, the agency chooses among the top three applicants. Those applicants not selected remain on the list for consideration for other vacancies. In addition to taking an exam, you may be required to attend an interview. Some jobs are not filled by examination; in these cases you are rated on the basis of your training and experience.

Advancement Possibilities and Employment Outlook

Federal government workers have many opportunities for advancement. Many jobs are filled by promotions from within agencies. Skilled workers can move up within an agency or be promoted to a job in another agency.

The employment outlook varies greatly, depending on the area of employment and the nature of individual jobs. However, little overall growth in the employment of federal workers is expected through the year 2006. Most openings will result from the need to replace workers who retire or transfer to jobs outside government service.

Working Conditions

Federal government workers generally work a 40-hour, 5-day week although at times they may be required to work overtime. Some workers do not have standard work schedules because of the nature of their job. Employees have a great deal of security in their work.

Earnings and Benefits

More than half of all federally employed workers are paid according to a system called the General Schedule. Most other workers are paid according to the Postal Service Schedule or the Federal Wage System. Under the General Schedule system, wages are set by Congress and applied nationwide. Each job is assigned to 1 of 18 grade levels according to the difficulty of the work and the training and experience required. Workers in the lowest grade, GS-1, earn a starting salary of about $13,000 a year. Most high school graduates with no related work experience start at GS-2, with a starting salary of about $14,900 a year. Those with a 2-year associate degree generally start at grade GS-4, with an entrance salary of about $19,600 a year. Those with a bachelor's degree generally start at grade GS-5 or grade GS-7, depending on their academic record. Starting salaries for these positions are about $22,100 and $27,300 a year, respectively. Most applicants with a master's degree or equivalent experience start at GS-11, with a salary of about $40,000 a year. Those in the highest grade, GS-15, earn an average salary of about $83,900 a year.

Skilled workers, manual laborers, and service workers are paid under the Federal Wage System at hourly rates. These rates are based on the prevailing rates for similar jobs in private industry and vary according to geographic location.

Federal government workers receive many benefits, including paid vacations, holidays, sick leave, low-cost life and health insurance, and retirement plans. In addition, some workers who continue their education in their free time are eligible for reimbursement.

Where to Go for More Information

American Federation of Government
   Employees
80 F Street, NW
Washington, DC 20001-1528
(202) 639-6435

Federally Employed Women
1400 I Street, NW, Suite 425
Washington, DC 20005
(202) 898-0994

National Federation of Federal Employees
1016 Sixteenth Street, NW
Washington, DC 20036
(202) 862-4400
www.nffehg@erols.com

Institutional Child Care Worker

Definition and Nature of the Work

There are hundreds of thousands of children in institutions for many different reasons. Sometimes children need a setting other than their own homes to overcome emotional problems they may have developed while living with their families. Abandoned children and those whose parents are unable to give them proper care may be placed in institutions by courts or social service agencies. Most of these children are placed in institutions until a good foster home can be provided. Children with physical and mental disabilities may also be institutionalized.

Institutional child care workers help these children by giving them care and guidance in their educational and leisure activities and helping them overcome disabilities. Children who live in institutions are usually between the ages of 6 and 18.

Generally, child care workers are in charge of a cottage with from 5 to 15 children of the same age. Sometimes a husband and wife team act as house parents. House parents in both public and charitable institutions live in the cottages with the children. The workers give the children some of the affection ordinarily provided by actual parents. They teach the children to care for their living quarters and see that they are well fed and clothed and in good health. In addition, child care workers follow the program for each child in their unit as it has been planned by medical doctors, psychologists, and other specialists. Child care workers help rehabilitate children both physically and emotionally.

Some institutional child care workers help children who are mentally retarded. Child care workers teach them to get along better with other people by living and learning in a group. Some of these children are trained for a job and return to live with their families. Many children with cerebral palsy, epilepsy, and sight and hearing difficulties also need institutional aid. They undergo various forms of therapy that help them deal with their particular disabilities.

Government agencies and private charities operate institutions for children. Child care workers work in homes for dependent and neglected children, in state schools for children who are mentally retarded, and in training schools for juvenile delinquents. They work in children's hospitals and in the pediatric units of general hospitals.

Education and Training Requirements

A high school education is the minimum requirement for child care workers. Your grades are not as important as your interest in children, in further education, and in child care training. Many 2-year junior and community colleges offer programs leading to an associate degree. Courses include topics such as group work, child and adolescent development, the techniques of child care, and problems faced by children in institutions. Students are supervised in field work in several different types of institutions where they work directly with children. In addition, courses are given in English, social science, science, health, and physical education.

Some state and voluntary institutions send their child care workers to a 2-year college for further training. Sometimes child care workers are employed part-time in the institution while they attend college at no cost. Some public agencies give 2 years off with pay for this training. Many institutions also have special

---

Education and Training
High school plus training

Salary Range
Average—$12,000
to $20,000

Employment Outlook
Very good

seminars and workshops that help workers learn how to care for institutionalized children.

Getting the Job

Your state mental health department can refer you to institutions seeking child care workers. You can write or visit these institutions to find out the beginning requirements for child care work. If you are a graduate of a 2-year college program, your college placement office can help you find a position. The fieldwork you have done at different kinds of institutions while you were in college will give you personal contacts for job applications. These contacts will also help you decide on the type of institution in which you would prefer to work. Volunteer work with children and summer camp jobs are assets for beginning child care workers.

Advancement Possibilities and Employment Outlook

Experienced child care workers who are graduates of a 2-year college program may become supervisors of several child care units. Some child care workers earn a bachelor's degree in psychology or social work in order to advance in the field. A few colleges have 4-year programs in the child care field for people who wish to become institution administrators.

The employment outlook for institutional child care workers is very good. There is a continuing demand by institutions for qualified child care workers. Both men and women are needed as house parents and for a variety of other child care duties.

Working Conditions

Child care workers usually work 40 hours a week and serve an 8-hour shift a day. In small rural communities they may have a longer workweek and take turns at different 8-hour shifts in the 24-hour day. However, they may be on call 24 hours a day in case of emergencies.

Child care workers must enjoy children and have warm personalities. They need a great deal of patience and an understanding of the problems that institutionalized children have to face. In addition, they must be familiar with the deprived cultural and economic conditions from which many of the children come.

Earnings and Benefits

There is a great variation in the salaries of child care workers, depending on the location of the work and the worker's experience and education. Many child care workers earn from about $12,000 to $20,000 a year. Untrained child care workers may receive less.

Public institutions usually pay higher salaries than charitable institutions. Nearly all institutions offer child care workers pension plans, health insurance, paid vacations and holidays, and sick leave.

Where to Go for More Information

American Federation of Teachers
555 New Jersey Avenue, NW
Washington, DC 20001
(202) 879-4440
www.aft.org

American Speech-Language-Hearing
   Association
10801 Rockville Pike
Rockville, MD 20852
(301) 897-5700
www.asha.org

Council for Exceptional Children
1920 Association Drive
Reston, VA 22091-1589
(703) 620-3660
www.cec.sped.org

Legal Assistant, Corporate

Definition and Nature of the Work

The growing complexity of laws governing private industry has made legal services increasingly costly for businesses. Rather than rely entirely on the services of attorneys, many businesses use corporate legal assistants to handle the legal tasks that do not require a lawyer's expertise. Corporate legal assistants, also called corporate paralegals or legal technicians, work for banks, insurance companies, manufacturers, and many other types of businesses.

Corporate legal assistants work under the supervision of a corporate attorney to research background material, write reports, and help prepare financial statements and tax returns. They may also prepare employee contracts, labor and management negotiations, stock option plans, contracts, and mortgages. Other tasks include indexing and summarizing documents and drafting organization documents such as calendars and agendas of board meetings.

The legal profession's use of computers and other technological equipment has grown immensely. Legal assistants are emerging as the trained operators of the computer terminals. Litigation assistants working on a large antitrust case, for example, must handle thousands of documents. Computer storage systems have decreased paperwork and made the storage and retrieval of documents much more manageable. Legal assistants can analyze and code documents and depositions, as well as search and retrieve data from the computer.

Education and Training Requirements

Many businesses require that their corporate legal assistants have specialized training in business law, legal procedures, and terminology. There are many formal

Many businesses require that their corporate legal assistants have specialized training in business law, legal procedures, and terminology.

paralegal training programs, ranging from 2-year programs to 4-year and post-graduate programs. The 2-year associate degree programs generally require that students have a high school diploma. The 4-year programs often require that students have a high school diploma and receive a passing score on an entrance examination. To enter paralegal programs offered by law schools, a bachelor's degree and high scores on standardized legal aptitude tests are usually required. Legal assistants who plan to work in business should, in addition, try to take courses in business law, personnel management, finance, or other subjects related to their future work. Legal assistants may take special courses in on-line database searching. Research databases facilitate thorough and fast legal research. A trained legal assistant can check legal citations and retrieve information. Companies that design legal research computers also employ legal assistants as market analysts, sales representatives, and systems programmers. The National Association of Legal Assistants began sponsoring a certification examination in 1976.

Getting the Job

The placement offices of business schools and legal training programs often post recruiting bulletins and job vacancy announcements for corporate legal assistants. Paralegal associations maintain job banks or referral services and can provide a list of firms in which jobs are available. Classified ads in newspapers and private and state employment agencies may also offer job leads. Another way to find work is to apply directly to those companies that hire corporate legal assistants.

Advancement Possibilities and Employment Outlook

Because law is an increasingly important element in modern business practice, corporate legal assistants often find that their skills form a good base for administrative positions of increased responsibility. Some corporate legal assistants use their specialized knowledge as the foundation for more advanced training at law school.

The employment outlook for corporate legal assistants is excellent through the year 2006. Corporate legal assistants may find work in insurance companies, estate and trust departments of large banks, and real estate companies. Because of the increasing costs of legal services, these workers will be in high demand to perform the auxiliary tasks associated with corporate legal matters. The growth of prepaid legal plans will also increase the number of jobs available.

Working Conditions

People employed as corporate legal assistants may have to handle confidential business information in the course of their work, so an ability to use discretion is important. Most of their work takes place in an office or in law libraries, but corporate legal assistants sometimes must travel to branch offices and other locations. Overtime work beyond the standard 35- or 40-hour workweek may occasionally be required.

Earnings and Benefits

Salaries vary, depending on education, training, experience, and type of employer. Most corporate legal assistants start at an annual salary of about $28,000 and after a few years of experience average $32,000. Benefits generally include paid holidays and vacations, health and life insurance, and pension plans.

Where to Go for More Information

American Bar Association
750 North Lake Shore Drive
Chicago, IL 60611-6281
(312) 988-5000
www.abanet.com

National Association of Legal Assistants
1516 South Boston Avenue, Suite 200
Tulsa, OK 74119-4013
(918) 587-6828
www.nala.org

Paralegal Aide

Definition and Nature of the Work

Paralegal aides assist lawyers with the preparatory work involved before hearings, trials, and corporate meetings. Their main responsibility is to perform legal research, and help organize and analyze data. Paralegal aides work under the supervision of a lawyer, a senior paralegal, or a senior legal assistant. Their work differs from that of legal secretaries, who focus primarily on the clerical functions in a law office, such as typing, filing, and receiving clients. Paralegal aides research public documents, records, and law books for materials that the lawyers will use in preparing their cases. They may prepare probate inventories (investigations of the validity of wills) and inheritance and income tax returns, or they may contact clients for information the lawyers need for specific legal cases. Paralegal aides also analyze and follow procedural problems that arise in different kinds of law cases. For example, many cases are settled out of court by the opposing attorneys. Paralegal aides may research a particular case to see whether it is to their client's advantage to settle out of court or go before a judge. Computerized legal research is another area where a paralegal aide may play an essential role. Paralegals now receive specialized training in searching on-line databases so that they can operate computer-assisted legal research systems.

Private law firms are the largest employers of paralegal aides. These workers are also employed by judges and various government agencies. The duties of paralegal aides vary.

Education and Training Requirements

Paralegal aides must have some knowledge of law, legal procedures, and legal terminology, and they must be able to apply this knowledge to their work. There are more than 800 paralegal training programs nationwide. Most of the programs are completed in 2 years and require a high school diploma for admission. Other training programs are given by 4-year colleges, universities, and business and law schools. For admission to a paralegal training program offered by a law school, a college degree and high scores on an entrance examination are usually required. The length of time for training may vary from a few months for a special course to 4 years or more. Courses include law office management, accounting, insurance, and torts. The American Bar Association approves those paralegal training programs that meet stringent quality criteria.

Paralegal aides who begin as legal secretaries can pick up valuable legal experience. They may take legal courses while working as legal secretaries in order to advance to the position of paralegal aide.

Getting the Job

You should register with your school placement office, where lawyers and law firms often send requests for paralegal aides. You can also apply directly to any law firm or lawyer for whom you would like to work. Paralegal associations maintain job banks and can provide listings of private and public employers. If you are interested in a government position, you should apply to take the necessary civil service test.

Advancement Possibilities and Employment Outlook

Individual law firms usually set their own standards for salary increases corresponding to the paralegal aide's experience and responsibilities. Moving from a small law firm to a larger one may provide better advancement possibilities. In a large law firm a paralegal aide may progress from researching minor legal matters to handling tasks of greater responsibility.

Experienced paralegal aides may advance to positions with supervisory responsibility over other legal assistants. Some paralegal aides advance by entering law school and becoming attorneys.

The employment outlook for paralegal aides is excellent through the year 2006. The demand for legal services continues to grow rapidly. Well-trained paralegal aides are needed to perform many tasks that will ease the workloads of lawyers. In addition to private law firms, consumer organizations, government agencies, and the court system also employ paralegal aides. The best opportunities will be for graduates of formal paralegal programs.

Working Conditions

Paralegal aides must be mature and responsible people. Their work requires intelligence and analytical ability. Those individuals who work in the legal field must exercise discretion and confidentiality. A keen interest in the law is necessary. Paralegal aides enjoy working with clients and take a special interest in many of the cases. They may attend formal meetings with clients and be present at court proceedings.

Most paralegal aides work full-time, although those who are training to be lawyers may work only part-time. Full-time paralegal aide work consists of 8-hour days, 5 days a week. However, sometimes an important case requires special attention, and paralegal aides may have to work overtime.

Where to Go for More Information

American Bar Association
750 North Lake Shore Drive
Chicago, IL 60611-6281
(312) 988-5000
www.abanet.com

National Association of Legal Assistants
1516 South Boston Avenue, Suite 200
Tulsa, OK 74119-4013
(918) 587-6828
www.nala.org

Earnings and Benefits

Earnings for paralegal aides depend on education, experience, employer, and location. Paralegal aides with 1 year or less of experience average $29,300 year. Experienced paralegal aides average about $32,900, and paralegal specialists working for the federal government can make up to $44,000. Many employers provide benefits that include paid vacations and holidays, life and health insurance, and pension plans.

Police Officer

Education and Training
High school plus training

Salary Range
Starting—$18,900
to $22,000
Average—$25,700
to $45,300

Employment Outlook
Fair

Definition and Nature of the Work

Police officers protect the lives and property of citizens. They work to prevent crimes, catch lawbreakers, and maintain order. In small towns police officers perform many duties. In large cities there is a more structured division of duty. Police officers may work as patrol officers on foot or in a squad car. They may be assigned to traffic control or crime prevention, or they may work as detectives who investigate crimes. Officers who work inside the police department may be assigned to work in the crime laboratory, with police records, or in the communications department. Filing reports of incidents is an important part of every officer's job. Officers who are involved in criminal cases testify at court trials and hearings.

Police officers are supervised by senior officers. The chain of command is modeled after that of the armed services. In large cities sergeants, lieutenants, and captains direct the work of squads or companies of officers. Ranking officers generally report to police chiefs or commissioners. In small towns the chief of police may be the only ranking officer.

Education and Training Requirements

There are no specific educational requirements for this position. Many police departments require at least a high school education. A few require some college education. Requirements generally specify that you be at least 21 years of age. In many communities you must meet minimum requirements for height and weight. In addition, you must have good eyesight.

Because most police departments fall under civil service regulations, you must pass a test for the job. You must also pass a strict physical examination. Police departments check the character and background of applicants. Senior officers screen applicants.

New recruits often go through formal classroom training in a police academy. After graduating they continue to train on the job with experienced officers for 3 to 12 months. In small communities there may be no formal training program. Officers are usually encouraged to continue their education by taking college courses in criminal justice.

Getting the Job

You can apply to take the civil service test for police officer. In many departments, if you have completed high school or are attending college in criminal justice, you can enter police work as a cadet or trainee while you are still in your teens. You may then be appointed to regular police work when you are 21 years old if you meet the necessary requirements.

Advancement Possibilities and Employment Outlook

For each promotion to a higher rank in the police department, officers must take a civil service test. A good work record or special honors help officers get ahead. Police officers who have investigation abilities may advance to detective. Other positions include sergeant, lieutenant, captain, and inspector.

Police officers in large cities have a definite division of duties. They may work as patrol officers assigned to either traffic control or crime prevention, as detectives who investigate crimes, or as officers in the crime laboratory.

The employment outlook for police officers is fair. The number of openings will depend on the amount of funding available to police departments. The total number of positions will rise slowly, and there will be openings to replace officers who retire or leave their jobs for other reasons. However, competition for jobs will be keen.

Working Conditions

Police work can be very dangerous. In addition, officers work outdoors in all kinds of weather. But despite the dangers police get a great deal of satisfaction from knowing how important their work is. Officers are guided by the rules of their departments, but they have a good deal of independence. They must make quick decisions while on duty and be tactful and patient with people who are in trouble.

Police protection is provided 24 hours a day. Therefore, police work in shifts. Officers usually rotate shifts. The scheduled workweek is 40 hours. However, officers are on call at all times for emergencies. Officers usually wear uniforms. Most police departments provide uniforms or uniform allowances. Many police officers belong to labor unions.

Where to Go for More Information

International Association of Chiefs of Police
515 North Washington Street
Alexandria, VA 22314-2357
(703) 836-6767

National Fraternal Order of Police
1410 Donelson Pike, Suite A-17
Nashville, TN 37217-2933
(800) 451-2711

Earnings and Benefits

Earnings vary, depending on location and experience. Recruits usually start at about $18,900 to $22,000 a year. Experienced officers may earn $25,700 to $45,300 a year. Those with higher rank earn more. Officers who work overtime receive premium pay or equal time off.

Benefits include paid health and life insurance, sick days, and vacations. Many officers are covered by pension plans that allow them to retire at half their pay after 20 or 25 years of service.

Shorthand Reporter

Education and Training
High school plus training

Salary Range
Varies—see profile

Employment Outlook
Good

Definition and Nature of the Work

Shorthand reporters are specialized stenographers who record all the words that are spoken during a legal or business proceeding. They record by writing in shorthand, which is a system of using symbols and abbreviations to take notes. Some shorthand reporters use a stenotype machine, which allows them to press more than 1 of the machine's 21 keys at a time. These combinations of letters represent sounds, words, or phrases. They may come out on a pad or roll of paper for the reporter to transcribe—or translate into words— later. They may also be stored on a computer disk and can be translated by a computer program.

About one-half of all shorthand reporters are *court reporters*. They work for courts at all levels, ranging from local traffic courts to the U.S. Supreme Court. They sit at a table near the witness, taking down every word either by hand or by machine. Because their records are official, speed and accuracy are essential. During a trial, shorthand reporters are often asked to read aloud from their notes. After the trial the reporter either translates the stenotype's computer disk or dictates the notes into a dictating machine for later transcription.

Hearing reporters perform similar tasks for government agencies. A hearing is similar to a trial. The parties are often represented by lawyers who plead the case and question witnesses. *Legislative reporters* work for federal or state legislatures, taking down the debates and speeches of the legislators.

General, or *freelance, reporters* are either in business for themselves or work for an agency of shorthand reporters. They are hired on a fee basis to cover arbitration hearings, trade association meetings, and the meetings of boards of directors and stockholders. Courts and government agencies often hire general reporters on a temporary basis. Recording depositions (pretrial examinations) is a major part of the general reporter's work.

Education and Training Requirements

A high school diploma or its equivalent is required to become a shorthand reporter. The major qualification for this type of work is exceptional stenographic skills. Most shorthand reporting jobs require at least 160 words of dictation a minute. Good typing is also important. To achieve these skills, most shorthand reporters attend either a 2-year or 4-year training program. About 300 postsecondary vocational and technical schools currently offer such programs. Some states require court reporters to be notary publics.

Most business and secretarial schools offer programs in shorthand reporting. A training program generally includes courses in shorthand, typing, transcribing, medical terminology, legal and Latin words and phrases, business law, English grammar and punctuation, editing, court procedure, and economics. Shorthand reporters are usually trained to use the stenotype machine rather than manual shorthand.

Getting the Job

Your school's placement office or your state employment service can help you find a job. You may find good opportunities while working for a freelance reporter who has already built up a large clientele.

The National Shorthand Reporters Association can furnish you with information about agencies and firms that need reporters. This service is free to members and nonmembers.

If you wish to work for one of the federal agencies, you should apply to take the federal civil service examination. You also need to take an examination if you wish to work for state courts or agencies. Many states require that you take a shorthand speed test for certification.

Advancement Possibilities and Employment Outlook

Under civil service regulations, shorthand reporters must accumulate experience and take another examination to advance. Those who wish to transfer from federal or state agencies to federal courts must meet the standards set by the courts.

The outlook for shorthand reporters is good. While employment is expected to grow more slowly than the average, there will be a steady demand for qualified shorthand reporters through the year 2006. Business and government expansion is projected to increase the number of hearings, trials, and conferences that must be recorded. There may be some competition for entry-level positions because of advances in transcribing testimony. Government budget constraints may also slow growth in demand somewhat.

Working Conditions

Good shorthand reporters can usually choose the type of work and the part of the country in which they would like to work. There are opportunities in all parts of the country and in foreign countries as well.

In large cities court reporters are generally employed by one court. In smaller, less populated areas where one judge serves many courts, the reporter travels the circuit. The court reporter's work is varied because there are so many different types of cases, ranging from a civil case, such as a case involving an automobile accident, to a criminal case, such as a murder trial.

Good organization, careful attention to detail, accuracy, speed, a sense of responsibility, and an even disposition are all extremely important. A reporter must be able to record all types of speech no matter how many distractions there are.

Sometimes there is a lull between assignments, when the work becomes routine. The reporter must be patient and flexible enough to adjust to both the slow and demanding paces.

Earnings and Benefits

Earnings vary widely according to the location and nature of the work. General stenographers average $18,300 to $22,000 a year. Court reporters earn the most, averaging between $23,100 and $30,000 a year. Some reporters with many years of experience can earn up to $50,000 a year. By working hard, freelance reporters can earn more than other types of reporters. However, because they are not permanently on staff, they are not eligible for employee-sponsored benefits such as insurance and pension plans. All federally employed shorthand reporters receive paid holidays and vacations, health insurance, and pension plans.

Where to Go for More Information

National Court Reporters Association
8224 Old Courthouse Road
Vienna, VA 22182-3808
(703) 556-6272
www.verbatimreporters.com

State Police Officer

Education and Training
High school plus training

Salary Range
Starting—$22,800
Average—$25,700
to $45,300

Employment Outlook
Fair

Definition and Nature of the Work

State police officers, or troopers, patrol and enforce laws on highways. Troopers issue traffic tickets, investigate highway accidents, administer first aid, direct traffic, call emergency services, and make out reports. They also help motorists by radioing for automobile mechanics and by giving directions and tourist information. Sometimes they check the weight of commercial vehicles and give the public information about highway safety.

In areas that do not have regular police forces, troopers often investigate crimes. They frequently assist city or county police with their cases. However, most of the troopers' work is restricted to highway matters.

Like members of city police forces, state troopers often specialize in certain areas of work. Some conduct fingerprint classification, pilot police aircraft, and do chemical and microscopic analyses of pieces of evidence for cases they are investigating. Others work in special units such as the mounted police or canine corps.

Education and Training Requirements

Most states require state police officers to have a high school education. In high school you should take courses in English, social science, government, chemistry, and physics. A course in driver education is also useful. State police officers sometimes continue their education while on the job. Many 2- and 4-year colleges now offer courses in criminology and police science.

All states provide recruits with a formal training program that generally lasts for several months. During this time recruits learn about state laws, procedures for accident investigation, and traffic control. They are also taught how to use a gun, administer first aid, and handle a car at very high speeds.

Getting the Job

To apply, you must be a U.S. citizen and, in most states, at least 21 years old. In some states you must pass a civil service examination. There may also be certain physical and personal requirements. Good eyesight, honesty, and a sense of responsibility are essential. You can go directly to the nearest state police headquarters, or you can apply to take a civil service test. You will be selected on the basis of your score on the civil service exam, a personal interview with an officer, and an investigation of your character.

In some states you can become a cadet when you graduate from high school. You will receive a salary as you attend classes to learn about police work. If you do a good job performing nonenforcement duties, you may become a trooper at age 21.

Advancement Possibilities and Employment Outlook

New recruits are required to serve a probationary period lasting from 6 months to 3 years. After this period they become eligible for promotion. In most states they must pass an examination to qualify for each advancement in rank. The ranks are from lowest to highest: private, corporal, sergeant, first sergeant, lieutenant, and captain. Most troopers begin as privates. If state police officers show administrative ability, they may become a commissioner or director.

The number of job openings for state police officers is expected to grow more slowly than in the past because of tight budgets in most states. Some openings will occur to replace experienced officers who retire or leave their jobs for other reasons. Stiff competition is expected in many states.

Working Conditions

State troopers work irregular hours because police protection is provided 24 hours a day. Troopers generally take turns working on three 8-hour shifts. Sometimes they must work weekends and holidays. In an emergency situation troopers must be ready to offer their services.

State troopers spend most of their time driving police cars and are exposed to all types of weather. Like other police officers, they are often exposed to dangerous situations and may have to risk their lives in the line of duty.

Work as a state trooper can be very rewarding. Troopers help many people by aiding stranded motorists and preventing accidents. At all times they must be tactful, patient, and alert.

Earnings and Benefits

Salaries vary from state to state. Beginning salaries for state police officers average about $22,800 a year. The annual salaries of experienced state police officers average about $25,700 to $45,300 a year, although some officers earn more. Earnings increase with advancement to higher ranks.

Most states provide officers with uniforms or an allowance for their purchase. Benefits usually include paid vacations, sick leave, health and life insurance, and pension plans.

Where to Go for More Information

International Association of Chiefs of Police
515 North Washington Street
Alexandria, VA 22314-2340
(703) 836-6767

National Fraternal Order of Police
1410 Donelson Pike, Suite A-17
Nashville, TN 37217-2933
(800) 451-2711

Teacher, Vocational Education

Education and Training
High school plus training

Salary Range
Average—$25,000
to $35,000

Employment Outlook
Very good

Definition and Nature of the Work

Vocational education teachers instruct students in vocational and occupational subjects that teach specific skills. These subjects may include secretarial skills, computer technology, cosmetology, drafting, commercial art, plumbing, automotive mechanics, practical nursing, and electronics. Vocational education teachers may work in public or private high schools, in community colleges, or in privately owned trade schools. They may also work in special teaching facilities run by noneducation organizations such as companies and labor unions.

Some teachers specialize in one subject, while others teach a variety of subjects. In addition to teaching the material and evaluating students' knowledge and performance, vocational teachers are sometimes responsible for placing students in actual work settings and monitoring their progress.

Education and Training Requirements

A college degree generally is not required for vocational education instructors, but they usually have to pass a licensing examination that verifies their expertise in the subject they plan to teach. Many have extensive job experience in their fields of instruction. Some teachers, especially those who are in rapidly changing technological fields, continue to take courses throughout their teaching careers.

Getting the Job

Jobs are often advertised in the newspapers. Some teachers break into the field as teaching assistants in vocational programs. These positions are sometimes given to vocational program graduates who place at or near the top of their class. These assistants divide their time between teaching and working in industry.

A vocational education teacher works with students in an automotive body shop classroom.

Advancement Possibilities and Employment Outlook

Vocational education teachers may advance to administrative positions such as principal or superintendent, but this move often requires additional education credentials.

Participation in adult education will continue to increase as more people realize the importance of lifelong learning for their success. The employment outlook is very good because the field currently is suffering from a lack of vocational teachers. This trend is apt to continue because qualified vocational education teachers can earn considerably more money for their expertise by working in industry, and many are choosing to do so. Opportunities should be best for part-time positions and in fields such as computer technology, automotive mechanics, and medical technology.

Working Conditions

The hours are fairly regular, but teachers usually have to prepare lessons and grade tests on their own time. Teachers whose place of employment follows the conventional 10-month school year do not work during the summer months. Most vocational teachers work with students who are there by choice, are highly motivated to learn, and often bring years of experience to the classroom. Therefore, vocational teachers normally do not encounter the behavioral or social problems that can sometimes be found when teaching younger students. Nevertheless, vocational teachers do have to deal with students at different levels of development and students who may lack effective study skills.

Earnings and Benefits

Vocational education teachers earn annual salaries ranging from $25,000 to $35,000. However, some experienced teachers can earn as much as $50,000 or more a year. Teaching assistants may earn as much as 90 percent of a teacher's salary. Benefits generally include vacations, sick pay, and health and life insurance. Some employers may offer tuition reimbursement programs for employees who wish to attend college.

Where to Go for More Information

American Vocational Association
1410 King Street
Arlington, VA 22314
(703) 683-3111
www.avaonline.org

Teacher's Aide

Definition and Nature of the Work

Teacher's aides provide clerical and instructional classroom support for certified teachers in schools. Their assistance enables teachers to devote more time to lesson planning and teaching. All teacher's aides work under the guidance and supervision of the classroom teacher or school administrator to whom they are assigned.

Noninstructional teacher's aides serve as general assistants for teachers. Their duties vary with their qualifications and the needs of the school in which they work. Noninstructional teacher's aides carry out many of the simple housekeeping tasks that need to be done in every classroom. They put the classroom in order before and after each class session. They pass out and put away supplies such as paper, pencils, and textbooks, and they prepare bulletin boards. Teacher's aides also help

Education and Training
Varies—see profile

Salary Range
Average—$8.50 to $9 an hour

Employment Outlook
Very good

An instructional teacher's aide demonstrates to preschool children how to prepare an art project.

with clerical tasks. They take attendance, keep the roll book, and make sure that health records are up to date. They do typing and filing in the school office and help students fill out library cards. They monitor children in study halls and during test periods. They also supervise students on the playground and as they board and leave the school bus.

Technical aides are in charge of audiovisual equipment such as television sets, film projectors, tape recorders, and stereo systems. They set up the equipment and operate it during the lesson.

Many schools that employ teacher's aides provide 1- or 2-week preservice training courses. This training helps the aides understand the tasks they will be performing in the school and introduces them to the educational policies of the school. Pretraining programs include information on understanding and working with children at different age levels and with different learning capabilities. In addition, most schools provide training while the teacher's aides are working. In-service training sessions may take the form of workshops or conferences that are held throughout the school year. During these meetings, teachers and aides discuss problems that arise in the classroom. For example, aides may be taught how to handle disciplinary problems.

Instructional teacher's aides help teach the classes. Those who play the piano aid in music instruction. Aides who can draw help in art classes. Teacher's aides who have some college training may take charge of the classroom while the teacher works with smaller groups, or the aides may work with individual students who have been absent or need special help. Sometimes instructional teacher's aides correct papers or tests by using the correction key supplied by the teacher. In many schools they help teach reading, math, spelling, and social studies.

Teacher's aides may be employed in preschool classrooms, in elementary schools, or in junior and senior high schools. They are typically concentrated in the early grades.

Education and Training Requirements

Teacher's aides have a wide range of educational backgrounds. Requirements vary in each school district, depending on the duties to be performed, the grade level at which the teacher's aide assists, and the type of school district. A high school diploma is needed for the job, and many schools require that aides have some college background. Generally, more training is required for jobs with more responsibility.

Newly hired teacher's aides usually are given some form of on-the-job training to prepare them for their duties. Some 2-year community colleges offer a teacher's aide program leading to an associate degree. These programs include courses in educational psychology and the history of education as well as courses in the materials and methods of teaching English, biology, math, art, and music. Some states have instituted certification procedures for teacher's aides.

Getting the Job

The best way to apply for a position as a teacher's aide is through the administration office of the school district in which you would like to work. Sometimes job openings for teacher's aides are listed with the state employment office, local newspapers, or job banks on the Internet. Applicants are interviewed by either the classroom teacher or a school administrator. Usually the tasks you will be expected to perform are clearly defined for you in a job specification sheet.

Advancement Possibilities and Employment Outlook

Advancement in the form of higher earnings and more responsibility usually comes with increased experience. Advancement possibilities for teacher's aides who further their education also are very good.

A number of teacher's aides advance by taking college courses leading to a bachelor's degree. Aides are then eligible to become fully certified professional teachers. Teachers acquire certification by passing a special examination that is given to all people seeking to teach in their state.

The employment of teacher's aides is expected to grow much faster than the average through the year 2006. As elementary and secondary school enrollments increase, so will the demand for teacher's aides. In addition, the turnover rate is relatively high in this profession, so many openings will occur to replace aides who leave their jobs. However, the job outlook is heavily dependent on the economy and the funds available for hiring. When school districts or local school boards have the necessary funds available, they can hire more teacher's aides. Some school districts receive government grants to finance teacher's aides' positions.

Working Conditions

Teacher's aides work the full school day, 5 days a week. The school year generally runs from September to June. Some teacher's aides assist teachers during the summer or find other jobs. Aides must enjoy working with children or young people. They should have good communication skills and be patient, fair, and understanding. Aides must also be able to work well with supervising teachers, school administrators, and parents. They have to be willing to follow the directions of supervisors. Many teacher's aides find their work rewarding because they have the satisfaction of helping all kinds of children progress in their education.

Earnings and Benefits

Salaries vary, depending on the location of the work and the qualifications and experience of the teacher's aide. The wages for teacher's aides whose duties include some instructional tasks average about $9 an hour. The earnings for teacher's aides involved in nonteaching activities average about $8.50 an hour.

Benefits are not always provided for teacher's aides. In school districts where they are available, benefits generally include paid holidays and vacations, medical and hospital insurance, and pension plans.

Youth Organization Worker

Education and Training
Varies—see profile

Salary Range
Average—$16,000
to $18,000

Employment Outlook
Fair

Definition and Nature of the Work

The YMCA down the street, the Girl Scout troop that meets in the church basement, and the teen center just opened in the civic center are all managed by youth organization workers. These workers are employed by many different organizations, from the Police Athletic League to the 4-H Club, but they all share the same goal of helping young people enjoy themselves and grow to become responsible adults.

Youth organization workers are employed full-time or part-time, as salaried employees or as volunteers. In large organizations, such as Hillel and the Boy Scouts of America, both full-time and part-time workers are employed. Full-time workers manage the organization on a daily basis. Executive directors raise funds, develop new programs, balance budgets, plan for new buildings, and supervise other workers. Activities and program directors plan specific programs for youths and organize other workers to help run these programs.

Education and Training Requirements

You need at least a high school education for most youth organization jobs. Most full-time activities and program directors have an associate degree or a bachelor's degree. Almost all executive directors have a bachelor's degree.

While in high school, you should take courses in English, math, science, and social studies. In college you should take courses in sociology, child psychology, recreation, public speaking, art, music, and physical education. Many youth organization workers earn a degree in recreation with a special emphasis in youth work.

During the summers you can gain valuable experience by working as a volunteer for any youth agency. You might work as a day camp counselor, a municipal recreation helper, or an aide in a church youth fellowship organization.

A youth organization worker plays chess with teenagers at a program sponsored by the city's department of recreation.

Getting the Job

You can apply directly to any youth agency for a job as a youth organization worker. Your school placement office may be able to help you find a job. You can also apply to the national or regional headquarters of organizations such as the Girl Scouts of America or the YMCA.

Advancement Possibilities and Employment Outlook

The possibilities for advancement in youth organization work are good. Most workers begin their career as an assistant to a program or recreation director. With experience, they are promoted to program or recreation director. Those who have obtained the required skill and training may be promoted to executive director of a youth agency.

There is a great need for youth organization workers. However, most youth organizations are funded through private grants and charitable donations. Opportunities in the field depend on available funds.

Working Conditions

Working conditions for youth organization workers vary. Some work a 5-day, 40-hour week. Others work mainly at night and on weekends. Workers generally spend a good deal of time outdoors, although youth organization executives may work indoors most of the time.

Youth organization workers generally must be in good physical condition because much of the work involves supervising recreation programs for youngsters. Workers must be patient, kind, and fun loving. Above all, youth organization workers must enjoy working with youngsters.

Earnings and Benefits

Salaries for youth organization workers vary widely and depend on the location and duties of the job and the experience of the worker. Many youth organization workers with a college degree earn average salaries of about $16,000 to $18,000 a year. Supervisors may earn $22,000 or more a year. Part-time workers and those without a college degree can expect to earn less. Youth organization workers generally receive benefits such as paid sick leave and vacations, life and health insurance, and retirement pensions.

Adult Education Worker

Definition and Nature of the Work

Adult education workers administer programs and teach evening classes for community members who are more than 18 years of age. Many teachers work for the evening division of public high schools. Others work for community colleges, private and religious organizations, and community groups.

The aim of the programs and range of subjects vary from one school to another. However, most schools offer basic adult and continuing education. Basic education courses are intended for older people who do not qualify for regular high school attendance. Teachers provide instruction in reading, writing, and mathematics. Some schools offer English as a second language. Enrollment in these courses can lead to a general equivalency diploma (GED), which is comparable to a high school diploma.

Continuing education is generally intended for people who have completed their basic education. Continuing education courses teach specific skills that range from typing to flower arranging. Schools often offer courses in topics such as literature, history, and Bible interpretation. The courses offered depend on the needs of the community.

Education and Training Requirements

Requirements vary by state and employer. Basic education workers who teach in public high schools may need teacher certification. Some basic education

Education and Training
College

Salary Range
Average—$19,200 to $44,800

Employment Outlook
Very good

Adult education workers teach a specific skill, such as computer programming, to adults in the community.

teachers need only a bachelor's degree. Administrators may need teaching experience and advanced degrees such as a master's or a doctoral degree in community education and administration.

Many continuing education programs, however, need workers with specific skills rather than those with academic degrees. A program that needs someone to teach ceramics is more likely to hire an experienced potter than a teacher with college training and little experience with ceramics.

Getting the Job

If you have a specific skill you would like to teach, write your local director of community schools or school board and propose a course. If you are interested in teaching basic education, you can write to the school board and ask about openings. Applications can be sent directly to the superintendent of schools. Teaching positions for private courses often become known by word of mouth. Openings are sometimes listed in local newspapers, in job banks on the Internet, and with the state employment service.

Advancement Possibilities and Employment Outlook

Continuing education teachers usually begin by working part-time. They may decide to pursue teaching on a full-time basis or become program administrators. Advancement to other kinds of teaching positions may require further education and perhaps certification in some cases. Basic education workers can also use their experience to become administrators. However, there are few administrative jobs.

The job outlook is very good. Many schools that want to put their facilities to best use are offering evening classes. More employers are demanding higher levels of academic skills, which will increase enrollment in classes that cover reading, writing, mathematics, and GED preparation. Participation in continuing education classes will continue to grow as the educational attainment of the population continues to grow. Workers need to stay current in their fields as technology advances and an increasing number of adults are enrolling in classes for personal enjoyment and enrichment.

Working Conditions

Many adult education personnel work part-time. They generally teach one or two courses a week. Most people teach in addition to holding a full-time job. They usually teach in the evening because both students and teachers generally work during the day.

Sessions usually last from 1 to 3 hours and courses meet from one to five times a week. Class sizes range from 3 to 60 students. Teachers may lecture or hold discussions or workshops. Classes are most often held in public high schools, community colleges, or at the facilities of community organizations. Some are conducted in prisons and private homes.

Earnings and Benefits

Workers are often paid by the hour, and their wages vary with each school, state, or private sponsor. Adult education workers often earn about $19,200 to $44,800 a year. In some programs teachers receive a flat fee per course. There are generally few, if any, benefits for part-time workers.

Where to Go for More Information

American Counseling Association
5999 Stevenson Avenue
Alexandria, VA 22304-3300
(703) 823-9800
www.counseling.org

National Community Education Association
3929 Old Lee Highway, Suite 91-A
Fairfax, VA 22030-2401
(703) 359-8973

National Education Association of the
    United States
1201 Sixteenth Street, NW
Washington, DC 20036-3290
(202) 833-4000
www.nea.org

City Manager

Definition and Nature of the Work

City managers are professional administrators who bring sound managerial practices to government. They work to make city governments operate with the same efficiency with which successful businesses are run. Managers keep their cities running smoothly from day to day despite legislative or political upsets that may occur. Elected officials such as mayors and city councils appoint and direct city managers to create and carry out policies. While managers may make proposals to the mayor or council, they are not authorized to take action on their own. Furthermore, they do not take sides publicly in political disputes. Most city managers are employed by the government of small and medium-sized cities—generally those with populations of 10,000 to 500,000 people.

City managers direct the various services provided by the city and administer government functions. They are in charge of preparing budgets, hiring administrative officers, and keeping records. They supervise department heads such as tax collectors, police commissioners, and the chiefs of fire protection, traffic, and sanitation. Managers may spend a great deal of their time proposing ways to cut or control the costs of services. Because many cities employ great numbers of unionized teachers, police officers, firefighters, and refuse workers, city managers may be heavily involved in labor relations and contract negotiations. City managers often meet with business and community groups to explain city policies and hear citizens' demands.

Education and Training
College

Salary Range
Average—$65,000

Employment Outlook
Fair

City managers take direction from and report to city council members on a broad range of issues, including budgets, record keeping, labor relations, and city policies.

City managers try to improve efficiency by using new methods and procedures. Because they deal with a broad range of problems, city managers must be familiar with many aspects of government and public works. They may call in consultants to advise on specific problems such as urban renewal. For example, the city council may direct the city manager to cut costs in the tax collection system. After reviewing the system and considering alternatives, the city manager decides to replace the existing method of billing taxes with a data processing system that uses computers. The city manager hires a consulting firm of computer experts to direct the change from one system to another. Before putting the plan into action, however, the manager must present it to the city council for approval.

Most city managers have assistant city managers and administrative assistants on their staff. In a small city there may be only a city manager and one administrative assistant. In a large city the manager may have an assistant city manager for each of several important departments, such as transportation and education.

Education and Training Requirements

You must have a college education to become a city manager. College courses in economics, sociology, statistics, urban planning, political science, finance, and management may prove useful. However, most city councils and mayors prefer to hire individuals who have a master's degree in public administration. Some graduate programs in the field require internships that last from 6 to 12 months in addition to other academic requirements. Internships give students a chance to work in city governments as assistants to city managers, enabling them to get practical knowledge in the field as well as work experience that may help them find jobs.

Recent graduates generally expand their skills by working as administrative assistants or assistant city managers. They are given more responsibility as they gain more experience.

Getting the Job

Internship jobs sometimes lead to permanent jobs after graduation. Your college placement office may be able to help you find a job in city management. Professional organizations and journals may list job openings for city managers. You may also apply directly to the manager of a city in which you would like to work.

Advancement Possibilities and Employment Outlook

Some city managers advance by taking jobs in larger cities in which the management problems are more complex and the work is more challenging. Others go into related fields. For example, some become teachers in colleges and universities.

As more cities employ city managers, qualified people will be needed in greater numbers to fill new positions. However, an increase in the number of qualified applicants available will create stiff competition for the available jobs through the year 2006. Applicants with a master's degree will have the best opportunities.

Working Conditions

City managers work long hours to serve the needs of their cities. They work under pressure to carry out the policies and programs of their governments. They are also in a position to feel pressure from civic groups and labor unions. Managers must be available when crises develop. City managers spend most of their time in the office. Their work involves a great deal of contact with the public and with others in government. Sometimes they travel to attend meetings and conferences.

Earnings and Benefits

Salaries vary, depending on the size of the city and the amount of responsibility. Most assistant city managers earn salaries ranging from about $25,000 to $35,000 a year. The average salary for city managers is about $65,000 a year. Annual salaries for managers of cities with more than 1 million inhabitants range up to $130,000 a year. In towns of 2,500 or less, city managers average $33,000 a year. Benefits include paid holidays and vacations, health insurance, and pension plans.

Where to Go for More Information

International City/County Management
   Association
777 North Capitol Street, NE, Suite 500
Washington, DC 20002-4201
(202) 289-4262
www.icma.org

United States Conference of Mayors
1620 I Street, NW, Fourth Floor
Washington, DC 20006
(202) 293-2352

College Student Personnel Worker

Definition and Nature of the Work

Education and Training	College
Salary Range	Varies—see profile
Employment Outlook	Fair

Modern colleges and universities are such large and complex institutions that they require staffs of trained workers to coordinate activities. College student personnel workers act as liaisons who reconcile the needs of the students with the requirements of the administration. College student personnel workers are active in every phase of college life. They carry out administrative policies in the daily operation of the school and keep the administration informed of the effect its policies have on the students. College student personnel workers also interpret student opinion to decision makers in the college or university.

Deans of students coordinate the administrative staff and assist college presidents in planning college policy. Deans evaluate both academic and nonacademic student programs. *College admissions officers* interview applicants and read their application forms and essays to decide whether the college will admit them. Admissions officers judge prospective students in terms of the needs of the individual college. Furthermore, they try to determine whether the school will meet the needs of the student. *Registrars* keep records of all student grades and transcripts. Since this is primarily an office job, registrars must be familiar with record-keeping methods, budgeting, and other office procedures.

College placement counselors help place students and alumni in jobs; they also help students determine career goals and the education required to meet those goals. Placement counselors administer occupational interest tests and interview students. They set up exhibits and interviews when corporation representatives visit the campus to recruit students. *Financial aid officers* help students obtain scholarships and government loans. *Student counselors* offer counseling services to students who are experiencing emotional difficulties because of academic or other problems. *Foreign student advisers* work with international students by helping them adjust to the college both socially and academically. *Student center staff members* help students plan programs and activities. Some student centers house dining facilities and bookstores in addition to recreational facilities. In such cases staff members are responsible for the maintenance of these facilities.

A college admissions officer is a type of college student personnel worker who interviews applicants to the college and determines whether the college will admit them.

Education and Training Requirements

College student personnel workers generally have at least a bachelor's degree. College and graduate school courses in administration, educational psychology, and student personnel work can prove extremely helpful. Workers with little or no experience usually start as assistants. People with graduate training in counseling or psychology generally work in the various counseling jobs. Higher administrative jobs often require a doctoral degree as well as several years of experience in higher education.

Getting the Job

Your college or graduate school placement office may have information on college student personnel positions. Your own college may have openings on its staff. Private employment agencies and newspaper want ads sometimes list these openings.

Advancement Possibilities and Employment Outlook

In large universities there are generally several members in a department or office such as the registrar's office. With experience, an assistant may become head of the department. Further education and experience can qualify workers for top-level posts such as dean of students or college president. College administrators sometimes go on to government posts in departments of education.

The job outlook for college student personnel workers is fair. Some new jobs will become available each year; there will also be replacement positions as workers retire or leave the field. However, staff reductions are expected overall because of tightened budgets and declining enrollments in many 4-year institutions. Competition among job seekers will be keen.

Working Conditions

Each college student personnel job is somewhat different from all others. However, all the jobs involve contact with students, so workers should enjoy working with people. Some staff members combine their administrative duties with teaching. Most college student personnel workers work at least 40 hours a week. Top-level positions require many extra hours for consultations, meetings, and attendance at college functions.

Earnings and Benefits

Salaries vary with the individual institution and the specific job. Annual salaries of college student personnel workers range from about $24,000 to $41,500 for student counselors to about $47,500 for admissions officers and registrars. Benefits include sabbatical leave in some schools, paid vacations, and health and retirement plans.

Criminologist

Definition and Nature of the Work

Criminologists study criminal laws, the social and psychological conditions that cause crime, the criminals themselves, and methods of rehabilitation. One branch of criminology, called criminalistics, develops ways to detect and solve crime. All criminologists work toward the same ends: to ensure that criminal laws are just and practical, to protect society, and to help criminals reenter society as useful citizens.

Criminologists use several procedures to study crime, to develop practical preventive methods, and to control and treat criminals. They study data about crimes, arrests, and convictions in order to determine the social background from which most criminals come. They ask—and attempt to answer—certain questions, such as Are most criminals poor? and Why do some members of a social class commit crimes? By understanding the role that social background plays in crime, criminologists can study ways to change social conditions so that crime can be diminished.

Some criminologists study the criminals themselves. Examining criminals' personal histories may reveal incidents that influenced them. Because of their knowledge of case histories, criminologists are able to suggest ways to help at-risk individuals before they turn to crime.

Other criminologists study the history and theories of crime and the nature of the criminal justice system. Criminologists investigate how people are affected by arrest or conviction. One aim of such investigation is to try to find ways to prevent someone who is sent to prison for a minor crime from being influenced by hardened criminals. Criminologists may point out that certain punishments do not prevent crime.

Education and Training
Advanced degree

Salary Range
Starting—$23,000
to $28,000
Average—$40,000
to $50,000

Employment Outlook
Fair

Criminologists study data about crimes, arrests, and convictions to learn about criminal actions and to suggest practical methods for controlling and treating criminals.

Criminologists interested in crime detection develop scientific methods to study clues. Lie detector tests and fingerprinting are advances made by crime researchers. When a crime is committed, these and other techniques are used by crime laboratory technicians to try to identify the criminal.

Criminologists work in a variety of places. They are employed by colleges and universities in teaching and research. Some are administrators of large social agencies or prisons. Some plan and direct juvenile and adult crime prevention projects. A few criminologists put their theoretical knowledge to practical use as police commissioners.

Education and Training Requirements

You will need a master's or a doctoral degree in subjects related to criminology. Some of these graduate courses include abnormal psychology, community studies, criminal law, the analysis of court cases to understand crime and justice, juvenile delinquency, police science, and statistics.

Getting the Job

Nearly all public and private agencies, universities, and colleges list their job openings with college or university placement services. You can also apply directly to the agencies or colleges that hire people in this field. Other good sources for job openings are professional organizations.

Advancement Possibilities and Employment Outlook

Advancement in the field of criminology depends on education and experience. A doctoral degree is generally required for a top position as a professor, director of a research department, administrator of a large social agency or special crime prevention project, or police commissioner.

There are comparatively few positions for criminologists. The number of new jobs in the field will depend on the amount of public funding for crime prevention projects and agencies.

Working Conditions

Criminologists in social agencies generally work in offices. Those who are involved in casework may do counseling or interview criminals. Those in the field of criminalistics work in laboratories. Administrators, such as police commissioners, may be in the public eye. Because of the public's concern about crime, administrators may be under a great deal of pressure. Criminologists must keep abreast of new developments in their field. They generally work more than 40 hours a week.

Where to Go for More Information

American Sociological Association
1722 N Street, NW
Washington, DC 20036
(202) 833-3410
www.asanet.org

National Council on Crime and
    Delinquency
685 Market Street, Suite 620
San Francisco, CA 94105
(415) 896-6223

Earnings and Benefits

Salaries of criminologists vary according to the responsibilities of the job and the size of the population served. Both training and experience affect their earnings. Beginning criminologists earn between $23,000 and $28,000 a year. Those with experience can earn from about $40,000 to $50,000 a year. Police commissioners, prison administrators, and others who administer public or private agencies or crime prevention projects earn higher salaries. Those who work as consultants on special projects are paid on a fee basis. Pension plans, health insurance, and paid holidays and vacations are generally available.

FBI Special Agent

Definition and Nature of the Work

Federal Bureau of Investigation (FBI) special agents investigate violations of U.S. laws and report their findings to the office of the U.S. attorney general. They investigate crimes such as kidnapping, extortion, espionage, bank robbery, fraud, and sabotage. To carry out their jobs, they talk to witnesses, observe the activities of their suspects, do research, and participate in raids.

Because their work is strictly investigative, special agents do not express opinions about the guilt or innocence of suspects. These decisions are left to lawyers employed by the federal government. If agents are called on to testify in court, they relay the information they have gathered. Because much of their work is confidential, they are not allowed to discuss it with any outsiders, including members of their families. On some assignments they may have to carry firearms.

Agents work from field offices located in the United States and Puerto Rico and from the national headquarters in Washington, DC. To uncover facts, they use the crime detection laboratory in Washington, where experts analyze blood, paint, and fragments that agents find at the scenes of crimes. There is also a fingerprint file that they use.

Some federal crimes such as tax evasion and counterfeiting are investigated by other agencies. However, agents may be called in for assistance. FBI agents also run character and security checks on many employees of the government.

Education and Training Requirements

To become an FBI special agent, you must be a graduate of a state-accredited law school or be a college graduate with a major in accounting. You may also be considered for a position as an FBI agent if you have a bachelor's degree in any discipline, with fluency in a foreign language useful to the bureau. A bachelor's degree in any discipline plus 3 years of full-time work experience, or an advanced degree plus 2 years of work experience may also qualify you to become an agent.

To become an agent, you must also be a citizen of the United States, between the ages of 23 and 37, and in good physical condition. Excellent eyesight and hearing are essential. Your background and character are investigated thoroughly, and you must pass physical, written, and oral examinations. The written examinations are similar to those required for employment by the federal civil service.

During the first year, which is probationary, agents receive 16 weeks of intensive training in Washington, DC, and at the FBI Academy in Quantico, VA. They learn self-defense, FBI rules and methods, fingerprinting, criminal law, and weapons use. When this training course is completed, they are assigned to one of the field offices for the remainder of the year, after which they are given permanent assignments.

Getting the Job

If you are interested in getting a job as an FBI special agent, write to the director of the FBI. In addition to sending a resume and cover letter, request information on vacancies, requirements, and employment applications.

Advancement Possibilities and Employment Outlook

Special agents are eligible for periodic salary increases. After demonstrating ability and proving that they are capable of assuming more responsibilities, agents may be promoted to supervisory or administrative positions.

Education and Training
College plus training

Salary Range
Starting—$33,800
Average—$55,600
to $66,100

Employment Outlook
Poor

Openings are limited. The rate of turnover in the FBI is very low. Each year some agents are hired because of expansion, but most people working as agents remain in their positions until retirement.

Working Conditions

FBI special agents must be ready for assignments in all places at all times. They are subject to call 24 hours a day. Because agents generally put in many extra hours, they are compensated with an annual bonus in a fixed amount.

The work can be both exciting and dangerous. Agents work alone or in small groups. Agents who can accept the responsibilities of the job find it a rewarding career. The work is seldom routine.

Earnings and Benefits

Beginning special agents earn about $33,800 a year. Many experienced agents earn $55,600 or more a year. Supervisory agents can earn $66,100 or more a year. Agents may earn an additional 25 percent a year in overtime pay. Benefits include paid holidays and vacations, medical insurance, and pension plans.

Foreign Service Worker

Education and Training
Varies—see profile

Salary Range
Varies—see profile

Employment Outlook
Poor

Definition and Nature of the Work

Foreign service workers represent the United States in countries with which we have diplomatic relations. The foreign service, a branch of the U.S. Department of State, includes officers and reserve officers as well as support staff members and specialists.

Foreign service officers interpret American foreign policy to the government of the foreign, or host, country and help foster friendly political and trade relations. They make periodic reports to their supervisors in the State Department on political activities, market conditions, public opinion, and all other important matters that affect U.S. policy. Sometimes foreign service officers help negotiate treaties and agreements between the United States and foreign governments. Such negotiations are entered into to protect American shipping, economic, and legal interests. Foreign service officers help ensure the welfare of Americans visiting or residing in the foreign country.

Foreign service officers can specialize in one of four areas of service: administrative, consular, commercial-economic, or political. However, most workers are knowledgeable in more than one field.

Officers with administrative duties plan, develop, and direct the operations of their offices. They are in charge of their post's expenses and budget, the acquisition and maintenance of government property, and the supervision of personnel. Consular officers assist Americans with problems they face in foreign countries, issue passports and visas to Americans abroad, and help foreigners who want to visit the United States obtain visas. Commercial-economic officers

This foreign service officer interprets American foreign policy to the government of Africa and helps to foster friendly political and trade relations.

promote U.S. business in foreign countries, analyze and report on foreign economic trends, and negotiate commercial and economic agreements. Political officers interpret U.S. foreign policy to other governments, promote understanding between the United States and foreign countries, and negotiate agreements.

Foreign service reserve officers perform similar tasks on a temporary basis. They work where they are needed most. Reserve officers usually have special skills that the department needs in fields such as agriculture, labor, economics, and finance.

Foreign service staff members provide the support needed to operate State Department offices in other countries. Workers include secretaries, nurses, communications and records assistants, and specialists in budget and fiscal problems.

Education and Training Requirements

Education requirements vary with the level of the job. A foreign service officer must be at least 21 years old and a U.S. citizen. Applicants must pass a written examination to be eligible for a foreign service appointment. Although there is no formal requirement that the applicant have a college degree, many candidates for foreign service officer positions have a bachelor's as well as a postgraduate degree.

To gain an appointment, candidates do not have to be fluent in a foreign language. After being hired, however, they must develop professional competence in at least one foreign language before the end of their initial 4-year probationary period on the job.

Education and training requirements for foreign service support staff members and specialists vary according to the nature of the job. Foreign service secretaries must type 40 words a minute and take dictation at 80 words a minute. They must also have 3 to 5 years of experience in general office clerical, secretarial, or administrative work. Education beyond high school may be substituted for part of the required experience. To work as a communications and records assistant, you need a minimum of 18 months of experience in the communications field. You will also be required to pass qualifying tests in typing, clerical, and verbal abilities. Staff members employed as diplomatic couriers, or mail carriers, generally are college graduates who have had military experience. All applicants and their dependents must pass comprehensive medical examinations to qualify for a foreign service appointment.

Getting the Job

You must apply directly to the Department of State. Foreign service officers must take a competitive examination, which consists of written and oral tests. The written test assesses the applicant's general intelligence, problem-solving abilities, writing skills, and knowledge of history, government, geography, commerce, administration, and economics. Candidates who pass the written test take the oral examination before a board of foreign service officers. The oral examination tests verbal ability. Board members ask questions on American culture, history, economics, politics, and foreign affairs. Foreign service reserve officers do not have to take the competitive examination.

Candidates accepted into the foreign service are trained to serve as workers in a particular area of the world. The training period may last up to 2 years or more, depending on the needs of the service and the officer's qualifications. It forms the initial part of the 4-year probationary appointment that newly hired candidates serve before they become commissioned officers. After several overseas assignments, foreign service officers specialize in one area and, if they wish, may return to school to expand their knowledge and skills.

Staff secretaries may take a 3- to 4-week training course and then be assigned overseas. Others may choose to work in Washington, DC, for 1 year before applying for an overseas assignment.

All applicants for foreign service positions are investigated thoroughly before employment. Candidates must be loyal to the American government.

Advancement Possibilities and Employment Outlook

The opportunities for advancement in foreign service are good. Officers may rise through the ranks of the foreign service. Promotions are based on ratings from superiors. Highly ranked officers may be appointed ambassadors. Staff workers are also promoted on the basis of their merit ratings. If they meet the necessary requirements, they may eventually become officers.

Positions in foreign service are highly coveted, and the field is comparatively small. As a result, competition for appointment as a foreign service officer is very stiff, with applicants far outnumbering available posts.

Working Conditions

Foreign service workers travel widely and meet many people of different nationalities. Maintaining relations with other countries is highly rewarding work, and members of the foreign service take great pride in their accomplishments. However, the work is physically and mentally demanding. Workers are under pressure much of the time. They are not always sent to the countries of their choice, and living conditions in some areas are substandard. Employees are on duty at all times, and work hours are often uncertain.

Earnings and Benefits

Beginning foreign service officers with bachelor's degrees earn between $18,000 and $28,000 a year. Experienced officers with special skills can earn $30,000 or more a year. Senior officers can earn up to about $88,000 a year. Support staff members often start at about $15,500 a year.

Foreign service workers receive benefits such as paid vacation and sick leave, a housing allowance if government housing is not available, and special compensations for certain types of duty.

Where to Go for More Information

American Foreign Service Association
2101 E Street, NW
Washington, DC 20037
(202) 338-4045

Diplomatic and Consular Officers, Retired
1801 F Street, NW
Washington, DC 20006-4497
(202) 682-0500
e-mail: dacor@ix.netcom.com

Fund-Raiser

Definition and Nature of the Work

Hospitals, charities, colleges, and other nonprofit institutions need a great deal of money to meet operating expenses. Professional fund-raisers organize fund drives and solicit contributions from corporations and individuals for these institutions. Politicians running for office often hire fund-raisers to solicit contributions from individual voters. Fund-raisers develop plans for fund drives, organize volunteers to ask for funds, and monitor the progress of fund drives at every step. They may meet with corporation officers, government officials, and community leaders who wish to help solicit funds or plan fund-raising programs.

Fund-raisers begin their work by figuring out how much money the institution or person needs. They add to this sum an estimate of the expenses of the fund drive itself to determine the goal for the fund-raising campaign. Once the fund-raising goal and budget are set, fund-raisers begin to plan the campaign. They must decide on the length of the campaign, slogans and other publicity, how funds will be solicited, and who will do the soliciting. Once the campaign is under way, fund-raisers must make sure it goes according to schedule. They regularly analyze the progress of the campaign, review its strong and weak points, determine who was successful in raising funds and who was not, and plan changes in the campaign to make it more successful in the future.

Fund-raisers work either on a consulting basis or full-time for one institution. Consulting fund-raisers work for firms that specialize in offering this service. Usually they are given temporary offices at the institution so that they can meet with management when necessary. Some fund-raisers take on several small-scale fund drives at the same time. Politicians generally employ consultants for short periods of time. Colleges and universities, large hospitals, and national charities often employ full-time fund-raisers. These professionals plan and supervise major campaigns.

Fund-raisers must be able to work well with other people. They have to be able to sell the public on the worthiness of their cause. They also need managerial skill to direct and inspire those who are soliciting funds. In addition, they must have a working knowledge of finance and tax laws so that they can explain to potential contributors the tax advantages of charitable or political contributions.

Education and Training
College

Salary Range
Average—$44,000

Employment Outlook
Good

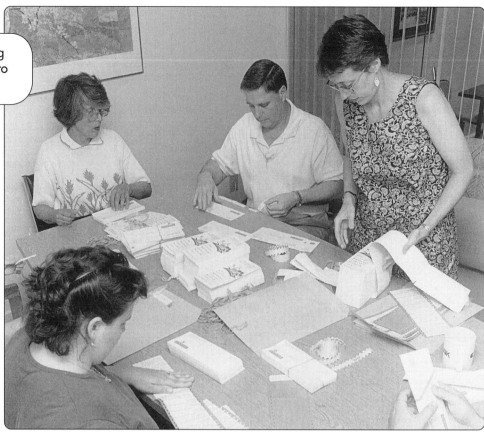

These fund-raisers are working on a mass mailing campaign to solicit money for a charity.

Education and Training Requirements

Most fund-raisers learn their skill by working as volunteers in fund-raising campaigns. However, a formal education is also important, and most fund-raisers have graduated from a 4-year college or university.

While in high school you should take college preparatory courses in English, mathematics, social studies, and a foreign language. College courses in accounting, business administration, economics, psychology, speech, and statistics are useful. Some colleges offer courses that relate directly to fund-raising. In addition, professional societies often hold seminars and workshops in fund-raising techniques.

Getting the Job

You can apply directly to fund-raising consulting firms and to institutions such as hospitals, colleges, and charities for a position as an assistant fund-raiser. You might also consider getting a job as a public relations worker because fund-raising is closely related to public relations. Your college placement office and state and private employment agencies may also be able to help you find a job. Newspaper want ads and Internet job banks may list entry-level jobs in fund-raising.

Advancement Possibilities and Employment Outlook

With experience, workers may become directors of fund-raising programs. Some become the heads of consulting firms or start their own firms. Fund-raisers may seek more challenging positions by taking on larger drives with bigger organizations.

The employment outlook for fund-raisers is good. Fund-raising is a relatively new and small field. Qualified fund-raisers will continue to be in demand in the future.

Working Conditions

Fund-raisers generally work irregular hours, including nights and weekends. They travel a great deal, especially when they are working on national campaigns. They must be able to work well with people, such as college presidents and volunteer solicitors. They must be able to work well under pressure and remain calm and organized to direct their campaigns successfully.

Earnings and Benefits

Salaries for fund-raisers vary according to the size and location of the institution and the fund-raiser's experience. Fund-raisers working in the Northeast tend to earn higher salaries. Earnings for fund-raisers average about $44,000 a year. Fund-raisers with a great deal of experience may earn $90,000 or more a year.

Fund-raisers employed by institutions and consulting firms usually receive paid holidays and vacations, health insurance, and pension plans. Self-employed fund-raisers must provide their own benefits.

Where to Go for More Information

American Association of Fund-Raising
    Counsel
25 West 43rd Street, Suite 820
New York, NY 10036
(212) 354-5799
www.aafrc.org

National Society of Fund Raising Executives
1101 King Street, Suite 700
Alexandria, VA 22314-2967
(703) 684-0410
www.nsfre.org

Government Inspector and Examiner

Definition and Nature of the Work

Government inspectors and examiners work for a variety of government agencies. Their duties vary within each agency and for each job. Generally, their job is to enforce the laws and regulations enacted by government agencies. Some government inspectors, however, oversee the work of the government agencies themselves; their job is to make sure the agencies are run honestly and efficiently. Inspectors and examiners work at all levels of government: federal, state, county, and municipal.

Many inspectors work on behalf of public health. Some *food and drug inspectors* work for the Department of Health, Education, and Welfare. They inspect food, drugs, and cosmetics to make sure that they are safe and fresh enough for public consumption. They travel to firms that manufacture, warehouse, or sell these products.

Because there are many different businesses, facilities, and organizations to be monitored, most inspectors specialize in a particular area. *Meat graders* and *grain inspectors* work for the Department of Agriculture to make certain that food products are safe to eat. They see that meat is handled and labeled according to government regulations. *Agricultural quarantine inspectors* are responsible for keeping potentially contaminated meats and produce away from good foods. Many of these inspectors work at U.S. ports of entry to make sure that contaminated foods do not enter the country.

Other inspectors work in the area of safety. For example, *aviation safety officers* investigate plane accidents. They also inspect facilities to see that the laws of the Federal Aviation Administration are followed. *Construction inspectors* see that buildings are erected according to approved blueprints.

Education and Training
Varies—see profile

Salary Range
Average—$32,800

Employment Outlook
Fair

Construction inspectors work on all levels of government to enforce laws and regulations and to ensure that buildings are erected according to approved blueprints.

A great number of inspectors are in charge of collecting taxes and enforcing tax laws. On the federal level these people work for the Department of the Treasury and the Internal Revenue Service. *Alcohol and tobacco tax inspectors,* for example, check the quantities of liquor and tobacco that are sold and collect the proper amount of tax monies.

Other inspectors handle claims and examine the use of funds. For example, many agencies, including the Social Security Administration, employ *claim examiners,* who see that people receive the correct benefits. There are *budget examiners* in all agencies who help plan and regulate the agencies' finances.

Education and Training Requirements

Requirements vary considerably. In general, applicants must be U.S. citizens and at least 18 years of age. To be hired they must pass a civil service examination. For a number of positions a bachelor's degree or specialized course work is required, although relevant work experience often can be substituted for part of the educational requirements.

Newly hired government inspectors and examiners are usually given on-the-job training under the guidance of an experienced worker. Some employees serve a probationary period before they become permanent employees.

Getting the Job

To become a government inspector, you should apply to take the necessary civil service test. Job bulletins for state, county, and municipal governments are usually available from the post office or state and local civil service commissions. For information about federal jobs contact your local Federal Information Center.

Advancement Possibilities and Employment Outlook

Workers generally advance by moving up the civil service ranks. They usually take a civil service test for each promotion. Inspectors and examiners may become supervisors or heads of their departments.

Employment of most government inspectors and examiners is expected to increase faster than the average through the year 2006. This growth reflects a growing public demand for safer products and a cleaner environment. Many job openings will occur when experienced examiners and inspectors retire or leave their jobs for other reasons.

Working Conditions

Many inspectors and examiners spend time traveling. Their actual working conditions vary with each department. Inspectors and examiners often work overtime or irregular hours. They are either paid extra for overtime or given the same number of hours off. Generally, government employees work a 40-hour week.

Earnings and Benefits

Inspectors and examiners earn anywhere from $24,800 to $59,300 a year. The average salary is about $32,800 a year. Workers receive periodic raises. Increases are also granted for merit. Federal government workers receive generous benefits, including travel expenses, paid vacations and holidays, sick leave, health and life insurance, and pension plans.

Where to Go for More Information

Food and Drug Administration
5600 Fishers Lane
Rockville, MD 20857
(301) 443-3170

Internal Revenue Service Worker

Definition and Nature of the Work

Internal Revenue Service (IRS) workers implement tax collection for the federal government. They work in the national office in Washington, DC, and in regional offices throughout the United States. IRS personnel hold a number of professional positions. *Internal revenue agents* are accountants. They examine the tax returns and accounting records of business and individual taxpayers to determine how much tax money is owed. Agents may question individual taxpayers or survey the accounting books of large enterprises. Several agents may cooperate on complex cases. Agents also advise taxpayers on accounting methods and assist government attorneys involved in tax cases.

Unlike auditors in business, IRS *tax auditors* are not accountants. Trained as experts in IRS regulations, they examine tax returns in cases where adherence to tax regulations is at issue. *Internal auditors* are accountants. They audit the operations of the IRS itself. *Revenue officers* collect delinquent, or late, taxes. *Special agents* investigate cases of suspected tax fraud and advise government attorneys of their findings.

Some IRS workers are lawyers. *Tax law specialists* interpret federal tax laws. They prepare informational and instructional publications for taxpayers and IRS workers. Tax law specialists are employed only in Washington, DC. *Estate tax attorneys* interpret laws relating to estate and gift taxes.

Education and Training
College plus training

Salary Range
Starting—$21,000
to $27,000
Average—$34,000
to $45,000

Employment Outlook
Good

Education and Training Requirements

Requirements vary, depending on the specific position. However, all professional IRS workers need at least a bachelor's degree. Internal revenue agents, internal auditors, and special agents need a background in accounting. Business courses are useful for tax auditors. Tax law specialists and estate tax attorneys need law degrees. To learn about the current requirements for specific job titles, you should contact the IRS recruitment office in the city in which you want to work. All IRS workers receive both formal and on-the-job training after they are hired.

Getting the Job

You may apply directly to the IRS recruitment office in the city in which you would like to work. In addition, you may need to take the federal civil service examination.

Advancement Possibilities and Employment Outlook

IRS workers can advance with further education and experience. Many go into administrative work. Internal revenue agents with a master's degree in accounting earn higher salaries. They can also go into private tax work. The employment outlook is generally good. Because the volume of tax returns grows larger each year, qualified workers are in demand.

Working Conditions

Internal revenue agents and special agents spend time both in the office and in the field. Meeting a wide variety of people is part of the job. Other IRS personnel work in the office and handle a great deal of paperwork. Tax work demands care, attention to detail, and a responsible attitude. A 40-hour workweek is standard.

Earnings and Benefits

Beginning internal revenue agents earn between $21,000 and $27,000 a year, depending on their academic record and experience. Experienced agents average about $34,000 to $45,000 a year. Benefits include paid holidays and vacations of 2 to 5 weeks, health and life insurance, and retirement plans.

Judge

Education and Training
Advanced degree

Salary Range
Varies—see profile

Employment Outlook
Fair

Definition and Nature of the Work

Judges administer federal, state, and local laws by overseeing the legal process in civil and criminal court cases. They preside over trials and hearings and rule on the admissibility of evidence. Judges also monitor the testimony of witnesses, settle disputes between counsels for the prosecution and the defense, and enforce rules and procedures. When standard procedures do not already exist, judges establish new rules based on their own knowledge of the law. They must ensure that all proceedings are fair and just and that they protect the legal rights of everyone involved.

Judges often conduct pretrial hearings to determine if the evidence warrants a trial. In criminal cases they must decide whether to hold the defendant in jail pending the trial or to set bail and other conditions for release. If the defendant

A judge confers with two lawyers over the admissibility of evidence. Judges administer federal, state, and local laws in civil and criminal court cases.

is found guilty, the judge is responsible for pronouncing the sentence. The judge must also instruct jurors on their duties and advise them of applicable laws. In nonjury cases the judge determines the verdict.

Outside the courtroom, judges work in their private offices, called chambers, where they read legal briefs and motions, research legal issues, hold hearings with lawyers, and write opinions. They also manage their courts' operations, which includes overseeing the administrative and clerical personnel.

There are different types of judges, whose duties vary depending on their jurisdictions and powers. Federal and state *general trial court judges* have jurisdiction over any case in their system. *Administrative law judges* are employed by government agencies to rule on appeals of such matters as an individual's eligibility for workers' compensation or the enforcement of health and safety regulations. *Appellate court judges* have the power to overrule decisions made by general trial court or administrative law judges if they find legal errors or a contradictory legal precedent. *Magistrates,* or *municipal court judges,* form the majority of state court judges. Most of their work involves small-claims cases, misdemeanors, and pretrial hearings.

Education and Training Requirements

Almost all judges have a law degree and several years of legal experience. Whereas many states permit nonlawyers to be administrative law judges and to hold limited-jurisdiction judgeships, a law degree is preferred. All federal and state trial and appellate court judges and administrative law judges must be lawyers. In addition, federal administrative law judges must pass an examination administered by the U.S. Office of Personnel Management.

Getting the Job

Judges are either appointed or elected to serve in federal, state, or municipal courts. The president, with Senate approval, appoints federal judges for life. The various federal agencies appoint federal administrative law judges, generally for life. About half of all state judges are appointed; the other half are chosen in statewide elections. Most state and municipal judges serve fixed terms. Limited-jurisdiction judges usually serve a term of 4 to 6 years, while some appellate court judges serve terms as long as 14 years.

Advancement Possibilities and Employment Outlook

Judges advance by moving into judgeships that extend their jurisdictions and powers. Administrative law judges may become trial court judges, then appellate court judges. They may eventually be elected or appointed to a state's highest court or, in a few cases, to the U.S. Supreme Court.

Employment opportunities for judges will be fair through the year 2006. Although public concerns about crime and the need for justice are likely to increase the demand for judges, cuts in government spending will slow job growth. Most job openings will be created because of the trend toward early retirement.

Working Conditions

Many judges work a standard 40-hour week, but about a third work more than 50 hours a week. Judges who preside over small-claims or family courts may work evening hours. Criminal arraignments may be held at any time.

Earnings and Benefits

Judges' annual salaries vary according to the type of judgeship. The average for full-time federal administrative law judges is $94,800; magistrates, $122,900; federal district court and claims court judges, $133,600; circuit court judges, $141,700; associate justices of the U.S. Supreme Court, $164,100; chief justice, $171,500.

Associate justices of the states' highest courts receive annual salaries ranging from $68,900 to $133,600. State intermediate appellate court judges receive annual salaries ranging from $79,400 to $124,200. Benefits for most judges include health and life insurance and a retirement plan.

Where to Go for More Information

American Bar Association
750 North Lake Shore Drive
Chicago, IL 60611-6281
(312) 988-5000
www.abanet.com

American Judges Association
National Center for State Courts
300 Newport Avenue
P.O. Box 8798
Williamsburg, VA 23187-8798
(757) 259-1841

Lawyer

Education and Training
Advanced degree

Salary Range
Varies—see profile

Employment Outlook
Good

Definition and Nature of the Work

Lawyers serve as both advocates and advisers. As advocates, they represent their clients in court by presenting supportive evidence. As advisers, they counsel their clients on their legal rights and obligations. Lawyers—also called attorneys and counsels—are experts in the law and its applications. They can interpret laws, apply laws to specific situations, and draft new laws. Lawyers draw up legal documents, handle out-of-court settlements, and represent their clients during trial. They may spend much of their time preparing arguments—both written briefs and oral arguments—to be presented in court. Much of their work involves researching precedents, which are earlier interpretations of a law and the history of judicial decisions based on that law. Lawyers use precedents to help support their cases in court. Many resources—from law libraries and public documents to computer databases and the Internet—are available to lawyers for research.

Many lawyers are specialists in certain areas of legal work. Criminal lawyers, for example, are hired by people facing prosecution for a crime. Public defenders are employed by the government to represent people who cannot afford to pay lawyers.

Civil law concerns disputes that do not involve criminal misconduct. Divorce suits and damages suits fall under civil law. Some lawyers handle only certain types of civil cases. Labor law concerns disputes between management and unionized workers. Patent law concerns disputes over the rights to inventions. International law is the system of treaties and informal agreements that govern nations' dealings with one another. Attorneys who practice real estate law handle the details of transactions that involve buying, selling, renting, and developing land and buildings.

Some lawyers practice corporate law. These lawyers advise corporations on their rights, responsibilities, and obligations in business transactions. They may also represent their companies in government investigations and hearings.

Most lawyers have private practices. They handle a wide range of legal problems. Some work for law partnerships or firms. Lawyers may also find employment with corporations and with federal, state, and local government agencies. Some lawyers become district attorneys or judges. Others teach law. Lawyers often enter other fields, such as politics, in which a legal background is helpful.

In addition to representing clients in a court of law, lawyers draw up legal documents and handle out-of-court settlements. They spend much of their time preparing arguments and researching precedents.

Education and Training Requirements

Most lawyers obtain a college degree and a law school degree. Helpful college courses include English, history, political science, economics, and social science. You may want to major in engineering if you hope to be a patent attorney, or in accounting if you are planning to be a tax lawyer.

Occasionally, students are offered early admission to law school after 2 or 3 years of college. But most students complete college before going on to complete 3 years of law school. A high school diploma, a college degree, and a good LSAT (Law School Aptitude Test) score are required for admission to law school. Law school courses include classes in contracts, property law, criminal law, and constitutional law. In the last 2 years of law school, students specialize in the areas of law in which they hope to work. Law school graduates may spend several months studying for the bar examination.

In order to practice law you must be admitted to the bar, or organization of lawyers, in the state in which you want to practice. In most states admission to the bar requires graduating from law school and passing the bar examination. In some states you are permitted to take the bar examination if you have substituted legal work experience for formal training. If you do not attend law school, you must study law on your own to prepare for the bar examination. In certain states graduates of "preferential" law schools located in the state may be admitted to the bar without taking the examination. Some state bars have cooperative arrangements with other states that enable lawyers who are members of one state bar to practice in another state without taking that state's bar exam.

Getting the Job

Law school placement offices can help graduates find jobs. Many law firms and corporations send representatives to law schools to recruit graduating students. Part-time or summer jobs during law school sometimes lead to permanent jobs after graduation. Students with good grades and students who have worked on the law reviews published by each law school have the best chance to be hired by top law firms. If you are interested in working for the government, arrange to take the necessary civil service test. Many corporations, including insurance companies, banks, accounting firms, and manufacturers, employ lawyers. Check the want ads of your local newspaper or job banks on the Internet for current openings.

Advancement Possibilities and Employment Outlook

Most beginning lawyers start in salaried positions as associates in law firms or as research assistants or law clerks to experienced lawyers or judges. After several years of experience, lawyers may become partners in their firms or set up their own practices. Some lawyers go into politics or become judges. Some become prosecutors or are elected district attorney.

Currently, about 622,000 lawyers are employed nationwide. The demand for lawyers will increase through the year 2006. However, with so many people entering the profession, admission to top law schools is difficult, and competition for available jobs is keen. Lawyers who want to work for law firms will find the best opportunities in big cities, while those who are interested in setting up their own practices will find more opportunities in small towns or suburban areas.

Working Conditions

Lawyers often work long hours when they are doing research and preparing for court cases. Lawyers in private practice can schedule their own workloads. Those who work for law firms are assigned cases and must often work overtime to prepare for court or to draw up legal documents. Lawyers are often involved in civic and community affairs. All lawyers must spend some time keeping up with new laws and court decisions in their areas of interest.

Earnings and Benefits

Many lawyers entering practice in some large law firms earn starting salaries ranging from about $30,000 to more than $50,000 a year. Beginning lawyers who are employed by the federal government start at salaries ranging from $27,800 to $33,600 a year, depending on their qualifications.

Lawyers who start their own practices right after graduating from law school generally earn very little for the first few years. After they get some experience and build their businesses, they can do quite well. The most experienced lawyers can earn anywhere between $130,000 and $1 million a year. They can charge yearly fees, or retainers, with extra charges for court appearances or special work. Sometimes they charge hourly fees or work on a percentage basis when lawsuits or estates are involved.

Associates in law firms work on a salary basis and receive raises as they take on more responsibilities. After some years of experience, they may become partners in their firms and receive a percentage of the firm's profits. Lawyers generally receive paid holidays and vacations, health and life insurance, and pension plans. Those in private practice must make their own insurance and retirement arrangements.

Where to Go for More Information

American Bar Association
750 North Lake Shore Drive
Chicago, IL 60611-6281
(312) 988-5000
www.abanet.com

Association of Trial Lawyers of America
1050 Thirty-first Street, NW
Washington, DC 20007
(202) 965-3500

National Association of Women Lawyers
American Bar Center
750 North Lake Shore Drive
Chicago, IL 60611
(312) 988-6186

Lawyer, Corporate

Definition and Nature of the Work

Corporate lawyers advise their clients or employers on their legal rights and obligations. As advocates, they may represent companies in both criminal and civil court cases. A self-employed corporate lawyer may advise several corporate clients. A corporate lawyer may also work in-house as a full-time employee of one company.

Whether serving as in-house or outside counsels, corporate lawyers are hired to keep a company out of trouble by anticipating and helping circumvent problems. They also keep their clients up to date on new business laws and regulations. Corporate lawyers advise on such matters as labor relations, employee contracts, tax issues, suits against the corporation, employee injury, patents, and contracts with suppliers of raw materials.

The head of a corporation's legal department may be called the general counsel and hold vice presidential status. The counsel is supported by legal staff.

Education and Training Requirements

A high school diploma, a college degree, and 3 years of law school are minimum requirements for work as a corporate lawyer. All law students take core courses in corporate law, trusts, tax, and insurance law. However, those interested in a corporate law specialty should also take relevant electives, such as creditors' rights, trade regulations, commercial transactions, and trial advocacy. To practice law, graduates must be admitted to the bar in the state in which they want to practice. In most states, admission to the bar requires graduating from law school and passing the bar examination.

Getting the Job

Job experience during law school will prove helpful for job hunting later. Typing briefs, working in the law school library, or searching records as a junior court clerk will give you job contacts and a firsthand view of the legal world. Many corporations send representatives to law schools to recruit graduating students. Check law journals and newspaper ads for corporate law vacancies.

Advancement Possibilities and Employment Outlook

The job outlook for corporate lawyers is good through the year 2006. Corporations are eager to protect themselves from skyrocketing damage suits, so it is worth their while to employ a team of legal advisers to keep them from expensive litigation. Corporate experience may later lead to a lucrative outside practice advising a number of corporate clients.

Working Conditions

Corporate lawyers are usually assigned their own offices with their own secretaries and access to legal research assistants and a legal library. They often work long hours, especially when they are preparing court cases. Lawyers who are employed by corporations with district branches may travel to various locations to investigate legal problems.

Education and Training
Advanced degree

Salary Range
Average—$50,000
to $80,000

Employment Outlook
Good

Earnings and Benefits

Average earnings range from about $50,000 to $80,000 a year for corporate lawyers. With experience and specialization, earnings can increase to $100,000 or more a year for a general counsel. Benefits for corporate lawyers usually include pensions, paid vacations and holidays, and health insurance.

Lawyer, Public Service

Education and Training
Advanced degree

Salary Range
Varies—see profile

Employment Outlook
Very good

Definition and Nature of the Work

Lawyers who work in public service may specialize in one of several areas, such as legal aid, government law, or environmental law. *Legal aid lawyers* offer legal services to people who cannot afford to pay for them. These services include giving legal advice; drawing up legal documents, such as contracts and wills; and representing the client in court proceedings. Legal aid lawyers may also work as legal consultants for public-interest organizations, such as the American Civil Liberties Union (ACLU) and the National Association for the Advancement of Colored People (NAACP).

Many lawyers work for state, federal, and local government agencies. *Government lawyers* draft regulations to implement laws, prosecute criminals, or work as judges and magistrates in the courts.

Environmental lawyers assist community groups in preparing injunctions against companies whose activities threaten environmental standards. Environmental lawyers are also consulted on major real estate transactions because buyers and lenders fear inheriting cleanup costs from previous toxic leaks or asbestos in buildings.

Education and Training Requirements

A high school diploma, a college degree, and a good LSAT (Law School Aptitude Test) score are required for admission to law school. Law school training usually takes 3 years and requires courses such as contracts, criminal law, and property law. The second and third years may be devoted to specialized courses for law in the public service sector. These include constitutional law, family law, and workers' compensation. Environmental lawyers should also take courses in environmental law and have a good technical grasp of environmental science.

To practice law, you must be admitted to the bar in the state in which you want to practice. In most states admission to the bar requires graduation from law school and passing the bar examination.

Getting the Job

During law training, students can assist attorneys undertaking pro bono work (services donated for the public good). Many law firms and government agencies send representatives to law schools to recruit graduating students. Students with good grades and those who have worked on law reviews published by law schools have the best chance to be hired. A civil service test is required for government jobs.

Two public service lawyers consult on a case. They work as legal consultants for public interest organizations.

Advancement Possibilities and Employment Outlook

Most public agency lawyers start as research assistants or law clerks to experienced lawyers or judges. After several years of experience, they may become district attorneys or heads of the legal department in a state or federal agency. From there, they may move to private law firms and use the valuable expertise and contacts they have gained in the public arena.

In recent years there has been a boom in environmental law, and there are now more than 14,000 lawyers in the field. The boom is expected to continue because of renewed attention to air pollution and landfill problems. Some environmental lawyers work for private law firms and build up the staff and reputation of the environmental department. Others work for the Environmental Protection Agency and such organizations as the Sierra Club and the Natural Resources Defense Council.

Working Conditions

Public service lawyers may be required to work long hours, especially during emergency situations. Outside of working hours, lawyers must spend time keeping up with new laws and court decisions in their areas of interest. Public service lawyers may also have to travel to carry out their legal duties in certain situations.

Earnings and Benefits

Public service lawyers may make a financial sacrifice when they accept jobs in government agencies or legal aid offices. Environmental lawyers earn only 55 to 80 percent of the standard $175 to $200 an hour received by other specialty lawyers. Salaries for government lawyers, for example, average about $62,000 a year. They also receive paid vacations and holidays, health and life insurance, and pension benefits.

Where to Go for More Information

American Bar Association
750 North Lake Shore Drive
Chicago, IL 60611
(312) 988-5000
www.abanet.com

Librarian, Public

Definition and Nature of the Work

Public librarians make information available to the community they serve. This information can be in the form of books, books on tape, compact discs, government documents, films, audiotapes or videotapes, and even computer software. Jobs range from selecting and ordering print and nonprint materials to using them in a variety of ways to serve the public. Some librarians may develop materials and programs especially designed to meet the needs expressed by their patrons. Librarians who work closely with the community are knowledgeable about the interests of their patrons. Some librarians do not work closely with the public. Others are administrators who work with government and community leaders. Public libraries and library systems vary widely in scope and size, according to the needs and financial resources of the community to which they are connected. Librarians' duties vary accordingly.

Large libraries offer librarians a chance to specialize. Among the librarians who have little contact with the public are *acquisitions librarians*. These librarians read reviews of new materials and often examine sample copies. They order and process new materials for the library and are familiar with companies that supply a variety of materials, including out-of-print books and videotapes. *Catalogers* describe books according to their subject matter and assign subject headings and classification numbers for card catalogs or on-line catalog terminals. Original cataloging is often unnecessary because it is readily available from the Library of Congress, the national library of the United States. Catalogers or their helpers prepare books for filing on shelves according to the system used by the particular library. The Dewey decimal and the Library of Congress classification systems are the ones most commonly used in public libraries.

Public librarians work in public libraries and have duties ranging from selecting and ordering materials to assisting library patrons with research.

Reference librarians, unlike catalogers, deal directly with library users. They help people research specific pieces of information by either looking up facts or referring people to useful sources. They handle reference questions in person and over the telephone. These librarians also use computerized information services to provide answers to questions or lists of book and periodical sources on particular topics. They may also be responsible for suggesting titles to be acquired for the reference collection. Reference librarians usually have a special desk in the reference or information section of the library.

Some librarians work with specific segments of the community. *Children's librarians* and *youth services librarians* are trained to meet the needs of young people. Librarians in the children's section often prepare displays and conduct weekly story hours designed to interest children in books and library services. They may also have film programs. Youth services librarians work mainly with junior and senior high school students, helping them learn to use libraries and their resources. They can aid young people in finding books for pleasure, vocational guidance, and reference for school-related projects.

Bookmobile librarians work from vans especially designed as mobile libraries. They travel to outlying neighborhoods that lack adequate library services. Librarians select books according to the needs of the community the bookmobile serves. They often supply books or other materials from a central library in response to requests from their bookmobile patrons. Other community outreach librarians may serve special groups, such as those living in nursing homes or housing projects.

Some libraries are staffed by only two or three people. These librarians may combine the duties of all of the above specialists. Large library systems are generally administered by sizable staffs. *Library administrators* are responsible for the operation and continued funding of their libraries.

Education and Training Requirements

Librarians generally need a master's degree in library science. Graduate programs usually last 1 year and include a summer of study. About 120 schools offer such programs, and currently 60 of these are accredited by the American Library Association. Library school students take basic courses in the history of books and printing, intellectual freedom, reference tools, and user services. Because most libraries now have automated systems, almost all library schools offer courses in information storage and retrieval, microcomputer technology, and the use of on-line information retrieval systems. Advanced courses may be taken in specialties such as children's or adult services; classification, cataloging, indexing, and abstracting; library administration; library automation; and archives. Some schools offer doctoral programs in library science. A doctorate is often a prerequisite for top administrators in large library systems. Undergraduate study in the liberal arts, including English, foreign languages, data processing, and business, may prove helpful. Also useful is part-time library work as a technical or clerical assistant. Some graduate schools offer 2-year work-study programs that enable students to get work experience while they are in school.

Getting the Job

Your school placement office can give you information about job openings and applications. Both private and state employment offices sometimes list library openings. Library associations in many states have job hot lines that list openings in a recorded telephone message. You can also write directly to public libraries in your area. Professional library journals and local newspapers list job openings in their want ad sections. The Sunday edition of the *New York Times* lists library positions that are available throughout the country.

Advancement Possibilities and Employment Outlook

Librarians can advance within their own library system, or they may choose to move to a larger or more specialized library. Most top-level jobs are administrative and often require a doctoral degree. Librarians with doctoral degrees may also become teachers of library science.

Employment of librarians is expected to grow more slowly than average for all occupations through the year 2006. This is the result of an anticipated reduction of local government expenditures for library services. The increased use of computerized systems may also contribute to a reduced need for librarians. Competition for positions should be stiff; most openings that become available each year will be to replace librarians who retire or leave the field.

Working Conditions

Public libraries, particularly newer facilities, are generally pleasant and quiet places to work. The specific duties affect the conditions of work. For example, catalogers spend most of their day working in one place, while reference librarians move about the library helping people find information. Reference librarians work under pressure when patrons need information quickly. Most librarians work between 35 and 40 hours a week, including some evenings and weekends.

Earnings and Benefits

Salaries of public librarians vary largely by location and size of library and by a librarian's level of education and experience. Starting salaries for graduates of library school master's degree programs accredited by the American Library Association average $28,700 a year in public libraries. The average annual salary for federal government librarians in all positions, including supervisory and managerial, is $50,400. Most public librarians can expect paid vacations of 3 or 4 weeks a year, as well as paid holidays, sick leave benefits, and health and pension plans.

Librarian, School

Definition and Nature of the Work

School librarians introduce students to the school library and teach them how to use it. Elementary schools, junior and senior high schools, and colleges and universities all employ school librarians. Librarians select and order books and other materials that will support the curriculum of the school or college. They are responsible for maintaining the collection so that items are easily accessible to their patrons. Frequently they are also responsible for audiovisual materials and equipment. They sometimes prepare exhibits.

Actual duties vary with the size of the library and the needs of the students. High school libraries are generally larger than those in elementary schools because older students need more extensive resources for research. Elementary and secondary school librarians may work alone, while librarians in colleges and universities may be part of sizable staffs that include other librarians, technical assistants, and clerks. In large libraries assistants catalog new books,

A librarian in a high school helps students locate specific sources for research papers. In some states these librarians must be certified both as librarians and as teachers.

shelve returned books, repair damaged books, and take care of bindery procedures. In small libraries these tasks are done by professional librarians.

Elementary school librarians teach basic library skills, often in regularly scheduled classes in the library. They may teach students how to distinguish among various kinds of books, such as fiction, nonfiction, poetry, and biography, and how to use the classification system for finding books in the library. They encourage use of the library for information and recreation, while making it an interesting and important part of the students' school day. In an effort to interest students in reading, librarians may conduct story hours for the younger students and arrange other special programs for those in the higher grades.

Secondary school librarians teach more sophisticated skills to older students. Most students begin to learn research techniques in junior and senior high school. Secondary school librarians may hold orientation sessions for individual classes to explain the use of card catalogs or catalog access terminals, reference books, and indexes to periodicals. They help individual students by suggesting specific sources or ways of finding information. Sometimes librarians set up exhibits designed to make students aware of some of the library's holdings. Such exhibits may coordinate with historical events or holidays. Some school libraries contain many audiovisual materials. The school librarian may need to have training in this area.

College and university librarians work in relatively large libraries suited to the research needs of both students and faculty. Libraries at this level usually have large staffs of librarians who work in a number of specializations. Librarians in technical services order, process, and catalog new materials. These procedures are generally automated to a greater or lesser degree, depending on the size and budget of the library. Librarians in user services work closely with students and faculty. They direct users to helpful sources and also find specific pieces of information. They often conduct bibliographic instruction classes to teach library research methods. Many new on-line computer services available for reference may require that librarians also be trained in computer information searching techniques. Some universities have separate libraries for the various disciplines offered by the institution. There may be, for example, one library for general use, one for technical and scientific subjects, and an art library that may include an extensive slide collection. Some academic librarians develop subject bibliographies to direct patrons to the many different sources and forms of information in the library. Often libraries exchange materials through on-line interlibrary loan networks to make still more information available to the academic community. Librarians who work in specialized libraries may need expertise in the subject in addition to a degree in library science. They are sometimes required to have a second master's degree in the subject field. Library administrators and head librarians supervise all library operations.

Education and Training Requirements

Elementary and secondary school librarians may need to be certified both as librarians and as teachers in their states. To be certified as a school librarian, you generally must earn either a bachelor's or a master's degree in library science and pass a written examination. Because educational requirements vary from state to state and change frequently, you should check the current requirements in your state before making any decisions.

Most college and university librarians have a master's degree in library science. Top administrative posts, however, generally go to those who have a doctoral degree. Librarians who work in large university libraries are frequently required to have a second master's degree in the subject area of the faculty they represent. Some academic libraries may also require proficiency in a foreign language. Rare book librarians may need special training in that field, as well as a second advanced degree. Because of the many automated systems in academic libraries, librarians should be familiar with computerized information retrieval systems and on-line catalogs.

Getting the Job

College and graduate school placement offices usually list library openings. You can apply directly to private schools and public school boards. Newspapers sometimes list openings for librarians; the Sunday edition of the *New York Times* advertises positions that are available throughout the country. The *Chronicle of Higher Education* is a good place to look for librarian openings in colleges and universities. Professional library journals also list job openings in the field, as do private employment agencies that specialize in education. Many professional associations have telephone hot lines that list openings on prerecorded messages.

Advancement Possibilities and Employment Outlook

School librarians can advance by furthering their education. Graduate programs offer both master's and doctoral degrees in library science. With higher degrees or with a second-subject master's degree, school librarians may transfer to large college or university libraries or become library administrators. School librarians may also become teachers at library schools. Competition will be keen in schools, colleges, and universities. Growth in the number of new positions will depend largely on the extent of public funding for education. Replacement positions will be available each year as librarians retire or leave the field. In certain urban areas, such as New York City, there will be a strong demand for children's and young adult specialists in school and public libraries through the year 2006.

Working Conditions

Libraries are generally quiet, pleasant places to work. Working hours vary with each school, but elementary and high school librarians usually work the same hours that teachers do, while college and university librarians often work 35- to 40-hour weeks with some evening and weekend hours.

Earnings and Benefits

Salaries vary with the individual school, its location, and the librarian's education and experience. Starting salaries average about $29,600 for public school librarians and $27,400 for college and university librarians. The average salary of experienced school librarians is about $37,900 a year. Benefits include paid holidays, long vacations, health insurance, and pension plans.

Librarian, Special

Definition and Nature of the Work

Special librarians make information on specific subjects available to people in industry, commerce, and government. These librarians acquire and organize data that are required by their employers. Special librarians may work in institutions as large as the National Library of Medicine or as small as a two- or three-person office. The growth of computer storage and retrieval of information has changed this field radically. Many positions deal primarily or even exclusively with research through on-line database searching. Special librarians help people find information and see that needed materials are easily accessible.

The main difference between special librarians and all other librarians is that special librarians serve a particular organization and specialize in the subject area that suits the needs of that organization. They work in public institutions as well as in private businesses, such as television stations, advertising agencies, and law firms. Some librarians work solely with medical books and periodicals in hospital libraries, while others work in museums with such materials as filmstrips, slides, prints, and art history books. In some libraries the librarian is responsible for translating material into English from a foreign language. Such a librarian may also abstract and index articles, research papers, or books. Because special librarians deal with one subject in depth, they must be very knowledgeable in that particular field. Sometimes they do research for their companies and present their findings in a report to the staff. They also assist staff members who are conducting research.

Special librarians are usually free to reorganize traditional library procedures to adapt them to their specialized needs. Many special libraries have several staff positions. They are supervised by a *head librarian,* who is in charge of planning the budget, hiring personnel, and handling important correspondence. *Library assistants* often do the routine tasks of filing, checking in materials, and taking inventory. Others work in circulation or take care of subscription and book orders. In small libraries one or two staff members can often handle all the duties.

Education and Training
Varies—see profile

Salary Range
Average—$33,100
to $37,400

Employment Outlook
Good

Special librarians specialize in a subject area that suits the needs of the organization for which they work. This special librarian works for a business and provides information on foreign cultures to company employees.

Education and Training Requirements

The education required of special librarians is entirely up to the employer. Most employers look for a master's degree in library science combined with a strong background or an advanced degree in a specific field. However, sometimes a high school diploma plus some experience is sufficient for the job. Writing skills and knowledge of computer operations are often necessary. Art museum librarians generally need a college major in art history and a master's degree in library science. Librarians in large technical libraries usually need a master's or doctoral degree in a relevant field and a library science degree.

Some graduate students take part in work-study arrangements that allow them to work part-time while attending school. Graduate study often includes foreign language courses, as well as the study of library procedures, on-line database searching, information science, and library automation. Volunteer and part-time or summer work in libraries can prove useful for people who plan to become librarians.

Getting the Job

The college placement office is a good source of job openings. The want ads in newspapers and professional journals may offer job leads. You can also apply directly to firms and agencies that have special libraries. Government jobs usually require that applicants take the necessary civil service examination. The Special Libraries Association has local telephone hot lines listing job openings in various parts of the country.

Advancement Possibilities and Employment Outlook

Advancement generally depends on the librarian's educational background and continuing education in the field. Librarians with a doctoral degree may advance to become head librarians or library administrators.

The employment outlook is good because of the increase in the number of special libraries. In some areas of the country there are more jobs than there are librarians qualified to fill them. This trend is expected to continue through the year 2006.

Working Conditions

The atmosphere in libraries is generally pleasant and quiet. Special librarians, however, must sometimes work under considerable pressure, especially when information is needed quickly. Librarians should be well-organized and knowledgeable people. Their workweek is typically 35 to 40 hours long.

Earnings and Benefits

Salary depends on the librarian's education and experience as well as on the budget limitations of the employing organization. Special librarians with 1 to 5 years of experience earn average annual salaries of about $33,100 to $37,400. Special library managers earn an average of $58,400 a year. Librarians can expect between 2 and 4 weeks of paid vacation and sick leave. Other benefits usually include health insurance and pension plans.

Where to Go for More Information

American Library Association
50 East Huron Street
Chicago, IL 60611
(312) 944-6780
www.ala.org/index.html

American Society for Information Science
8720 Georgia Avenue, Suite 501
Silver Spring, MD 20910-3602
(301) 495-0900
www.asis.org

Special Libraries Association
1700 Eighteenth Street, NW
Washington, DC 20009-2508
(202) 234-4700
www.sla.org

Marriage and Family Counselor

Definition and Nature of the Work

Marriage and family counselors offer therapy to people who are having relationship problems. Counselors help clients understand themselves and their feelings toward specific people in their lives. The aim of counseling is to help clients use their new understanding to develop better relationships. Many counselors work in mental health centers and clinics, in hospitals, and for social service agencies. Others have private practices.

Marriage counselors use many approaches in conducting their sessions. They usually speak with a couple at the same time, although they may have some sessions with the husband or wife alone. Some marriage counselors see married couples in groups. They may also see groups of husbands or groups of wives. Whatever method is used, the goal is the same. Many marital problems arise because the couples are not communicating properly and therefore do not understand each other's needs. Counselors strive to increase this understanding. Perhaps a couple is considering divorce when they come to the counselor. The counselor will work to see whether a reconciliation is possible. If it is not possible, the counselor may suggest a trial separation.

Education and Training
College

Salary Range
Starting—$25,000 to $30,000
Average—$36,000 to $45,000

Employment Outlook
Very good

Family counselors work with entire families or with individual family members. Even when a counselor speaks with only one person, the orientation of the therapy includes the client's parents and siblings or spouse and children. Here, too, the counselor encourages the client to communicate with others, with the hope that this will improve troubled relationships.

The nature of counseling work varies, depending on the particular place of employment. Counselors in private practice, for example, may specialize in one or two kinds of problems. Such counselors may refer clients to other counselors if clients' problems are outside their area of expertise. Counselors who work in clinics may work in teams. They may consult with their colleagues on special cases. Some clinics employ counselors with special qualifications to take on the most difficult cases.

Education and Training Requirements

An increasing number of states have instituted formal licensing requirements for marriage and family counselors. Most marriage and family counselors have a master's degree in mental health counseling, psychology, or social work. Some counselors with a bachelor's degree work for social service agencies.

While in college, you should take courses in sociology, social work, psychology, and modern foreign languages. To get a position for which there is stiff competition, graduate work is necessary. Many schools offer graduate programs in marriage and family counseling. Some counselors specialize in social work and psychology.

Getting the Job

Newspapers, job banks on the Internet, and professional journals advertise counseling positions in their classified sections. School placement offices list openings, too. Applicants can also write directly to local agencies, hospitals, and clinics. If you wish to work for a government agency, apply to take the necessary civil service test. Many students make future job contacts while doing fieldwork for courses in social work and psychology.

Advancement Possibilities and Employment Outlook

Marriage and family counselors can become self-employed or work as directors of departments or agencies. They can also further their training by getting a doctoral degree or by taking further postgraduate courses. Counselors who have a great deal of experience may become trainers and teachers of new counselors. Rapid job growth is projected for marriage and family counselors through the year 2006.

Working Conditions

Counselors work in offices where they can speak with their clients in private or in groups. Some counselors in private practice have offices in their own homes. Working hours vary because many counselors combine part-time jobs in social service agencies with private practice. Agency work often includes 2 or 3 evenings a week, especially in marriage counseling, because many clients work during the day. Counselors in private practice can regulate their own schedule, although they, too, usually have some evening and weekend sessions.

The work can be very demanding. Counselors must always give their complete attention to their clients' difficulties.

Earnings and Benefits

Pay scales vary considerably. Beginning counselors employed in public agencies or clinics often earn starting salaries ranging from about $25,000 to $30,000 a year, depending on their educational background. Experienced counselors with a master's degree generally earn $36,000 to $45,000 a year. Counselors in private practice also often have higher earnings once they become established. Benefits for counselors employed by government agencies or other large public or private organizations usually include paid holidays and vacations, health insurance, and pension plans.

Where to Go for More Information

American Association for Marriage and
    Family Therapy
1133 Fifteenth Street, NW, Suite 300
Washington, DC 20005-2710
(202) 452-0109
www.aamft.org

Parole Officer

Definition and Nature of the Work

Parole officers help people who have served time in prison make their transition back into a free society. They work with prisoners who are eligible for parole. Parole is the conditional release of prisoners from prison before their sentences have been completed. Prisoners become eligible for parole after they show progress in rehabilitation programs. Such progress is demonstrated by obeying prison rules, performing prison jobs well, and completing therapy programs. The prison parole boards decide which prisoners have made enough progress to be released. They try to identify those prisoners who will not repeat their crimes. Most parole officers work for state parole departments. Some officers are employed by counties or at the federal level by the U.S. Board of Parole.

Some parole officers work inside correctional institutions. They prepare reports for the parole board. These reports include the details of the prisoners' lives before prison, of their prison years, and of their home situations. The officers try to give the parole board some idea of whether the prisoners' families will be helpful to the released prisoners. Parole officers provide information about the job prospects a prisoner might have if released. Based on the parole officers' reports and interviews with the prisoners and their families, the board chooses certain prisoners for release.

Other parole officers work in the field with parolees, or prisoners who have been released. They may be assisted by parole aides or parole officer trainees. When ex-convicts are released back into society, the first thing they need to do is find work. Parole officers help place their clients in jobs. They also lend emotional support to parolees as they meet the challenges of returning to their communities. For example, ex-convicts are often held suspect by employers, coworkers, and neighbors. Parole officers try to help parolees by talking to their employers and explaining to them that the parolees need a chance to make a living if they are to function as honest citizens. Other ex-convicts may have financial problems. Parole officers familiarize themselves with community services and welfare benefits so that they can direct ex-convicts to agencies that can provide further support.

Even once they are out of prison, parolees generally continue with rehabilitation programs such as basic education, job training, or therapy. Participating in these programs is often an important condition of their release. Parole officers assist clients in finding schools and job training or therapy programs. For instance, former drug addicts may need to be enrolled in programs that help them stay off drugs. In addition, parolees can also be placed in halfway houses or community

Education and Training
College plus training

Salary Range
Starting—$20,000
to $30,000

Employment Outlook
Good

centers where people on parole live together in small groups to share their experiences and lend each other support. These halfway houses are sometimes supervised by parole officers with the help of drug therapists, psychiatrists, and social workers.

Parolees must visit their officers regularly so that their progress can be evaluated. Parole officers question their clients at these sessions to make sure that they are not breaking the parole rules in any way. If a parolee breaks the rules, such as by violating a law or by associating with bad company, the parole officer may recommend that the parole be revoked. Then the parole board may send the parolee back to prison.

Education and Training Requirements

You generally must have a bachelor's degree to become a parole officer. A major in sociology, psychology, criminology, or corrections is appropriate. In addition, many agencies, including the U.S. Board of Parole, require 1 or 2 years of experience in a correctional institution or other social agency or a master's degree in sociology or psychology. Parole officer trainees work under the supervision of experienced parole officers and the senior parole officer.

Getting the Job

Contact state, federal, or county parole boards to ask about job openings. Arrange to take the required federal or state civil service test. If you do fieldwork for college courses in social work, you may come in contact with people who can help you find a job when you graduate. Job openings are often listed at college placement offices.

Advancement Possibilities and Employment Outlook

Advancement opportunities are good for parole officers. There are many chances for qualified people to advance to jobs as administrators and department heads. They may become the directors of special projects or units.

The need for new parole officers will be great because of the increasing numbers of people who are serving prison terms and will become eligible for parole. However, opportunities depend on the extent of public funding. Many states and counties as well as the federal government are expected to expand their parole departments through the year 2006, if funding permits.

Where to Go for More Information

American Correctional Association
4380 Forbes Boulevard
Lanham, MD 20706-4322
(301) 918-1800
www.corrections.com/aca

American Federation of State, County and
Municipal Employees
1625 L Street, NW
Washington, DC 20036
(202) 452-4800

National Council on Crime and
Delinquency
685 Market Street, Suite 620
San Francisco, CA 94105
(415) 896-6223

Working Conditions

Field parole officers do much of their work independently. They interview clients and go out into the community to find jobs for parolees. All parole officers are under pressure to present a positive image of the parole system to the community. They often spend much time advising, encouraging, and evaluating parolees. Caseloads may be heavy. Officers often work more than 40 hours a week. They sometimes make evening or weekend appointments with parolees who work or who have emergency problems.

Earnings and Benefits

Earnings vary, depending on the location of the employer. Beginning parole officers average about $20,000 to $30,000 a year. Supervisors and directors earn much higher salaries. Most parole officers receive paid holidays and vacations, health insurance, and pension plans.

Political Consultant

Definition and Nature of the Work

Political consultants, in some cases called lobbyists, work behind the scenes to promote the election of certain candidates or the interests of certain groups. The political consultant plans a campaign strategy, coordinates the campaign staff, and arranges meetings to publicize the candidate or cause.

A political consultant uses media advertising, press releases, fund-raising drives and other activities to help introduce the politician and his or her ideas to the voting public. The consultant functions as a public relations specialist, a salesperson, and a manager all in one. The goal is to "sell" the public on the politician that he or she represents.

Political consultants do not only represent people. A corporate lobbyist, for example, may specialize in representing a company to the federal or state government. Lobbyists try to persuade government officials to understand their company's problems, and they may advise and participate in marketing the company's products to government departments. They often try to sway governmental policy or congressional votes to work in favor of the company they represent. Lobbyists also discuss such issues as taxation and regulation with members of Congress and other senior officials.

> **Education and Training**
> Advanced degree

> **Salary Range**
> Starting—$26,000
> to $31,000
> Average—$50,000
> to $75,000

> **Employment Outlook**
> Very good

Political consultants meet with politicians to promote the election of certain candidates or the interests of certain groups.

Education and Training Requirements

If you are interested in becoming a political consultant, you should take college courses in political science, communication, English, and foreign languages. Other useful fields of study are economics, business, law, and sociology.

Volunteer work for local politicians or interest groups will give you experience and helpful contacts. A master's degree in government policymaking or public administration may be supplemented by part-time work on a campaign staff or in a legislator's local office.

Getting the Job

Volunteer and part-time work during school and college will be a good springboard for finding full-time employment. Jobs in the personnel and public relations divisions of companies may lead to corporate lobbying positions. Many trade and professional associations have well-established lobbying offices and regularly hire new personnel.

Advancement Possibilities and Employment Outlook

As local, state, and federal political contests become more complex, candidates increasingly rely on campaign consultants to manage their overall organization. While there may be more jobs at the local level during election time, state and federal representatives often employ full-time political consultants in Washington, DC, and the state capitals.

Corporate lobbying has been on the rise since 1980. Smaller companies that cannot afford full-time lobbyists hire outside lobbyists who are experts on specific issues. Specialization has opened up new advancement possibilities for many political consultants who have set up their own political consulting firms.

The outlook for political consultants is very good. However, competition will be keen for those in beginning positions or those who are starting their own consulting firms.

Working Conditions

Political consultants work at an energetic pace, arguing the case of their candidate or cause. They spend a considerable amount of time on the telephone and in face-to-face contact with legislators and other officials. They must have excellent communications and interpersonal skills. During an election campaign the consultant often travels ahead of the candidate, organizing meetings, interviews, and publicity. The job is varied and often requires evening and weekend work.

Earnings and Benefits

Entry-level political consultants may receive payment for out-of-pocket expenses and low wages. Starting salaries range from $26,000 to $31,000 a year. However, as word of energetic and successful strategies gets around, candidates and corporations will offer higher wages and benefits. A Washington, DC, lobbyist for a corporation may receive $50,000 to $75,000 or more a year. Political consultants who work for corporations also receive health insurance, and pension and vacation benefits. Self-employed consultants must arrange these benefits for themselves.

Probation Officer

Definition and Nature of the Work

When someone breaks the law or is charged with juvenile delinquency, a court may place that person on probation instead of or in addition to administering a prison sentence. Probation officers are appointed by the courts to provide these people with guidance and counseling. Officers generally work in the adult, juvenile, or family divisions of probation departments. Some officers work for state or county courts. Others work at the federal level in the Probation Office of the U.S. District Court.

Individuals who have been convicted of a crime may also be placed on probation. They are assigned to a probation officer, with whom they must consult regularly. The officer evaluates a client's activities and may make recommendations such as entering a job-training program or enrolling in a school. Clients on probation must obey certain rules, such as avoiding bad company and informing the probation officer of any change of address. If clients violate the rules of probation, officers report it to the judge. The judge may then revoke the probation, extend the period of probation, or impose a fine. Sometimes probation officers go to court to present information to the judge.

Some of the probation officers' clients are not on probation. For example, juveniles or children may be placed under an officer's supervision if they have done something that is wrong but would not be considered a crime if done by an adult.

Pretrial investigations are an important part of probation officers' work. Many people accused of crimes are investigated before they are brought to trial. The officers must decide whether it is in the best interest of society and the individuals to hold a trial. Because trials are very costly, court systems try to find alternative ways of dealing with alleged criminals. Probation officers interview the alleged

Education and Training
College plus training

Salary Range
Starting—$20,000
to $30,000

Employment Outlook
Good

After interviewing each divorcing parent, this probation officer in a family division will make recommendations to the judge for custody, living, and visitation arrangements for the children.

criminals, their families, and their coworkers. The officers may believe that it is unlikely the accused will ever commit another crime. They may then recommend to the judge that these people be placed under supervision instead of going to trial. The officers hope that their direction will prevent their clients from being accused of a crime again.

Probation officers also conduct the presentence investigations. They investigate the character, background, and criminal record of people who have been tried and convicted of crimes before. Then they make recommendations to the judge concerning sentences. Officers may recommend prison sentences, probation, or a combination of the two. Probation officers must consider possible harmful effects on society if certain people are not imprisoned.

Probation officers often conduct bail investigations. People who are arrested may be released pending trial if they pay a sum of money to the court. A portion of the money, called bail, is returned if they appear at the trial. Probation officers may make bail recommendations, such as high, low, or no bail, depending on whether or not the officers think it is likely that the accused will appear at the trial.

Officers who work in family divisions may conduct custody investigations. In cases in which a couple is separating or getting a divorce, both parents may want the children. Officers interview members of the family and recommend custody, living, and visitation arrangements to the judge.

Some probation officers who work in large offices may specialize in one aspect of probation work such as job placement. Some officers work in rural districts where there are few clients. These officers often work on all kinds of probation problems. Clients on probation are sometimes placed in halfway houses, where they live together and work or go to school in the community. Some probation officers work in these halfway houses along with other professionals such as psychiatrists and social workers.

Education and Training Requirements

You must have a bachelor's degree to become a probation officer. Preferred majors are sociology, psychology, and criminology. Many probation offices and courts require that you have 1 or 2 years of experience working in a social welfare agency or correctional institution. Some offices prefer to hire people with a master's degree in one of the behavioral sciences. Probation officers are trained on the job by experienced officers.

Getting the Job

Most jobs in probation are at the county level. Contact your local probation office for information on job openings. You must pass a civil service test to get the job. If you are interested in working for probation offices at the federal level, arrange to take the necessary civil service exam. Then contact the federal probation offices to ask about current openings. Also check for job listings with your college placement office.

Advancement Possibilities and Employment Outlook

There are good advancement opportunities in probation work. Officers receive regular promotions and salary increases by passing civil service tests. Probation officers may go on to supervise other probation officers, or they may become the chief probation officer or the director of a probation department. Some probation officers go on to related jobs in government.

The employment outlook for probation officers is good because many officers will be needed to handle the increasing number of cases coming before the courts. Increased opportunities for probation officers, however, depend on public funding.

Working Conditions

Probation officers generally work 40 hours a week. Their hours may be irregular. They sometimes make weekend or evening appointments with probationers who work. The probation officer's job can be emotionally demanding because the officer must help clients solve a wide range of personal problems.

Earnings and Benefits

Salaries vary widely, depending on experience and location. The state, county, and federal governments have different pay scales. Beginning salaries for probation officers average about $20,000 to $30,000 a year. Benefits include paid holidays and vacations, health and life insurance, and retirement plans.

Where to Go for More Information

American Federation of State, County and
  Municipal Employees
1625 L Street, NW
Washington, DC 20036
(202) 452-4800

National Council on Crime and
  Delinquency
685 Market Street, Suite 620
San Francisco, CA 94105
(415) 896-6223

Rehabilitation Counselor

Definition and Nature of the Work

Rehabilitation counselors help people with disabilities deal with the personal, social, and vocational effects of their condition. They help determine the training, support, and opportunities their clients need to lead more self-sufficient and normal lives both at home and on the job. Rehabilitation counselors assist individuals who have mental, emotional, or physical handicaps. Many counselors work for publicly funded agencies. They may also be employed by hospitals, schools, and rehabilitation facilities.

It is the counselor's responsibility to evaluate the strengths and limitations of a person with a disability and to arrange for a rehabilitation program that is suited to his or her needs, interests, and capabilities. This program may include medical care, occupational therapy, and job placement. To find a suitable program for their client, counselors study medical and job histories and confer with doctors and therapists. They also talk to the client and his or her family.

The work requires patience, perseverance, and initiative. The ability to interact well with people is essential because a rehabilitation counselor must be able to relate not only to clients but also to their families and prospective employers.

Education and Training
College plus training

Salary Range
Starting—$18,600
to $25,000

Employment Outlook
Excellent

Education and Training Requirements

Some employers hire counselors with a bachelor's degree in rehabilitation services, counseling, psychology, or a related field. However, many employers require that their counselors have a master's degree in rehabilitation counseling, counseling and guidance, or counseling psychology. The Council on Rehabilitation Education (CORE) accredits graduate programs that include a minimum of

A rehabilitation counselor works with a visually impaired woman to teach her how to use special equipment to do her work.

2 years of study and 600 hours of supervised clinical internship experience. An increasing number of employers also require rehabilitation counselors to be nationally certified. Certification standards are set by the Commission on Rehabilitation Counselor Certification.

Getting the Job

Because roughly one-third of all rehabilitation counselors are employed by public service organizations, vacancies may be listed in state or federal civil service bulletins. Doing volunteer work in the field will give you some experience and may provide some useful contacts for permanent employment.

Advancement Possibilities and Employment Outlook

Counselors may become directors of rehabilitation programs or self-employed consultants. The employment outlook is excellent, with rapid job growth expected through the year 2006. The trend toward helping people with disabilities become more independent and productive is likely to continue. Moreover, both the government and private industry are showing an increased commitment to helping individuals with disabilities become members of the workforce.

Working Conditions

The job generally entails some fieldwork, such as visiting the homes of clients and meeting with members of the business community to promote employment for those with disabilities or to locate training programs for them. Rehabilitation counselors are sometimes assigned to the job sites of employees with disabilities to help them get used to their new work situation. Although counselors generally work conventional hours, they may perform a diverse range of tasks, from preparing marketing presentations for corporations to locating voice boards to help clients speak. Therefore, a good counselor must be highly versatile.

Earnings and Benefits

Entry-level annual salaries vary from about $18,600 to $25,000. Experienced counselors in the highest-paying positions may earn more than $40,000 a year.

Rehabilitation counselors who are employed by government agencies or private businesses usually receive paid vacations and holidays and medical insurance. Self-employed counselors must provide their own benefits.

Where to Go for More Information

American Rehabilitation Association
1910 Association Drive, Suite 200
Reston, VA 20191
(703) 648-9300

National Rehabilitation Association
633 South Washington Street
Alexandria, VA 22314-4109
(703) 836-0850

Religious Vocation

Definition and Nature of the Work

Education and Training
Advanced degree

Salary Range
Varies—see profile

Employment Outlook
Varies—see profile

Clergy members serve as spiritual leaders to the millions of Americans who follow a religious faith. There are many religions in this country, each with its own sects or denominations. However, Protestants, Catholics, and Jews constitute the three largest religious groups. Their spiritual representatives are Protestant *ministers,* Catholic *priests,* and Jewish *rabbis.* Most Protestant and Jewish denominations permit women to serve as ministers or rabbis, but the Catholic Church does not ordain women as priests. Members of the ordained Christian clergy and the Jewish rabbinate are the religious leaders of the community. They are responsible for the sacred activities of their religious group.

Ministers, priests, and rabbis perform many services that are common to all denominations. They preside over religious services, conduct weddings and funerals, counsel members of their congregations, and deliver sermons. Other activities are based on the beliefs and practices of the individual religions. Rabbis, for example, read the Torah, and priests hear confessions. Ministers, priests, and rabbis are sometimes assisted by members of their congregations. Some religious groups are assisted by *deacons.*

The duties of ministers, priests, and rabbis vary. They may participate in interfaith services, organize community activities, and work with community leaders on secular, or nonreligious, matters such as raising funds for building a hospital.

Not all high-ranking religious vocations involve working with a congregation. Some priests, for example, work as teachers or scholars. Various aspects of social work are open to people desiring religious vocations. There is also missionary work, which involves providing religious and social assistance to developing societies overseas. *Chaplains* serve people's spiritual needs at armed services bases and in hospitals and schools.

There are religious vocations other than those of ministers, priests, and rabbis. Roman Catholic *nuns* are members of religious orders. Frequently, they work as teachers. Their other jobs include nursing and social service work. Roman Catholic

brothers belong to religious communities. They serve as teachers and counselors and may perform other jobs, including maintenance work. A great number of lay employees—people who have no formal authorization for their religious vocations—assist in clerical matters, social work, and administration.

Education and Training Requirements

Requirements vary according to the particular faith and specific vocation. Most clergy have completed at least a bachelor's degree, but many denominations require an additional program of theological study. To be ordained as a rabbi, a student must complete a 4- or 5-year course of study in a seminary. Many Protestant denominations require a bachelor's degree and study at a theological school, although some have no formal education requirements. Preparation for the priesthood usually consists of college and an additional 4 years of study at a theological seminary. Regardless of education requirements, all ministers, priests, and rabbis must have a thorough knowledge of the rites and beliefs of their group.

Training for religious vocations may begin in high school. Prospective priests study Latin. Those interested in Jewish vocations study Hebrew. All religious vocations emphasize modern-language study. Many individuals seeking religious vocations attend high schools and colleges with religious affiliations, but this is not a requirement.

Those interested in religious vocations who do not wish to become ministers, priests, or rabbis will not need as much formal education. The range of jobs is too broad to generalize about the requirements. As a rough guide, however, lay employees require the same training as those performing similar tasks without religious affiliation. For example, the educational requirements for someone interested in working for a Christian youth group will be the same as those for a secular social worker with similar responsibilities.

Getting the Job

Many people who are interested in religious vocations are assigned to their positions by religious officials. People interested in a religious vocation should contact their religious leaders for career counseling. Many people begin by working as assistants in their own congregations. Lay employees, such as social workers, who perform jobs similar to those in the secular world generally find jobs the same way their secular counterparts do.

Advancement Possibilities and Employment Outlook

As priests, rabbis, and ministers become more experienced, they take on greater responsibilities. Priests may become bishops or cardinals. Religious teachers may advance within their colleges or seminaries to more prestigious teaching positions. Lay workers and members of the clergy sometimes assume administrative jobs in religious institutions.

The employment outlook for both rabbis and Catholic priests is favorable through the year 2006 because of a current shortage in the number of ordained clergy in these groups. There is more competition expected for Protestant ministers because of slow growth in church membership and a large number of qualified candidates. Graduates of theological schools will have the best prospects. There are additional opportunities in social institutions with religious affiliations.

Working Conditions

Conditions vary according to the faith and vocation. Clergy who have been "called" to their vocation have to understand that they are not just choosing a career but a way of life. As the most important representatives of their religion, they are held very strictly to the high moral standards set by their faith and community. While some laypeople may only work part-time, rabbis, priests, and ministers are involved with their vocations 24 hours a day. Religious vocations may involve working in majestic cathedrals, ghettos, jungles in foreign countries, hospitals, or any other place a religious message is needed.

The living situations also vary. Catholic priests, nuns, and brothers are not permitted to marry. They usually live with others of their order. A good part of the day is spent working with people, but time is also needed for prayer, meditation, and study.

Earnings and Benefits

Salaries range widely for the three religious groups. Many members of the clergy receive free housing, utilities, and benefits such as health and retirement plans.

Catholic priests receive an average salary of $11,000 a year in addition to free room and board in the parish rectory. Protestant ministers receive an average income of $30,000 a year. Rabbis can earn anywhere from $45,000 to $75,000 a year, including benefits. Salaries differ not only among the religious groups but within them. For example, in all groups, individual congregations of wealthy churches or temples can afford to pay more to their clergy than can smaller congregations. Priests, ministers, and rabbis can also earn extra income by performing special services such as marriages.

Where to Go for More Information

Association of Theological Schools in the United States and Canada
10 Summit Park Drive
Pittsburgh, PA 15275-1103
(412) 788-6505
www.ats.edu

National Council of the Churches of Christ in the U.S.A.
475 Riverside Drive, Room 880
New York, NY 10115-0050
(212) 870-2141

School Administrator

Definition and Nature of the Work

School administrators direct all aspects of school life. They work on several levels: as administrators for the federal government or the state government, as superintendents working for local school boards, and as principals of individual schools.

Federal and *state school administrators* work in government departments of education. Federal administrators develop academic standards and programs and allocate funds to the schools. State administrators interpret state policy governing school lunches, teaching standards, and student transportation. They run large education departments with many staff members.

School superintendents head a school district that is made up of several schools. District size varies considerably; districts may include from 2 to 800 schools. Superintendents carry out the school board's decisions on such matters as budget, hiring procedure, curriculum, and the expansion of facilities. They also keep track of their districts' needs and examine school policies to see that they are both efficient and effective. Superintendents may help the school board draw up the district's budgets or make budgeting decisions with state and federal school administrators.

Superintendents are in charge of setting and administering their district's policies on hiring and curriculum management. For example, superintendents may decide what textbooks will be used in classes. Superintendents of small districts work closely with each school and its faculty; those who are responsible for many schools have contact primarily with their staff of assistant superintendents.

School principals administer individual schools. Principals draw up their school's budget and see that the school's policies on curriculum, discipline, and teaching are carried out. Principals are also in charge of the school's physical maintenance. In addition, they maintain contact with students and parents. Depending on the size of their school, principals may have a staff of assistant principals in charge of curriculum or discipline for various grades. Like superintendents, school principals represent their school to the community. They may write papers for publication, distribute school awards, and attend meetings and conferences. As administrators they serve as links between the school and the community.

Education and Training Requirements

Educational requirements vary. Administrators should combine teaching experience with training in school administration. Most administrators have had college courses in education, economics, business, and sociology.

In most cases administrators need a master's degree in educational administration plus at least 2 years of teaching experience. Although not all principals have a master's degree, most have taken courses in school administration. Some urban school principals are required to have a doctoral degree. These requirements vary according to the grade level and location of the school. Many school principals work as assistant principals for several years before advancing. School district superintendents usually are required to have completed graduate study in educational administration, preferably at the doctoral level. Both superintendents and principals must meet the specific certification requirements that are set by the state in which they are employed.

A school principal is a type of school administrator whose duties include drawing up the school's budget, enforcing the school's policies, directing the school's physical maintenance, and maintaining contact with students and parents.

Getting the Job

Openings for school principals and superintendents are announced by local school boards. State departments of education and both public and private placement bureaus also list openings in educational administration. If you are interested in working for the state or federal government, you should apply to take the appropriate civil service examination. Inexperienced civil service workers generally begin in middle-management positions and advance to higher government posts through experience and length of service, and by taking further examinations.

Advancement Possibilities and Employment Outlook

School principals may become school superintendents. Superintendents may go on to more challenging jobs in larger districts or with the state or federal government. The top posts in government are generally filled by appointment. Outstanding workers in the civil service may be chosen for these jobs. Administrators on all levels may apply and be chosen to head special and experimental programs for government and for private companies that create educational materials.

Little growth in the employment of school administrators is expected through the year 2006. The number of available positions may decrease somewhat in some areas as school systems are reorganized. Most openings will occur to replace administrators who retire or leave their jobs for other reasons. Competition among job seekers is likely to be keen.

Working Conditions

School administrators generally work long hours. Principals are often expected to be at school when there are after-school functions such as concerts or sporting events. Superintendents spend extra time attending meetings and traveling. All administrators are on call in case of emergencies; their jobs carry pressure as well as prestige. They are often called on to make difficult decisions. Administrators should enjoy working with people. They must also be efficient and responsible in their work.

Earnings and Benefits

Salaries vary with the individual administrator's education and experience, as well as with the location and size of the school or district. Salaries for principals in public schools currently average $67,400 a year. Superintendents average about $70,000 a year. School administrators can expect paid holidays and vacations of between 2 and 4 weeks a year. They also receive health insurance and pension plans.

Where to Go for More Information

American Association of School
   Administrators
1801 North Moore Street
Arlington, VA 22209
(703) 528-0700
www.aasa.org

American Counseling Association
5999 Stevenson Avenue
Alexandria, VA 22304-3300
(703) 823-9800
www.counseling.org

National Education Association of the
   United States
1201 Sixteenth Street, NW
Washington, DC 20036-3290
(202) 833-4000
www.nea.org

School Counselor

Education and Training
College plus training

Salary Range
Starting—$25,000
Average—$38,500
to $45,000

Employment Outlook
Fair

Definition and Nature of the Work

School counselors help students make decisions that affect their personal and academic development. They help students choose the courses they will take. They also work with students who are experiencing personal and family problems. Often counselors may meet with parents and parent groups. Sometimes they provide students with special services such as drug and alcohol programs or conflict resolution sessions. School counselors, who are sometimes called guidance counselors, work in both public and private schools. They work at the elementary, junior high, and senior high school level. Counselors work as part of a team that includes classroom teachers, school psychologists, school nurses, and community groups.

Counselors who work in junior and senior high schools may spend much of their time helping students decide what they will do after high school graduation. As early as junior high school, students must choose courses that will enable them to get the training they need for the jobs they want. For example, students who plan to learn a trade may need a technical background, while business courses may best suit the career plans of others. Counselors encourage students to set goals and stick to them. To understand students' interests and abilities, counselors may administer tests such as occupational interest tests. If students wish to attend college after high school, counselors advise them on both their academic and extracurricular activities. They also provide students with scholarship information, training manuals, and catalogs of undergraduate schools.

Counselors who work in elementary schools work mainly with students who have special problems getting along in the classroom. Usually classroom teachers refer such students to counselors for guidance. Counselors also provide special assistance to students with physical handicaps and to those from troubled families. Students who get into trouble in the community may also be counseled.

In addition to speaking to students individually, counselors may hold group sessions. In some schools guidance is a regularly scheduled class. Counselors may use this time to present specific materials to the class, or they may allow the students to choose the subject for discussion.

Education and Training Requirements

Before making any definite plans that affect your schooling, check the educational requirements in your state. All states require school counselors to be certified, but certification standards vary widely from state to state and change frequently. Some states also require teaching certification. A bachelor's degree is required and an undergraduate major in psychology, education, or the liberal arts is useful. More counselors are participating in graduate-level counselor programs, which are usually in the education or psychology department of colleges and universities. Students in these programs may study group dynamics, human growth and development, testing, counseling, and statistics.

Getting the Job

Graduate school placement offices usually have a list of job openings. You can also write directly to the superintendent of schools in the district in which you would like to work. In addition, professional associations and journals may offer job leads. Newspaper want ads and job banks on the Internet may also list openings. Private employment agencies that specialize in placing workers in educational jobs may be able to help you. In some areas counselors are assigned to schools when they are certified.

Both public and private schools employ school counselors to help students make personal and academic decisions and to work with students who are experiencing personal and family problems.

Advancement Possibilities and Employment Outlook

School counselors are already at the top of their profession. Some specialize in a certain area of guidance, such as vocational counseling. They may become the coordinator for their school in their area of expertise. Others take on supervisory jobs or become administrators for the school system.

Limited employment growth for school counselors is expected through the year 2006 because of budgetary constraints. Counselors should expect to face considerable competition for jobs.

Working Conditions

Full-time school counselors work longer hours than teachers do because they often meet with students and parents before and after school. Some counselors work part-time or combine counseling with teaching duties. Generally, counselors have their own offices so that they can conduct their interviews in private. Counselors must be able to relate well to all kinds of people. Patience, resourcefulness, and stability are important qualities for school counselors.

Because the school year runs from September to June, counselors may take the summer months as paid vacation. Some counselors use this opportunity to earn extra money during the summer by working in their schools or at other jobs. Counselors also have long winter and spring breaks. Many school counselors belong to labor unions.

Where to Go for More Information

American School Counselor Association
801 North Fairfax Street, Suite 310
Alexandria, VA 22314
(703) 683-2722
www.schoolcounselor.org

Earnings and Benefits

Starting salaries for school counselors average $25,000 a year but vary, depending on the counselor's qualifications and geographic location. Experienced school counselors earn from $38,500 to $45,000 a year. Benefits include paid holidays and vacations, sick leave, health insurance, and retirement plans.

School Media Specialist

Education and Training
Advanced degree

Salary Range
Average—$27,400
to $37,900

Employment Outlook
Fair

Definition and Nature of the Work

School media specialists advise school personnel on the use of nonprint media. Films, audiotapes, filmstrips, film loops, and slide presentations are all nonprint media. School media specialists may work either for an individual school or for a school district. Those who work in individual schools help teachers plan programs for their classes. For example, a media specialist may consult with a history teacher about the maps, tapes, and filmstrips available for an American history project. Media specialists also help plan the school's curriculum. They conduct workshops for teachers on the use of media in the classroom. They know what equipment is available for school use from the state and district offices. They also supervise the purchase of equipment and resources for the school. Many specialists work in school libraries.

Specialists at the district level have administrative duties. They plan the use of audiovisual materials for all the schools in a given district. They also make policy decisions about the use of media in schools. For example, they may help

A school media specialist advises a teacher on the use of nonprint media that will assist in the curriculum.

school superintendents make presentations to school boards. Sometimes they are in charge of the schools' libraries as well.

School media specialists are experts on the tools and techniques of media production and presentation. Some media specialists use their training and experience to produce new educational materials for publishing firms.

Education and Training Requirements

Requirements vary widely from state to state. Furthermore, requirements change frequently. Before you decide on a course of study, be sure to check the requirements of the state in which you want to teach. School media specialists generally need a master's degree in educational media or a master's degree in another field of education and course work in media. In some states, teacher certification, teaching experience, and work experience as a media specialist are required.

Getting the Job

Your school placement office may be able to help you find a job. Private employment agencies that specialize in the field of education may offer job leads. Want ads in local newspapers and job banks on the Internet may list openings. In some areas you are assigned to a post when you are certified. You can also apply directly to school boards.

Advancement Possibilities and Employment Outlook

Specialists can advance from positions at the school level to posts at the district level or to jobs as heads of media for several school districts. Those with a doctoral degree can find jobs as college teachers. Some specialists advance to state posts in the department of education. They may become directors of curriculum or media programming.

Little growth is anticipated in the employment of school media specialists through the year 2006. Opportunities in this relatively small field will depend largely on the extent of public funding for education. However, corporations that maintain in-house libraries may offer some additional job opportunities for the media specialist.

Working Conditions

Many specialists who work at the school level combine media work with teaching. Their schedule follows that of other teachers. Sometimes their work involves handling heavy projection equipment. District media specialists and state workers work less often in the actual production of programs. However, their hours may be longer because they often attend late meetings and conferences.

Earnings and Benefits

Salaries vary with each state. School workers earn salaries comparable to those of teachers. District supervisors earn slightly higher wages. School media specialists currently earn salaries ranging from $27,400 to $37,900 a year. Benefits generally include paid holidays and vacations, health insurance, and pension plans. Media specialists often may receive tenure during their years as full-time teachers. Tenure protects employees from being fired without exceptional cause.

Where to Go for More Information

Association for Educational
    Communications and Technology
1025 Vermont Avenue, NW, Suite 820
Washington, DC 20005
(202) 347-7834
www.aect.org

International Communications Industries
    Association
11242 Waples Mill Road, Suite 200
Fairfax, VA 22030
(703) 273-7200
www.usa.net/icia

National Education Association of the
    United States
1201 Sixteenth Street, NW
Washington, DC 20036-3290
(202) 833-4000
www.nea.org

Social Worker

Education and Training
Advanced degree

Salary Range
Varies—see profile

Employment Outlook
Very good

Definition and Nature of the Work

Social workers offer guidance and counseling to people with problems related to poverty, sickness, family matters, and individual crises. They work in a variety of settings, including public welfare agencies, private social service agencies, school systems, hospitals, clinics, and recreation and rehabilitation centers. Social workers' clients range from children who have family or school problems to elderly people who have no one to care for them to people who are unemployed or have inadequate housing.

Social workers provide a number of services, including finding foster homes for children and helping families who have been victimized by floods and other disasters. Sometimes social workers work with their clients to obtain government funds and services. They may help clients seek treatment for illness, obtain additional education, and find homemaking services when needed. Social workers may also conduct courses on child care and begin legal action in cases of child abuse.

Social workers who are employed in school systems counsel students who are having difficulties. In trying to discover the root of a particular problem, they meet with the student and his or her parents and teachers. If social workers cannot handle the case, they refer it to an appropriate agency. Many work in conjunction with juvenile courts. Social workers employed by hospitals help patients adjust to disabilities. They also counsel patients' families. A small number of social workers are employed as teachers or researchers.

There are three approaches to social work: casework, group work, and community organization work. Most social workers use a combination of these methods. Caseworkers have conferences with individuals and families. For instance, they may help families stricken by the death of a parent. Group work involves helping people who have problems in common through recreation, guidance, and rehabilitation. Social workers meet with groups of unwed mothers, alcoholics, drug addicts, and elderly people to help them solve their problems through discussions and well-planned activities. Through community organization work, social workers set up religious, civic, and political groups that are needed in an area of a city or town. For example, they may set up programs to find jobs for idle high school students.

One special group of social workers are *psychiatric social workers*. They may work at the same agencies and institutions as other social workers, but their emphasis is on psychological problems. Psychiatric social workers are usually members of a team of specialists. In most agencies they work under the direction of a psychiatrist or psychologist.

Education and Training Requirements

For most positions, a master's degree in social work is required, although a limited number of jobs are available for those with a bachelor's degree. Social workers who teach or do research generally hold a doctoral degree.

When in college, you should major in sociology, psychology, or another social science and take courses in related areas, such as economics, child studies, education, and political science. Graduate school study often consists of courses in human growth and development, social welfare policies, and methods of social work. Most graduate schools offer work-study programs that will enable you to get work experience in an agency, hospital, or school.

All states have licensing, certification, or registration laws regarding social work, although requirements vary from state to state. New social workers generally learn from experienced workers for the first few months on the job. After 2 years of supervised experience, you may be eligible for membership in the Academy of Certified Social Workers, which is administered by the National Association of Social Workers. Membership is not required, but it is prestigious.

Psychiatric social workers must have a master's degree in psychiatric social work. Their academic requirements are similar to those of social workers, but there is a heavier concentration in psychology. A good part of their training during graduate school is spent in fieldwork supervised by clinical psychologists.

Getting the Job

Your school placement office may be able to help you find a job. You can also apply directly to agencies for which you would like to work. Newspaper want ads, job banks on the Internet, and professional journals offer job leads. Private employment agencies that specialize in placing professional workers may help you. If you are interested in a government job, apply to take the necessary civil service test. Many job contacts are made by students doing fieldwork for college courses.

Advancement Possibilities and Employment Outlook

Experienced social workers holding a master's degree may become senior caseworkers, case supervisors, or chief social workers. They may also take on administrative jobs. Those holding a doctoral degree may become university teachers or researchers.

The outlook for social workers is very good, with employment projected to grow faster than the average through the year 2006. Many openings will occur to replace workers who retire or leave their jobs for other reasons. Competition may exist in major metropolitan areas, however. Job prospects will be best for holders of graduate degrees.

Working Conditions

Social workers are employed in many places. Cities, suburbs, and rural areas all need social workers in schools, hospitals, offices, agencies, jails, and courts. While social work is generally challenging and fulfilling, at times it can be quite frustrating. Many people are afraid to share their problems, and some cases may be difficult to handle. Frequently, important work cannot be accomplished because agencies do not have the money for supplies and services. Social workers must be mature and sensitive to handle their responsibilities. Although they usually work 35 to 40 hours a week, they are sometimes required to work overtime to meet with clients, attend community meetings, and handle emergencies. Social workers generally receive compensatory time off for extra hours worked.

Earnings and Benefits

Salaries vary widely with education, experience, and location. Social workers with a bachelor's degree earn an average of $25,000 a year. Those with a master's degree earn an average of $35,000 to $40,000 a year. Federal government workers make $45,000 or more a year. Social workers in teaching, research, and administrative positions, as well as those employed by cities and large urban counties, earn considerably more than those employed by state agencies. Benefits generally include paid holidays and vacations, health insurance, and pension plans.

Where to Go for More Information

American Federation of State, County and
   Municipal Employees
1625 L Street, NW
Washington, DC 20036
(202) 452-4800

National Association of Social Workers
750 First Street, NE, Suite 700
Washington, DC 20002-4241
(202) 408-8600

Teacher, College

Education and Training
Advanced degree

Salary Range
Varies—see profile

Employment Outlook
Varies—see profile

Definition and Nature of the Work

The job of teacher at the college and university level involves much more than just teaching. As experts in their subject area, college teachers set the standards for the research conducted in their discipline. They also write articles and books in addition to teaching classes on the graduate and undergraduate levels. Teachers work at 2-year junior and community colleges, 4-year colleges and universities, and graduate and professional schools. Some teach in evening and continuing education programs.

Colleges and universities are composed of many different departments, such as literature, history, music, psychology, and chemistry. Most teachers work in one department and specialize in one phase of their discipline. They usually teach from two to four courses each semester. Teachers often combine many different methods of teaching, but most use some form of lecture and discussion. In addition, teachers read student papers and correct examinations. They hold office hours so that students may discuss their work and serve as advisers to students who are majoring in their department. Some teachers combine teaching with administrative duties. For example, a physics teacher at a small college might also be the dean of students. Other college teachers work-part time as consultants to educational organizations and other groups that can use their special knowledge.

Although all college teachers may be called professors in the general sense, there are distinct ranks in the profession. *Instructors* are at the lowest level; they usually have no job security and may have no voice in determining curriculum or setting university policy. Instructors usually teach undergraduates. *Assistant professors* and *associate professors* are more experienced. They teach undergraduates and, at some schools, graduate students. They may be active in university administrative affairs and set the curriculum for their own courses. *Full professors* are the most highly ranked teachers. They may serve as department heads as well as teach.

Education and Training Requirements

College teachers must have a master's or a doctoral degree. Many 2-year junior and community colleges hire teachers who have a master's degree. Many 4-year colleges and universities employ master's degree holders as instructors, but they usually expect these teachers to complete their doctoral degree. Many teachers finish the requirements for their doctoral degree while they work. A doctoral degree is generally required for full-time positions in colleges or universities.

A master's degree generally requires between 1 and 3 years of graduate work beyond college. To complete a doctoral degree, between 2 and 6 years of work beyond the master's are required. High school and college courses in foreign languages are helpful because many graduate programs require that students be able to read foreign languages. Graduate students take in-depth courses in their field. For a master's degree, a master's thesis and written and oral examinations may be required. Requirements for a doctoral degree include more course work, oral examinations, and a book-length paper, called a dissertation, which is based on original research.

Many graduate students work as teaching assistants for at least 1 year. Some teach their own classes. Others lead small discussion groups or conduct laboratory classes that are part of a professor's large lecture classes. Teaching assistantships provide graduate students with financial aid and college teaching experience.

Getting the Job

Your school placement office may be able to help you find a teaching position. Often professors help their students find jobs. Because they know teachers at other colleges, they are in a good position to know about openings before they are announced. You can apply directly to teaching institutions for jobs. Professional journals often list openings in a specific field, as do newspaper want ads. The *Chronicle of Higher Education,* a weekly newspaper, also lists hundreds of positions. You may be able to find a job through a private employment agency that specializes in placing teachers.

Most college teachers work in one department and specialize in one phase of their discipline. In addition to teaching classes, they conduct research on their specialty and write articles and books.

Advancement Possibilities and Employment Outlook

Instructors may become assistant professors, associate professors, and then full professors after many years of experience. Teachers usually need a doctoral degree to obtain positions as associate professors. The requirement for promotion varies from place to place; some colleges look for excellence in teaching, while others require teachers to write extensively for publication. Experienced and well-qualified teachers often are given tenure at their colleges. Having tenure generally constitutes a permanent appointment; tenured professors cannot be dismissed without exceptional cause. Professors can also advance by accepting jobs at more prestigious colleges or by becoming department heads. They may choose to take administrative posts; for example, some become college presidents.

More than 860,000 people work as full- or part-time college teachers. The employment outlook varies with each field. However, employment of college and university faculty is expected to increase as fast as the average through the year 2006 as enrollments in higher education increase. The number of people holding doctoral degrees has increased as well, so there are more people competing for teaching jobs. Most openings arise when teachers advance, retire, or leave the field. Because some colleges and universities are facing financial difficulties, there has been a trend of hiring more part-time faculty. With uncertainty over future funding, many colleges and universities are cutting back and even eliminating some academic programs or departments. Teaching prospects are best in computer science, engineering, and business—fields that offer appealing nonacademic job opportunities and attract fewer applicants for academic positions. Teachers in the sciences, as well as those with administrative skills, generally will also have good opportunities.

Working Conditions

Most teachers spend from 12 to 16 hours a week in class. Their schedules change each semester. Office hours, faculty meetings, advising, and class preparation account for between 30 and 40 additional hours a week. Teachers enjoy a certain degree of freedom because they can arrange their own schedules around their class time. Because the academic year runs from September to May, teachers may use the other months to do research or take summer teaching jobs. Because research projects, especially those in the sciences, may be funded by private and government money, teachers may have to compete for available funds. In colleges in which the pressure to publish is strong, research may take up much of the teacher's time. Teachers with established reputations may be asked to spend semesters as visiting professors at other colleges. Many college teachers belong to labor unions.

Earnings and Benefits

Salaries vary widely with rank and with the individual college. By rank, the average for instructors is $30,800 a year; assistant professors, $40,100; associate professors, $48,300. Salaries for full professors range from $52,000 to more than $67,000 a year. Some teachers increase their income by working as consultants.

Benefits also vary. Teachers are usually paid over a 12-month period that includes the time they do not teach. Most receive health insurance and pension plans. Some colleges offer tenured teachers sabbatical leave every seventh year. During leaves, professors are relieved from teaching duties to devote all of their time to research. Some colleges provide housing at reduced prices.

Where to Go for More Information

American Association of University
   Professors
1012 Fourteenth Street, NW, Suite 500
Washington, DC 20005-3465
(202) 737-5900
www.aaup.org

American Council on Education
1 Dupont Circle, NW, Suite 800
Washington, DC 20036-1193
(202) 939-9300
www.acenet.edu

National Education Association of the
   United States
1201 Sixteenth Street, NW
Washington, DC 20036-3290
(202) 833-4000
www.nea.org

Teacher, Elementary and Preschool

Definition and Nature of the Work

Elementary and preschool teachers instruct children from the nursery school level through the sixth grade. Preschool teachers work with the young children in nursery schools and kindergartens. *Nursery school teachers* teach children who are 2 to 4 years old. These teachers concentrate on the social skills; they teach children to share and communicate with others their own age. They also help children learn practical skills, such as tying their own shoes. Nursery school teachers keep their pupils occupied with activities that include music, games, and storytelling.

Kindergarten teachers have many of the same goals for their 5-year-old pupils. They help them learn to play and communicate with others. In kindergarten, students are introduced to subjects they will pursue in later grades. They learn arithmetic by means of counting games and begin to read the letters on building blocks. Teachers at the preschool level have little difficulty keeping their students occupied. Their aim is to provide constructive outlets for their students' curiosity. Because young children generally attend school for only a few hours each day, teachers may have two separate classes—one in the morning and one in the afternoon.

Elementary school teachers usually have the same class for the whole school day. They teach students the basic skills they will need throughout their school years: reading, writing, arithmetic, and simple concepts in science. Some teachers who participate in team-teaching programs specialize in one subject, such as science or arithmetic, which they teach to several groups of students. A few teachers, such as *remedial reading teachers,* are specialists who work with small groups of students who need special attention.

Bilingual teachers are another type of specialist. They concentrate on improving their students' English-language skills. They may also teach other subjects in their students' native language. *ESL* (English as a second language) *teachers* teach English to students who have very limited exposure to the language. *Special education teachers* teach students with physical or mental handicaps. Special education teachers usually teach diverse groups because students are placed in special education classes regardless of grade. *Homebound teachers* give lessons to students who are unable to attend school regularly because of health problems. Teachers of the homebound go to students' homes to teach.

Teachers on both the preschool and elementary levels may attend meetings of the school board and parent-teacher association. Furthermore, teachers meet regularly with parents to tell them about their children's progress and to determine how students' home environments affect their development in school.

Education and Training Requirements

Teachers who work in public schools must be licensed or certified in the state in which they teach,

Many public elementary schools employ teachers who specialize in one subject, such as art, music, or computers. These teachers must be certified in the state in which they teach.

although specific requirements vary from state to state. In some states private and parochial school teachers must also be certified to work. Certification requirements in most states include minimum educational standards as well as satisfactory performance on written examinations. Kindergarten and elementary school teachers need a bachelor's degree, including course work in education and student-teaching experience. Some school districts require a master's degree. Nursery school teachers generally need at least a bachelor's degree as well as experience working in early childhood education.

Because requirements vary, you should know the standards in your state and the preferences of local school boards before making any decisions regarding your education. Teachers who work in special areas of education generally need the most training.

Getting the Job

Your college placement office may help you find a teaching position. Some teachers' associations also offer help in finding academic positions. You can write directly to the superintendents of school districts in which you want to teach. In some school districts, teachers are assigned to schools when they pass the certification examinations. Newspaper want ads and job banks on the Internet often list openings for teachers.

Advancement Possibilities and Employment Outlook

As teachers become more experienced, they may find advancement in the form of higher pay. Some become specialists in areas such as remedial reading. Teachers may also become the directors of special educational projects in their school districts. Others advance to administrative positions such as teacher supervisors or principals. They might even decide to teach at colleges of education. These positions sometimes require further education. Nursery school teachers may go on to teach kindergarten and elementary classes if they complete the necessary educational requirements.

The employment outlook for elementary and preschool teachers varies with geographic area and subject specialty. Openings will occur to replace teachers who retire or leave their profession for other reasons. Many inner cities, with schools plagued with crime and overcrowding, have trouble attracting enough teachers. Moreover, school districts often have difficulty hiring teachers in certain subject areas such as math and the sciences. Efforts to recruit minority teachers are expected to increase, especially as the demand for bilingual teachers to teach ESL grows.

Overall employment of elementary and preschool teachers is expected to grow as fast as the average. School enrollment of 5- to 13-year-olds is projected to increase through the year 2006. The hiring of teachers is usually dependent on state and local expenditures, but with a growing public demand to improve the quality of education, there should be an increase in the teacher workforce. The supply of teachers may also increase as a result of reports of improved job prospects and greater teacher involvement allowed in determining school policy.

Working Conditions

Working conditions vary from school to school. The job can be tiring, even for teachers who love children. The pace of activity is especially high in the early grades. Unruly students can make teaching difficult. However, teachers can find great personal satisfaction by watching their students make progress and knowing that they are shaping young lives.

Nursery school teachers may work only half a day. Elementary school teachers usually work with the same class the whole school day, whereas kindergarten teachers generally work with two classes, one in the morning and one in the afternoon. Although preparation periods are built into the workday, teachers also spend extra time preparing lessons and grading papers at home. Teachers sometimes attend late-day meetings, and parent-teacher conferences are almost always scheduled in the evenings, when parents return from work. Because the school year runs from September to June, teachers may have to look for positions in summer schools or find other jobs. Some spend their summers taking courses to improve their skills. Many teachers belong to labor unions.

Earnings and Benefits

Salaries vary widely, depending on a school's location and a teacher's education. Public elementary school teachers earn an average of about $32,000 to $38,000 a year. Experienced teachers may earn as much as $45,000 a year. Salaries of preschool and kindergarten teachers average about $19,000 to $26,000 a year. Private school teachers generally earn less than public school teachers. Benefits vary, but elementary and preschool teachers can usually expect paid holidays and vacations, health insurance, and pension plans.

Where to Go for More Information

American Federation of Teachers
555 New Jersey Avenue, NW
Washington, DC 20001
(202) 879-4400
www.aft.org

National Association for the Education of Young Children
1509 Sixteenth Street, NW
Washington, DC 20036-1426
(202) 232-8777
www.naeyc.org

National Education Association of the United States
1201 Sixteenth Street, NW
Washington, DC 20036-3290
(202) 833-4000
www.nea.org

Teacher, Secondary School

Definition and Nature of the Work

Secondary school teachers instruct students in junior and senior high schools. They conduct classes in academic subjects or teach courses such as mechanical drawing and woodworking in which specific skills are learned. In addition, they meet with other teachers to plan courses that use new methods and materials. They also are often involved with organizing extracurricular activities such as sports and social groups. Teachers work as part of a team that includes school administrators, school counselors, and school psychologists. Teachers work closely with parents and parent groups and with community and social work agencies.

Junior high school teachers instruct students in the 7th, 8th, and 9th grades, while *high school teachers* teach the 10th, 11th, and 12th grades. In some school districts, junior high schools have been replaced by middle or intermediate schools, which students enter at a somewhat earlier age. *Intermediate school teachers* may teach the 5th through 8th grades.

Secondary school teachers generally teach between four and seven classes a day. Teachers usually conduct classes only in their field of interest. English, mathematics, science, and history are academic subjects taught in all schools. Some teachers specialize in foreign languages, computer sciences, music, or art. In addition to subject classes, teachers may be assigned to homeroom classes and study halls. In homeroom, attendance is taken and school business handled.

Education and Training
College plus training

Salary Range
Average—$38,600

Employment Outlook
Very good

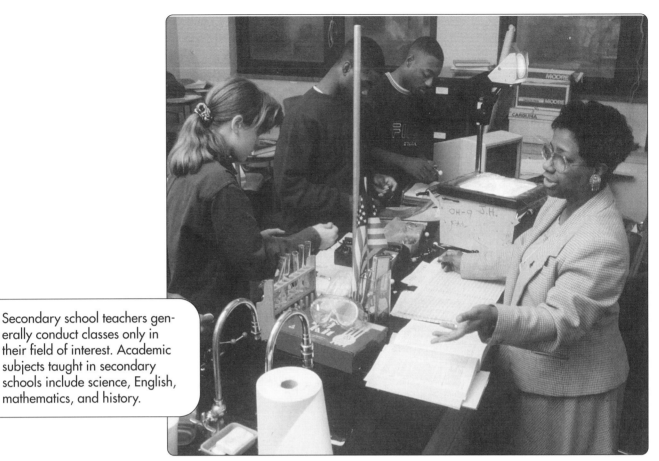

Secondary school teachers generally conduct classes only in their field of interest. Academic subjects taught in secondary schools include science, English, mathematics, and history.

Teachers in study halls must maintain order so that students can study in a quiet atmosphere.

Physical education teachers teach gym classes. These teachers concentrate on improving students' strength and motor skills. Teachers may administer physical fitness and posture tests and set up exercise programs to meet students' needs. Specific sports such as softball, basketball, and tennis may also be taught. Physical education teachers generally serve as coaches for one or more sports teams after school hours.

Some secondary school teachers have special skills in certain areas of teaching. *Special education teachers* teach students with physical or mental handicaps. *ESL* (English as a second language) *teachers* teach English to students who have very limited exposure to the language. *Bilingual teachers* work to improve their students' skills in English. They may also teach other subjects such as mathematics and history in their students' native language. *Homebound teachers* give lessons to students who are unable to attend school regularly because of health problems. Teachers of the homebound go to students' homes to teach.

Education and Training Requirements

Teachers who work in public secondary schools must be certified in their state; in some states private and parochial school teachers also must be certified. Certification requirements include a bachelor's degree, usually in the subject to be taught, student-teaching experience, and course work in education. Many states now require teachers to possess or be working toward a master's degree at the time of certification. Requirements vary from state to state and change frequently. Check the requirements in your state before making any decisions that affect your schooling. Usually teachers must pass written and sometimes oral examinations to be certified.

Getting the Job

Your school placement office may list job openings. You can also apply directly to the principal of a school or superintendent of a district in which you would like to teach. Some professional journals and teachers' organizations list job openings. Private employment agencies that specialize in education may offer job leads. Newspaper want ads and job banks on the Internet may also list openings. In some areas teachers are assigned to schools when they are certified.

Advancement Possibilities and Employment Outlook

Teachers may become heads of their departments. They may also take on administrative and counseling duties as school counselors, assistant principals, principals, and school superintendents. Most of these positions require at least a master's degree; some require a doctoral degree as well.

About 1,400,000 people are employed as secondary school teachers in the United States. Employment is expected to grow faster than the average because of a strong increase in the enrollment of 14- to 17-year-olds through the year 2006. Competition for jobs may be keenest in suburban areas, however. Jobs will be most plentiful in central cities and rural areas. Teachers in the natural and physical sciences, mathematics, special education, and vocational subjects are likely to find jobs more easily than teachers in other fields.

Working Conditions

Working conditions vary somewhat with each subject taught. While most teachers work with 10 to 30 students per class, music teachers may work with 1 student at a time. Teaching is physically strenuous; most teachers stand most of the day and may suffer from voice strain. Hours vary, but most teachers are in school between 9:00 A.M. and 3:00 P.M., Monday through Friday. Teachers also work at home, and some spend additional time at school attending meetings and supervising extracurricular activities such as drama productions or sports events. Secondary school teachers usually do not work during the summer months; many use this free time to earn additional income. Many teachers belong to labor unions.

Earnings and Benefits

Teachers' salaries vary with education, length of service, and location of the school. The average annual salary for public secondary school teachers is about $38,600. Urban schools tend to pay higher salaries than those in rural areas. Teachers with a master's or doctoral degree earn much more than those who have only a bachelor's degree. Private school teachers generally earn less than public school teachers. In some schools, teachers receive extra pay for coaching sports and working with students in extracurricular activities.

Teachers receive unusually long paid vacations and holidays, as well as health insurance and pension plans. Teachers may earn extra income during the summer working in the school system or in other jobs.

Where to Go for More Information

American Counseling Association
5999 Stevenson Avenue
Alexandria, VA 22304-3300
(703) 823-9800
www.counseling.org

American Federation of Teachers
555 New Jersey Avenue, NW
Washington, DC 20001
(202) 879-4400
www.aft.org

National Education Association of the
   United States
1201 Sixteenth Street, NW
Washington, DC 20036-3290
(202) 833-4000
www.nea.org

Urban and Regional Planner

Definition and Nature of the Work

Urban and regional planners are responsible for determining the best use of a community's land and resources for residential, commercial, and recreational purposes. Urban planners design new communities and develop programs for revitalizing and expanding existing cities. Regional planners are engaged in the same kind of work on a much larger scale; their work involves states, large regional areas, and sometimes entire countries. Planners renovate slums, expand cities, modernize transportation systems, and devise ways to distribute properly public facilities such as schools and parks. Their major concern is to unify the social, economic, and physical development of an area so that it will be functional for its citizens. Planners also find ways to attract industries to move to an area in order to create jobs for residents.

Urban and regional planning projects generally begin with a request from a city or state official to develop a new community or renovate an area that is run-down. Planners gather information about the area's economic and social climate, projected population growth or decline, and plans for industrial development. To get a cross section of public opinion, planners meet with representatives of community groups, government, public agencies, and labor and business organizations. Planners consider the area's current problems as well as needs that are likely to arise in the future. For example, an expected rise in an area's population will create a need for more electrical power. Foreseeing this need, planners try to determine ways in which the necessary power can be generated without creating pollution.

Whereas urban planners design new communities and develop programs for improving cities, regional planners do the same type of work on a much larger scale for states, regions, or even entire countries.

Once the data are collected, teams of planners study the information and arrive at decisions. Then they draw up proposals and submit them to the area's planning commission or to government officials for approval. If approval is given, construction or renovation begins. Planners usually supervise the work through its completion. Projects may take many years to complete.

Most planners work for city, county, state, federal, or regional agencies. Some work for large construction companies and architectural firms. Others work as consultants or hold teaching or research positions. Planners also work for international organizations that plan projects in developing nations.

Education and Training Requirements

Most entry-level jobs in federal, state, and local government agencies require a master's degree in urban or regional planning. Related areas of study include urban design and landscape architecture. Some employers may consider applicants with equivalent work experience. A bachelor's degree in an accredited planning program combined with a master's degree is good preparation for a job. In college it is best to major in architecture, public administration, landscape architecture, or civil engineering. Courses in related fields such as political science, economics, and geography are also helpful.

With a bachelor's degree in architecture or engineering, you may be able to earn a master's degree in 1 year. Many programs take 2 to 3 years to complete. In graduate school you will learn to analyze and solve planning problems. You will also have the opportunity to do part-time fieldwork in an office or agency.

Recent graduates expand their skills on the job. Generally, they begin by working on small projects under the supervision of experienced workers. As planners gain practical experience they take on more responsibility.

Getting the Job

Most people begin work at a city, state, or federal agency. Many cities have planning commissions with technical staffs and special agencies for urban renewal or neighborhood conservation programs. For a government job you must pass a civil service test and meet the necessary educational and experience requirements. There are many opportunities for regional planners in other countries. Private employment agencies that specialize in placing professionals may be able to help you find a job. You can also apply directly to private and international organizations for which you would like to work.

Advancement Possibilities and Employment Outlook

Urban and regional planners can advance to project director positions. Some choose to take on more challenging projects that offer them greater responsibility.

The job outlook for urban and regional planners is fair, with employment expected to grow more slowly than the average through the year 2006. There is a growing demand for experts trained in environmental, economic, and energy planning. However, increases in the number of people entering this relatively small field may result in stiff competition for available jobs. There have also been government cutbacks and regulations on commercial development. Opportunities will be best with nongovernmental initiatives and more affluent, rapidly growing communities.

Working Conditions

Urban and regional planning is highly rewarding work. Workers find satisfaction not only in knowing that they help others but also in seeing projects through from conception to the physical reality. There are, however, some disadvantages. Lack of funds or disapproval from government officials can be discouraging. Planners must be patient because their ideas may take many years to implement. Planners must be both creative and flexible when proposals have to be modified to suit the government's needs. They must be able to handle detail as well as have the tenacity to follow problems through until they are solved. Planners work both indoors and outdoors. They generally work 35 to 40 hours a week, although those in positions of great responsibility may work many more hours. Consulting planners set their own hours.

Earnings and Benefits

Salaries vary widely with education, experience, and the location of the work. Salaries are generally higher in larger cities. Urban and regional planners with less than 5 years of experience average $30,000 a year. Those with between 5 and 10 years of experience earn an average of $39,000 a year. Planners employed by the federal government earn an average of $57,000 a year. The most experienced planners can earn as much as $65,000 a year, depending on the size of the company for which they work. Consultants' fees are paid on an hourly basis and generally depend on a consultant's previous experience and reputation. Benefits generally include paid holidays and vacations, health insurance, and pension plans.

Where to Go for More Information

American Federation of State, County and
 Municipal Employees
1625 L Street, NW
Washington, DC 20036
(202) 452-4800

American Planning Association
122 South Michigan Avenue, Suite 1600
Chicago, IL 60603-6107
(312) 431-9100
www.planning.org

United States Government Federal
 Information Center
Phone number in local directory.

Vocational Counselor

Education and Training
College

Salary Range
Average—$35,800

Employment Outlook
Very good

Definition and Nature of the Work

Vocational counselors, also called employment counselors, help people find employment that suits their needs and skills. They provide a link between people looking for work and employers. Because people are not always aware of their capabilities, counselors often help clients decide on career goals. To do this, counselors must have an awareness of their clients' potential and also know what skills are in demand in the job market. Unlike agents who work for profit-making employment agencies, these counselors work for organizations that provide vocational counseling free of charge. Counselors work in state employment offices, veterans' programs, colleges and universities, and private and government-sponsored social service agencies. Counselors who work with people who have mental or physical disabilities are called *rehabilitation counselors*. In colleges and universities they may be called *college placement counselors*.

Counselors first interview their clients to find out about their education, past work experience, skills, and interests. They may also evaluate personality traits in an effort to match clients with the type of work that they would be good at and enjoy. Counselors sometimes administer achievement, aptitude, and occupational preference tests. In state employment offices and some other agencies, an employment interviewer collects this information for the employment counselor, who advises the clients. In some agencies the counselor performs all of these duties.

Some people are fully qualified for employment, and it is up to the counselors to contact prospective employers. This is often the case in college placement offices.

Clients who seek help from social service organizations, on the other hand, usually have had some difficulty in finding or holding jobs. Counselors may work with these clients over a period of several months. Such clients may have a handicap or be considered too old to start a job. They may lack sufficient training or have a history of alcoholism or drug abuse. Some have faced prejudice because of their race or gender. Those who have been out of work for a long time may be too discouraged to do well at employment interviews. Counselors work to solve the problems of the particular individual. They may place clients in training programs that will help them develop marketable skills. Counselors themselves may coach clients so that they are able to perform well at interviews. Sometimes counselors may refer clients to social service organizations that can provide more specific assistance. For example, a counselor might refer a client with a physical handicap to a physical rehabilitation center.

School counselors in junior and senior high schools sometimes serve as vocational counselors. They may help students find part-time or summer jobs or place them in full-time positions after graduation. However, these counselors concentrate on preparing students for the job market. They help students choose careers and get the education and training they need for the jobs they want.

Education and Training Requirements

A bachelor's degree is the minimum requirement for vocational counselors, although many employers require a master's degree in vocational counseling and guidance, social work, sociology, or a related field. Many agencies seek to have at least one staff member with a doctoral degree in a counseling-related field. A background in interviewing and testing procedures is useful. Most agencies give on-the-job training to teach new workers counseling methods and to acquaint them with the goals and procedures of the particular agency. Experience in personnel and administrative work may be helpful.

Getting the Job

The school placement office may help you find a job. You can also write directly to agencies for which you would like to work. Professional journals and organizations often list job openings in their publications. State and private employment agencies, newspaper want ads, and job banks on the Internet may offer job leads. If you are interested in a government job, apply to take the appropriate civil service test.

Advancement Possibilities and Employment Outlook

Vocational counselors may take on supervisory or administrative jobs in their agencies. Those who work in schools and colleges may move up to higher positions in the school administration. Some become consultants to government and industry. Others teach counseling in colleges and graduate schools. Counselors may be required to have a doctoral degree to teach in colleges or to reach the highest administrative jobs.

The outlook for vocational counselors is very good. Employment is expected to grow as a result of increasing school enrollments. However, opportunities in this field can be affected by changes in federal funding. Applicants are likely to face some competition for counseling jobs.

Working Conditions

Counselors must be able to communicate clearly and listen carefully. They must be aware of the changing employment scene as well as of various training programs.

Where to Go for More Information

American Counseling Association
5999 Stevenson Avenue
Alexandria, VA 22304-3300
(703) 823-9800
www.counseling.org

American Federation of State, County and
   Municipal Employees
1625 L Street, NW
Washington, DC 20036
(202) 452-4800

To keep up with their field, counselors may spend many extra hours reading papers and bulletins. They generally work in small offices where they can talk with people in private. Sometimes counselors leave the office to talk to employers or to visit training centers. Vocational counselors work 35 to 40 hours a week. Sometimes they put in extra hours during the evening or on weekends.

Earnings and Benefits

Salaries vary with experience, level of education, and the size and location of the employer. Full-time vocational counselors earn an average salary of $35,800 a year. The most experienced counselors can earn as much as $45,000 or more. Benefits generally include paid holidays and vacations, health insurance, and pension plans.

Books

Exploring the Working World

The Adams Job Almanac. Holbrook, MA: Adams Media Corp., annual.

American Almanac of Jobs and Salaries, John W. Wright. New York: Avon Books, biennial.

American Salaries and Wages, 4th ed., Helen S. Fisher. Detroit, MI: Gale Research, Inc., 1997.

America's Top Jobs for College Graduates, J. Michael Farr. Indianapolis, IN: JIST Works, 1997.

America's Top Jobs for People Without College Degrees, J. Michael Farr. Indianapolis, IN: JIST Works, 1997.

America's Top Technical and Trade Jobs, J. Michael Farr. Indianapolis, IN: JIST Works, 1997.

The Big Book of Jobs. Lincolnwood, IL: VGM Career Horizons, 1997.

Career Discovery Encyclopedia, Holli Cosgrove, ed., 6 vols. Chicago: Ferguson, 1997.

CareerSmarts: Jobs with a Future, Martin Yate. New York: Ballantine Books, 1997.

The Complete Guide for Occupational Exploration, J. Michael Farr. Indianapolis, IN: JIST Works, 1993.

The Complete Guide to Public Employment, 3rd ed., Ronald Krannich and Caryl Rae Krannich. Manassas Park, VA: Impact Publications, 1995.

The Harvard Guide to Careers, 5th ed., Martha P. Leape and Susan M. Vacca. Cambridge, MA: Harvard University Press, 1995.

Job Hunter's Sourcebook. Detroit, MI: Gale Research, Inc., biennial.

Jobs '98 (title changes annually), Kathryn Petras, Ross Petras, and George Petras. New York: Simon & Schuster, annual.

Jobs Rated Almanac, Les Krantz. New York: World Almanac, 1995.

Joyce Lain Kennedy's Career Book, Joyce Lain Kennedy and Darryl Laramore. Lincolnwood, IL: VGM Career Horizons, 1997.

The National JobBank, 1998 (title changes annually). Holbrook, MA: Adams Media Corp., annual. (The *JobBank* series also includes editions for several major U.S. cities and regions.)

Occupational Outlook series. Washington, DC: United States Government Printing Office. Briefs, separately published.

Occupational Outlook Quarterly. Washington, DC: Occupational Outlook Service, Bureau of Labor Statistics. Quarterly publication.

Recommended

Occupational Outlook Handbook, United States Department of Labor. Washington, DC: United States Government Printing Office, revised biennially. Expands on the *Dictionary of Occupational Titles.* Groups jobs into similar categories. Discusses the nature of the work, the employment outlook, and earnings.

VGM's Careers Encyclopedia, 4th ed. Lincolnwood, IL: VGM Career Horizons, 1997. A one-volume guide to 180 careers.

Professional Careers Sourcebook, 4th ed. Detroit, MI: Gale Research, Inc., 1996.

The Quick Internet Guide to Career and College Information, Anne Wolfinger. Indianapolis, IN: JIST Works, 1997.

A Student's Guide to Career Exploration on the Internet, Elizabeth H. Oakes. Chicago: Ferguson, 1998.

Vocational Careers Sourcebook, 2nd ed. Detroit, MI: Gale Research, Inc., 1996.

Education and Training Opportunities

American Universities and Colleges, 15th ed. Hawthorne, NY: De Groyter, 1997.

America's Lowest Cost Colleges, Nicholas A. Roes. Barryville, NY: NAR Publications, biennial.

America's Top Internships, Mark Oldman and Samer Hamadeh. New York: Random House, annual.

Barron's Guide to Graduate Business Schools, Eugene Miller, ed. Hauppauge, NY: Barron's Educational Series, revised regularly.

Barron's Guide to Law Schools. Hauppauge, NY: Barron's Educational Series, revised regularly.

Barron's Guide to Medical and Dental Schools, Saul Wischnitzer and Edith Wischnitzer, eds. Hauppauge, NY: Barron's Educational Series, revised regularly.

Bear's Guide to Earning College Degrees Non-Traditionally, 11th ed., John Bear. Benicia, CA: C&B Publishing, 1994.

Chronicle Vocational School Manual. Moravia, NY: Chronicle Guidance Publications, annual.

College Applications and Essays, 3rd ed., Susan D. Van Raalte. New York: Macmillan, 1997.

The College Costs and Financial Aid Handbook, The College Board Staff. New York: The College Board, annual.

College Financial Aid for Dummies, Herm Davis and Joyce Lain Kennedy. Foster City, CA: IDG Books Worldwide, 1997.

College Financial Aid Made Easy, Patrick L. Bellatoni. Berkeley, CA: Ten Speed Press, annual.

The College Guide for Parents, 3rd ed., Charles J. Shields. New York: The College Board, 1995.

The College Handbook. New York: The College Board, annual.

College Planning for Gifted Students, 2nd ed., Sandra L. Berger. Reston, VA: Council for Exceptional Children, 1994.

The Complete Book of Colleges. New York: Random House, annual.

Ferguson's Guide to Apprenticeship Programs, C. J. Summerfield and Holli Cosgrove, eds. 2 vols. Chicago: Ferguson, 1994.

Getting into College, Pat Orovensky. Princeton, NJ: Peterson's, 1995.

Recommended

The following four sources are basic directories of information on colleges and universities. They include general information on each school, its address, a listing of the programs offered, the size of the institution, and costs for tuition.

Barron's Top 50: An Inside Look at America's Best Colleges, Tom Fischgrund, ed. Hauppauge, NY: Barron's Educational Series, revised regularly.

The College Blue Book. New York: Macmillan, revised regularly.

Lovejoy's College Guide, Charles T. Straughn II and Barbarasue Lovejoy Straughn, eds. New York: ARCO, revised regularly.

Peterson's Guide to Four-Year Colleges. Princeton, NJ: Peterson's Guides, revised regularly.

The Gourman Report: A Rating of Undergraduate Programs in American and International Universities, Jack Gourman. Los Angeles, CA: National Education Standards, revised regularly.

Help Yourself: Handbook for College-Bound Students with Learning Disabilities, Erica-Lee Lewis. New York: Random House, 1996.

Index of Majors and Graduate Degrees. New York: The College Board, annual.

Insider's Guide to the Colleges, Yale Daily News Staff, ed. New York: St. Martin's Press, annual.

The Internship Bible. New York: Random House, annual.

Internships for 2-Year College Students. West Hartford, CT: Graduate Group, annual.

Internships Leading to Careers. West Hartford, CT: Graduate Group, annual.

Lovejoy's College Guide for the Learning Disabled, Charles T. Straughn. New York: ARCO, revised regularly.

The National Guide to Educational Credit for Training Programs, American Council on Education. Phoenix, AZ: ACE/Oryx Press, annual.

The 100 Best Colleges for African-American Students, Erlene B. Wilson. New York: Plume, 1998.

Free Money for College: A Guide to More Than 1000 Grants and Scholarships for Undergraduate Study, 4th ed., Laurie Blum. New York: Facts on File, 1996.

Peterson's College Money Handbook. Princeton, NJ: Peterson's, annual.

Peterson's Competitive Colleges. Princeton, NJ: Peterson's, annual.

Peterson's Guide to Graduate and Professional Programs: An Overview. Princeton, NJ: Peterson's, annual.

Peterson's Guide to Two-Year Colleges. Princeton, NJ: Peterson's, annual.

Petersons's Internships. Princeton, NJ: Peterson's, annual.

A Student's Guide to College Admissions: Everything Your Guidance Counselor Has No Time to Tell You, 3rd ed., Harlow Unger. New York: Facts on File, 1995.

Vocational Education: Status in 2-Year Colleges and Early Signs of Change. Upland, PA: Diane Publishing Company, 1994.

Career Goals

Adventure Careers, Alex Hiam and Susan Angle. Franklin Lakes, NJ: Career Press, 1995.

Career Anchors: Discovering Your Real Values, Edgar H. Schein. San Diego, CA: Pfeiffer & Co., rev. 1993.

The Career Atlas, Gail Kuenstler. Franklin Lakes, NJ: Career Press, 1996.

The Career Guide for Creative and Unconventional People, Carol Eikleberry. Berkeley, CA: Ten Speed Press, 1995.

Careers for the Year 2000 and Beyond: Everything You Need to Know to Find the Right Career. Piscataway, NJ: Research and Education Association, 1997.

Recommended

What Color Is Your Parachute? Richard N. Bolles. Berkeley, CA: Ten Speed Press, revised annually. One of the best sources for career changers and job hunters. Workbook style with exercises to identify skills and interests. Provides comprehensive list of sources including books, agencies, and associations.

Choices for the High School Graduate: A Survival Guide for the Information Age, Bryna J. Fireside. Chicago: Ferguson, 1997.

Choosing a Career Made Easy, Patty Marler and Jan Bailey Mattia. Lincolnwood, IL: VGM Career Horizons, 1997.

Chronicle Career Index 1994-95, Harriet Scarry, ed. Moravia, NY: Chronicle Guidance Publications, 1994.

The College Board Guide to Jobs and Career Planning, 2nd ed., Joyce Slayton Mitchell. New York: The College Board, 1994.

College Majors and Careers: A Resource Guide for Effective Life Planning, 3rd ed., Phil Phifer. Chicago: Ferguson, 1997.

Dr. Job's Complete Career Guide, Sandra "Dr. Job" Pesmen. Lincolnwood, IL: VGM Career Horizons, 1996.

Finding Your Perfect Work: The New Career Guide to Making a Living, Creating a Life, Paul Edwards and Sarah Edwards. New York: Putnam, 1996.

Graduate to Your Perfect Job in Six Easy Steps, Jason R. Dorsey. Austin, TX: Golden Ladder Productions, 1997.

Green at Work: Finding a Business Career that Works for the Environment, Susan Cohn. Washington, DC: Island Press, 1995.

The Job Seeker's Guide to Socially Responsible Companies, Katherine Jankowski. Detroit, MI: Gale Research, Inc., 1995.

Jobs for People who Love Travel: Opportunities at Home and Abroad, Ronald L. Krannich and Caryl Rae Krannich. Manassas Park, VA: Impact Publications, 1995.

The Off-the-Beaten-Path Job Book: You Can Make a Living and Have a Life! Sandra Gurvis. Seacaucus, NJ: Carol Publishing Group, 1995.

The Parent's Crash Course in Career Planning: Helping Your College Student Succeed, Marcia B. Harris and Sharon L. Jones. Lincolnwood, IL: VGM Career Horizons, 1996.

The PIE Method for Career Success: A Unique Way to Find Your Ideal Job, Daniel Porot. Indianapolis, IN: JIST Works, 1996.

The Right Job for You: An Interactive Career Planning Guide, J. Michael Farr. Indianapolis, IN: JIST Works, 1997.

Success 2000: Moving into the Millennium with Purpose, Power, and Prosperity, Vicki Spina. New York: Wiley, 1997.

Getting the Job and Getting Ahead

The Adams Electronic Job Search Almanac. Holbrook, MA: Adams Media Corp., 1997.

Almanac of American Employers, Jack W. Plunkett. Galveston, TX: Plunkett Research, Ltd., biennial.

CareerXroads: The Directory to Jobs, Resumes, and Career Management on the World Wide Web. Kendall Park, NJ: MMC Group, 1996.

The Complete Idiot's Guide to Getting the Job You Want, Robert Bly. New York: Alpha Books, 1996.

Electronic Job Search Revolution: How to Win with the New Technology that's Reshaping Today's Job Market, Joyce Lain Kennedy and Thomas J. Morow. New York: Wiley, 1996.

Getting Hired: A Guide for Managers and Professionals, Richard J. Pinsker. Menlo Park, CA: Crisp Publications, 1994.

Getting the Job You Want . . . Now! David H. Roper. New York: Warner Books, 1994.

Great Jobs Abroad, Arthur H. Bell. New York, McGraw Hill, 1997.

Government Job Finder, 1997-2000, Daniel Lauber. River Forest, IL: Planning/Communications, 1997.

The Guide to Internet Job Searching, Margaret Riley, Frances Roehm, Steve Oserman, and the Public Library Association. Lincolnwood, IL: VGM Career Horizons, 1996.

Hoover's Directory of Human Resources Executives. Austin, TX: The Reference Press, revised regularly.

How to Get a Job in . . . (series for major U.S. cities). Chicago: Surrey Books, Inc., annual.

How to Hit the Ground Running in Your New Job, Lynda Pritchard Clemens and Andrea Trulson Dolph. Lincolnwood, IL: VGM Career Horizons, 1995.

International Job Finder, 1997-2000, Daniel Lauber. River Forest, IL: Planning/Communications, 1997.

Job Hunter's Yellow Pages: The National Directory of Employment Services. Harleysville, PA: Career Communications Inc.

Job Search Organizer, Hal Weatherman. Lincolnwood, IL: VGM Career Horizons, 1997.

Job Search 101: Getting Started on Your Career Path, Monica R. Fox and Pat Morton, eds. Indianapolis, IN: JIST Works, 1997.

Job Seeker's Guide to Private-Public Companies, Charity A. Dorgan, ed. Detroit, MI: Gale Research, Inc., 1995.

Jobsmarts for Twentysomethings, Bradley G. Richardson. New York: Vintage Books, 1995.

National Job Hotline Directory, Sue A. Cubbage. River Forest, IL: Planning/ Communications, annual.

Non-Profits & Education Job Finder, 1997- 2000, Daniel Lauber. River Forest, IL: Planning/Communications, 1997.

Peterson's Hidden Job Market. Princeton, NJ: Peterson's, annual.

Professional's Job Finder, 1997-2000, Daniel Lauber. River Forest, IL: Planning/Communications, 1997.

Using the Internet and the World Wide Web in Your Job Search, Fred Edmund Jandt and Mary B. Nemnich. Indianapolis, IN: JIST Works, 1996.

The Very Quick Job Search: Get a Better Job in Half the Time, J. Michael Farr. Indianapolis, IN: JIST Works, 1996.

The Work-At-Home Sourcebook, 6th ed., Lynie Arden. Boulder, CO: Live Oak Publications, 1996.

Recommended

Knock 'Em Dead: The Ultimate Job Seeker's Handbook, Martin J. Yate. Holbrook, MA: Adams Media Corp., 1997. Helps job seekers identify their strengths and improve their interview techniques. Also gives practical advice on networking, handling tough interview questions, and negotiating salaries.

Resumes and Interviews

Better Resumes for Executives and Professionals, 3rd ed., Robert F. Wilson. Hauppauge, NY: Barron's Educational Series, 1996.

The Complete Idiot's Guide to the Perfect Resume, Susan Ireland. New York: Alpha Books, 1996.

The Complete Resume Guide, 5th ed., Marian Faux. New York: Macmillan USA, 1995.

Cover Letters for Dummies, Joyce Lain Kennedy. Foster City, CA: IDG Books Worldwide, 1996.

Cover Letters: Proven Techniques for Writing Letters that Will Help You Get the Job You Want, Taunee Besson and National Business Employment Weekly. New York: Wiley, 1995.

Developing a Professional Vita or Resume, 3rd ed., Carl McDaniels. Chicago: Ferguson, 1997.

Get Hired!: Winning Strategies to Ace the Interview, Paul C. Green. Austin, TX: Bard Books, 1996.

Information Interviewing, 2nd ed., Martha Stoodley. Chicago: Ferguson, 1997.

Interviewing, Arlene S. Hirsch and National Business Employment Weekly. New York: Wiley, 1994.

Job Interviews That Mean Business, 2nd ed., David R. Eyler. New York: Random House, 1996.

The Resume Handbook, 3rd ed., Arthur Rosenberg and David Hizer. Boston: Adams Media Corp., 1996.

The Resume Kit, 3rd ed., Richard H. Beatty. New York: John Wiley & Sons, 1995.

Resume Power: Selling Yourself on Paper, Tom Washington. Bellevue, WA: Mount Vernon Press, 1996.

Resume Writing Made Easy, Lola M. Coxford. Scottsdale, AZ: Gorsuch Scarisbrick, 6th ed., 1997.

Resumes for Dummies, Joyce Lain Kennedy. Foster City, CA: IDG Books Worldwide, 1996.

Resumes that Knock 'Em Dead, 3rd ed., Martin Yate. Holbrook, MA: Adams Media Corp., 1998.

Resumes for Better Jobs, 7th. ed., Lawrence D. Brennan. New York: ARCO, 1998.

Your Resume: Key to a Better Job, 6th ed., Leonard Corwen. New York: Macmillan, 1995.

Recommended

Damn Good Resume Guide, 3rd ed., Yana Parker. Berkeley, CA: Ten Speed Press, 1996. Describes how to write a functional resume.

The New Perfect Resume, Tom Jackson and Ellen Jackson. New York: Doubleday, 1996. A CD-ROM version is also available.

Mid-Career Options

Beat the Odds: Career Buoyancy Tactics for Today's Turbulent Job Market, Martin Yate. New York: Ballantine Books, 1995.

The Career Trap: Breaking Through the 10-Year Barrier to Get the Job You Really Want, Jeffrey G. Allen. New York: AMACOM, 1995.

The Complete Idiot's Guide to Changing Careers, William Charland. New York: Alpha Books, 1998.

The Complete Idiot's Guide to Freelancing, Laurie Rozakis. New York: Alpha Books, 1998.

How to Hold it All Together When You've Lost Your Job, Townsend Albright. Lincolnwood, IL: VGM Career Horizons, 1996.

Kiplinger's Survive and Profit from a Mid-Career Change, Daniel Moreau. Washington, DC: Kiplinger Books, 1994.

Out of Uniform: A Career Transition Guide for Ex-Military Personnel, Harry N. Drier. Lincolnwood, IL: VGM Career Horizons, 1995.

Second Careers: New Ways to Work After 50, Caroline Bird. Boston: Little, Brown, 1992.

Toxic Work: How to Overcome Stress, Overload, and Burnout and Revitalize Your Career, Barbara Bailey Reinhold. New York: Plume, 1997.

Equality of Opportunity

The Black Resource Guide, 10th ed. Washington, DC: Black Resource Guide, 1992.

Cracking the Corporate Closet, Daniel B. Baker, Sean O'Brien Strub, and Bill Henning. New York: HarperBusiness, 1995.

Equal Opportunity. Hauppauge, NY: Equal Opportunity Publications, published 3 times a year.

Financial Aid for Minorities. Garrett Park, MD: Garrett Park Press, 1994.

Financial Aid for the Disabled and Their Families, 6th ed., Gail A. Schlachter and R. David Weber. San Carlos, CA: Reference Services Press, 1996.

Successful Job Search Strategies for the Disabled: Understanding the ADA, Jeffrey G. Allen. New York: Wiley, 1994.

Women and Work, Susan Bullock. Atlantic Highlands, NJ: Humanities Press, 1994.

Recommended

Career Change: Everything You Need to Know to Meet New Challenges and Take Control of Your Career, David P. Helford. Lincolnwood, IL: VGM Career Horizons, 1995.

Change Your Job, Change Your Life: High Impact Strategies for Finding Great Jobs into the 21st Century, Ronald L. Krannich. Manassas Park, VA: Impact Publications, 1997.

Recommended

The Big Book of Minority Opportunities, 6th ed., Willis L. Johnson, ed. Chicago: Ferguson, 1995. Directory of organizations that have special programs to help minorities meet their educational and career goals.

The Big Book of Opportunities for Women, Elizabeth A. Olson, ed. Chicago: Ferguson, 1996. Directory of organizations that have special programs to help women meet their educational and career goals.

Coping with Sexual Harassment, Beryl Black, ed. New York: The Rosen Publishing Group, rev. 1992. Helpful in giving direct ways to respond to and prevent sexual harassment at work.

Lists and Indexes of Career and Vocational Information

The Career Guide: Dun's Employment Opportunities Directory. Parsippany, NJ: Dun and Bradstreet Information Services, annual.

Chronicle Career Index. Moravia, NY: Chronicle Guidance Publications, annual.

Dictionary of Holland Occupational Codes (DHOC), 3rd ed., Gary D. Gottfredson and John L. Holland. Lutz, FL: Psychological Assessment Resources, 1996.

Dictionary of Occupational Titles, 4th ed. United States Department of Labor. Washington, DC: United States Government Printing Office, 1991. Supplemented by *The Classification of Jobs According to Worker Trait Factors* (Elliott & Fitzpatrick, 1992) and *Selected Characteristics of Occupations Defined in the Revised Dictionary of Occupational Titles* (Claitors Pub. Div., 1993).

Where the Jobs Are: A Comprehensive Directory of 1200 Journals Listing Career Opportunities, S. Norman Feingold and Glenda Ann Hansard-Winkler. Garrett Park, MD: Garrett Park Press, 1989.

Internet Sites

Sites with Extensive Links

Career Resource Center
www.careers.org

Catapult
www.jobweb.org/catapult/catapult.htm

Job Hunt: A Meta-List of On-Line Job-Search Resources and Services
www.job-hunt.org

Job Search and Employment Opportunities: Best Bets

asa.ugl.lib.umich.edu/chdocs/employment/

Online Career Center (OCC)
www.occ.com

JIST Works
www.jist.com

The Riley Guide: Employment Opportunities and Job Resources on the Internet
www.dbm.com/jobguide

What Color Is Your Parachute Job Hunting Online
washingtonpost.com/parachute

Career Development Resources

Career Assistance from the Online Career Center
www.occ.com/occ/CareerAssist.html

Career Magazine
www.careermag.com

Kaplan's Career Center
www.kaplan.com/career

Online Information and References

AT&T Toll-Free Internet Directory
www.tollfree.att.net

Beatrice's Web Guide—Careers
www.bguide.com/webguide/careers

The Best Jobs in the USA Today
www.bestjobsusa.com

CareerMart
www.careermart.com

Federal Jobs Digest
www.jobsfed.com

GaleNet
galenet.gale.com

Infoseek Guide—Jobs & Careers
guide-p.infoseek.com/Careers

Job Finders Online
jobfindersonline.com

Occupational Outlook Handbook
stats.bls.gov/ocohome.htm

StudentCenter
www.studentcenter.com

U.S. Bureau of Labor Statistics Home Page
stats.bls.gov/blshome.htm

US News Online Colleges and Career Center
www4.usnews.com/usnews/edu/home.htm

Wall Street Journal Interactive Division
careers.wsj.com

Yahoo! Business and Economy
www.yahoo.com/Business

Job Databases and Resume Posting

America's Job Bank
www.ajb.dni.is/index.html

CareerCity
www.careercity.com

CareerMosaic
www.careermosaic.com

CareerPath
www.careerpath.com

Career Site
www.careersite.com

CareerWeb
www.careerweb.com

e-span
www.espan.com

JobBank USA
www.jobbankusa.com

Job Trak
www.jobtrak.com

Job Web
www.jobweb.org

The Monster Board
www.monster.com

World Wide Web Employment Office
www.harbornet.com/biz/office/annex.html

Audiovisual Materials

The following titles include, where possible, the developer's name and location or else the name and location of a distributor. Audiovisual titles may be available through several distributors.

Exploring the Working World

The Career Builders series. Video. New York: Educational Design, Inc.

Career Cluster Decisions. Video; guide. Bloomington, IL: Meridian Education Corp.

Career Exploration: A Job Seeker's Guide to the OOH, DOT, and GOE. Video. Bloomington, IL: Meridian Education Corp.

Career Plan. Video; guide. Bloomington, IL: Meridian Education Corp.

Career Planning: Putting Your Skills to Work. Video; guide. Mt. Kisco, NY: Guidance Associates.

Career Planning Steps. Video. Charleston, WV: Cambridge Educational.

Career S.E.L.F. Assessment: Designing a Self-Directed Job Search. Video. Charleston, WV: Cambridge Educational.

Career Self-Assessment: Where Do You Fit? Video; guide. Mt. Kisco, NY: Guidance Associates.

Careers for the 21st Century series. Video; guide. Bloomington, IL: Meridian Education Corp.

Careers Without College. Video. Charleston, WV: Cambridge Educational.

Connect on the Net: Finding a Job on the Internet. Video. Charleston, WV: Cambridge Educational.

Educational Planning for Your Career. Video. Bloomington, IL: Meridian Education Corp.

The JIST Video Guide for Occupational Exploration series. Video. Indianapolis, IN: JIST Works.

Jobs for the 21st Century. Video; guide. Mt. Kisco, NY: Guidance Associates.

Learning for Earning. Video; guide. Bloomington, IL: Meridian Education Corp.

School-to-Work Transition. Video; guide. Bloomington, IL: Meridian Education Corp.

Skills Identification: Discovering Your Skills. Video. Indianapolis, IN: JIST Works. *working Towards a Career.* Video. Bloomington, IL: Meridian Education Corp.

Your Aptitudes: Related to Learning Job Skills. Video. Bloomington, IL: Meridian Education Corp.

Your First Cruise: A Beginner's Guide to the Internet. Video. Charleston, WV: Cambridge Educational.

Your Future: Planning Through Career Exploration. Video. Bloomington, IL: Meridian Education Corp.

Your Interests: Related to Work Activities. Video. Bloomington, IL: Meridian Education Corp.

Your Life's Work series. Video. Indianapolis, IN: JIST Works.

Your Temperaments: Related to Work Situations. Video. Bloomington, IL: Meridian Education Corp.

Your 21st Century Employability Skills series. Video. Calhoun, KY: NIMCO, Inc.

Getting the Job and Getting Ahead

Ace the Interview. Video. Columbus, OH: Career Paths/MarkED.

The Art of Effective Communication. Video; guide. Indianapolis, IN: JIST Works.

Career Change: Meeting the Challenge. Video. Arlington Heights, IL: Library Cable Network.

Common Mistakes People Make in Interviews. Video. Columbus, OH: Career Paths/MarkED.

Dialing for Jobs: Using the Phone in the Job Search. Video. Indianapolis, IN: JIST Works.

Directing Your Successful Job Search. Video, guide. Charleston, WV: Cambridge Educational.

Extraordinary Answers to Common Interview Questions. Video. Charleston, WV: Cambridge Educational.

From Pink Slip to Paycheck: The Road to Reemployment series. Video. Indianapolis, IN: Park Avenue/JIST Works.

Getting a Job series. Video. New York: Educational Design, Inc.

How to Be a Success at Work series. Video. Indianapolis, IN: JIST Works.

Interview Power. Video. Columbus, OH: Career Paths/MarkED.

Interview to Win Your First Job. Video. Indianapolis, IN: Park Avenue/JIST Works.

Job Search and Job Survival series. Video. New York: Educational Design, Inc.

JobSearch: The Right Track. Video. Bountiful, VT: ECLECON.

Job Survival Kit. Video. Charleston, WV: Cambridge Educational.

Job Survival Skills: Working with Others. Video. Mt. Kisco, NY: Guidance Associates.

Kennedy's Career Secrets. Video. Arlington Heights, IL: Library Cable Network.

Making It on Your First Job. Video or laserdisc; guide. Charleston, WV: Cambridge Educational.

Mastering Change: How to Be "Change Skilled" and Thrive in Turbulent Times series. Video; workbook. Harleysville, PA: Career Commmunications Inc.

Maximizing Your Public Image. Video. Hinesburg, VT: Image Vision.

The Resume Remedy. Video. Indianapolis, IN: JIST Works.

Shhh! I'm Finding a Job: The Library and Your Self-Directed Job Search. Video; workbook. Charleston, WV: Cambridge Educational.

Successful Job Hunting: The Inside Scoop on Finding the Best Jobs. Video. Charleston, WV: Cambridge Educational.

Survival Skills for the World of Work series. Video. New York: Educational Design, Inc.

Take This Job and Love It. Video. Bloomington, IL: Meridian Education Corp.

Ten Ways to Get a Great Job. Video. Charleston, WV: Cambridge Educational.

Tough Times: Finding the Jobs. Video. Bloomington, IL: Meridian Education Corp.

The Very Quick Job Search Video. Indianapolis, IN: JIST Works.

The Video Guide to JIST's Self-Directed Job Search series. Video. Indianapolis, IN: JIST Works.

Your Public Image: Conducting Yourself in the Business World. Video. Hinesburg, VT: Image Vision.

Computer Software

The following titles include, where possible, the developer's name and location or else the name and location of a distributor. Software titles may be available through several distributors.

Ace the Interview: The Multimedia Job Interview Guide. CD-ROM for Macintosh or Windows. Charleston, WV: Cambridge Educational.

Adams JobBank FastResume Suite. CD-ROM for Windows. Holbrook, MA: Adams Media Corp.

Barron's Profiles of American Colleges on CD-ROM. Windows or Macintosh. Hauppauge, NY: Barron's.

The Cambridge Career Counseling System. Diskettes for IBM. Charleston, WV: Cambridge Educational.

Career Area Interest Checklist. Diskettes for IBM or Apple. Bloomington, IL: Meridian Education Corporation.

Career Compass. Diskettes for IBM or Apple II. Bloomington, IL: Meridian Education Corporation.

Career CompuSearch. Diskettes for IBM or Apple. Bloomington, IL: Meridian Education Corporation.

Career Counselor. CD-ROM for Windows. New York: Kaplan Educational Centers.

Career Directions (English and Spanish versions). Diskettes for Apple II. Charleston, WV: Cambridge Educational.

Career Finder. Diskettes for IBM DOS, Windows, or Macintosh. Bloomington, IL: Meridian Education Corporation.

Career Match. Diskettes for IBM or Macintosh. Charleston, WV: Cambridge Educational.

Career Movies: The Best of the DOT (Dictionary of Occupational Titles). CD-ROM for Macintosh or Windows. Charleston, WV: Cambridge Educational.

Career Toolbox. CD-ROM for Windows. Orem, UT: Infobusiness, Inc.

CD-ROM Version of the Occupational Outlook Handbook. Charleston, WV: Cambridge Educational.

Create Your Dream Job. CD-ROM for Windows or Macintosh. Columbus, OH: Career Paths/MarkED.

Discovering Careers and Jobs. CD-ROM. Detroit, MI: Gale Research, Inc.

Encyclopedia of Careers and Vocational Guidance. CD-ROM for Windows or Macintosh. Chicago: Ferguson.

Getting into College (U.S. News and World Report). CD-ROM. Portland, OR: Creative Multimedia.

Hoover's Company and Industry Database on CD-ROM. Austin, TX: The Reference Press.

Interview Skills for the Future. CD-ROM for Windows or Macintosh. Charleston, WV: Cambridge Educational.

JIST's Electronic Enhanced Dictionary of Occupational Titles. CD-ROM for Windows. Indianapolis, IN: JIST Works.

JIST's Multimedia Occupational Outlook Handbook. CD-ROM for Windows. Indianapolis, IN: JIST Works.

Job Search Skills for the 21st Century. CD-ROM for Windows or Macintosh. Charleston, WV: Cambridge Educational.

MSPI: Exploring Career Goals and College Courses. Diskettes for IBM or Macintosh. Charleston, WV: Cambridge Educational.

Multimedia Career Center. CD-ROM for Windows or Macintosh. Charleston, WV: Cambridge Educational.

The Multimedia Career Path. CD-ROM for Windows or Macintosh. Charleston, WV: Cambridge Job Search.

The Multimedia Guide to Occupational Exploration. CD-ROM for Windows or Macintosh. Charleston, WV: Cambridge Educational.

Multimedia Take this Job and Love It. CD-ROM for Windows or Macintosh. Charleston, WV: Cambridge Educational.

The Perfect Resume. CD-ROM for Windows. Torrance, CA: Davidson.

Resume Express: The Multimedia Guide. CD-ROM for Windows or Macintosh. Charleston, WV: Cambridge Educational.

Resume Revolution: The Software Solution. Diskettes for Windows or Macintosh. Charleston, WV: Cambridge Educational.

The Ultimate Job Source, 2.0. CD-ROM for Windows. Orem, UT: Infobusiness, Inc. *What Color Is Your Parachute?* CD-ROM for Windows. Boston: BumbleBee Technology.

General

Books

America's Top Medical, Education, and Human Services Jobs, 3rd ed., J. Michael Farr. Indianapolis, IN: JIST Works, Inc., 1996.

Becoming a Helper, Marianne Schneider Corey and Gerald Corey. Florence, KY: International Thomson Publishing, 1997.

Careers for Caring People and Other Sensitive Types, Adrian A. Paradis. Lincolnwood, IL: VGM Career Horizons, 1995.

Careers for Good Samaritans and Other Humanitarian Types, 2nd ed., Marjorie Eberts and Margaret Gisler. Lincolnwood, IL: VGM Career Horizons, 1998.

Choosing a Career in the Helping Professions, Pat Tretout. New York: The Rosen Publishing Group, 1997.

Great Careers for People Who Like Working with People, Helen Mason. Detroit: UXL, 1994.

Great Jobs for Sociology Majors, Stephen Lambert. Lincolnwood, IL: VGM Career Horizons, 1997.

Jobs and Careers with Nonprofit Organizations, Ron Krannich. Manassas Park, VA: Impact Publications, 1998.

Non-Profits and Education Job Finder, 1997–2000, Daniel Lauber. River Forest, IL: Planning Communications, 1997.

100 Jobs in Social Change, Harley Jebens. New York: Macmillan General Reference, 1997.

Opportunities in Nonprofit Organization Careers, Adrian A. Paradis. Lincolnwood, IL: VGM Career Horizons, 1994.

Washington Information Directory. Washington, DC: Congressional Quarterly, annual.

Internet Sites

Academe This Week
chronicle.merit.edu/.ads/.links.html

Air Base
www.airforce.com

American Library Association
www.ala.org/education

Army Recruiting
www.goarmy com

Community Career Center
www.nonprofitjobs.org

Council for the Support and Advancement of Education Job Classifieds
gopher://gopher.case.org/11/currents

Federal Jobs Database (Job Web)
www.jobweb.org/search/Jobs/advanced.cfm

Federal Jobs Digest
www.jobsfed.com

FedWorld Federal Jobs Search
www.fedworld.gov/jobs/jobsearch.html

Government Job Resource
www.statejobs.com

Job Search from Library Journal Digital
classifieds.bookwire.com/ljdigital.classifieds

Job Search: The GSLIS Job Placement Database (library and information science)
www.lis.uiuc.edu/gslis/people/students/jobsearch.html

Jobs in Government
www.jobsingovernment.com

JobWire (education)
www.jobweb.org/jobwire.htm

The Law Employment Center
www.lawjobs.com

Legal dot Net
www.legal.net

Library of Congress
lcweb.loc.gov

Local Government Job Net
www.lgi.org

Marine Corps Recruiting
www.marines.com

Ministry Connect
www.ministryconnect.org

National Association of Paralegal Associations Career Center
www.paralegals.org/Center/home.html

Navy Jobs
www.navyjobs.com

Official Army National Guard Recruiting Site
www.1800goguard.com

The Police Officer's Internet Directory
www.officer.com

The Riley Guide—Government, Law, Nonprofits, and Social Services
www.dbm.com/Jobguide/social.html

Social Work and Social Services Jobs Online
128.252.132.4/jobs/

Teach for America
www.teachforamerica.com

U.S. Department of Justice
www.usdoj.gov/careers/careers.html

University of Minnesota College of Education's Job Search Bulletin
gopher://rodent.us.umn.edu:11119/

West's Legal Director
www.wld.com

Yahoo! Library and Information Services Careers
www.yahoo.com/Reference/Libraries/Employment

Audiovisual Materials

African-American Role Models. Video series with segments on firefighter, police officer, and substance abuse counselor. Bloomington, IL: Meridian Education Corp.

Career Options With Math, Science, and Technology. Video series with segments on attorney and special education teacher. Bloomington, IL: Meridian Education Corp.

Enter Here: Government and Public Administration. Ten videos. Charleston, WV: Cambridge Educational.

Enter Here: Personal, Family and Community Services. Ten videos. Charleston, WV: Cambridge Educational.

Humanitarian Careers. Video. Indianapolis, IN: JIST Works, Inc.

Leading and Influencing Careers. Two videos. Indianapolis, IN: JIST Works, Inc.

Protective Careers. Video. Indianapolis, IN: JIST Works, Inc.

Public and Personal Service. Video. Bloomington, IL: Meridian Education Corp.

Success Stories in the World of Work: Multicultural Role Models. Video series with segments on biology professor, FBI agent, fighter pilot, firefighter, police officer, and teacher. Bloomington, IL: Meridian Education Corp.

Women of Achievement. Video series with segments on attorney, legislative aide, and police officer. Bloomington, IL: Meridian Education Corp.

Armed Services

Books

America's Top Military Careers: The Official Guide to Occupations in the Armed Forces, 2nd ed., United States Department of Defense. Indianapolis, IN: JIST Works, Inc., 1997.

Barron's Guide to Military Careers, Donald B. Hutton. Hauppauge, NY: Barron's, 1998.

Opportunities in Military Careers, Adrian Paradis. Lincolnwood, IL: VGM Career Horizons, 1994.

Audiovisual Materials

Innerview: Military. Video. Fresno, CA: Edgepoint Productions.

Law Enforcement

Books

Careers in Law Enforcement: Interviewing for Results, James Nelson. West Hartford, CT: The Graduate Group; 1995.

Careers in Law Enforcement and Security, Paul Cohen and Shari Cohen. New York: The Rosen Publishing Group, 1994.

Careers Without College: Emergencies, Linda Peterson and Peggy J. Schmidt. Princeton, NJ: Petersons Guides; 1993.

Choosing a Career in Law Enforcement, Claudine G. Wirths. New York: The Rosen Publishing Group, 1996.

Federal Careers in Law Enforcement, Russ Smith, ed. Kirkwood, MO: Impact Christian Books, 1996.

Guide to Law Enforcement Careers, Donald B. Hutton and Anna Mydlarz. Hauppauge, NY: Barron's Educational Series, 1997.

Law Enforcement Career Guide: A Practical Guide to Finding Police Employment, 5th ed., Jackye Bundschu. Winter Haven, FL: Harvest Communications, 1993.

100 Best Careers in Crime Fighting: Law Enforcement, Criminal Justice, Private Security, and Cyberspace Crime Detection, Mary Price Lee, Richard S. Lee, Carol Beam, and Carol Dilks. New York: Macmillan General Reference, 1998.

Opportunities in Law Enforcement and Criminal Justice Careers, James Stinchcomb. Lincolnwood, IL: VGM Career Horizons, 1996.

Seeking Employment in Criminal Justice and Related Fields, 2nd ed., J. Scott Harr and Karen M. Hess. St. Paul, MN: West Publishing Company, 1996.

Audiovisual Materials

Innerview: Corrections. Video. Fresno, CA: Edgepoint Productions.

Innerview: Law Enforcement. Video. Fresno, CA: Edgepoint Productions.

Legal Work

Books

Best Resumes for Attorneys, Joan Fondell and Mary J. Russo. New York: John Wiley & Sons, 1994.

Careers in Law, Gary Munneke. Lincolnwood, IL: VGM Career Horizons, 1997.

Careers in the Law: Paralegal Workbook, Charles P. Nemeth. Cincinnati, OH: Anderson Publishing Company, 1995.

Careers Without College: Paralegal, Kathryn A. Quinlan. Mankato, MN: Capstone Press, 1998.

From Here to Attorney: The Ultimate Guide to Excelling in Law School and Launching Your Legal Career, Robert J. Arnett III, Arthur Coon, and Michael DeGeronimo. Belmont, CA: Professional Publications, 1993.

How to Find a Job as a Paralegal: A Step-By-Step Job Search Guide, 3rd ed., Marie Kisiel. St Paul, MN: West Publishing Company, 1996.

How to Land Your First Paralegal Job: An Insider's Guide to the Fastest-Growing Profession of the New Millennium, 2nd ed., Andrea Wagner. Upper Saddle River, NJ: Prentice-Hall, 1997.

Life Outside the Law Firm: Non-Traditional Careers for Paralegals, Karen Treffinger. Albany, NY: Delmar Publishers, 1995.

National Directory of Legal Employers, 1998–1999: 22,000 Great Job Openings for Law Students and Law School Graduates, National Association for Law Placement. New York: Harcourt Brace Legal and Professional, 1998.

Opportunities in Law Careers, Gary A. Munneke. Lincolnwood, IL: VGM Career Horizons, 1994.

Paralegal: An Insider's Guide to One of Today's Fastest Growing Careers, 3rd ed., Barbara Bernardo. Princeton, NJ: Petersons Guides, 1997.

Paralegal Career Guide, 2nd ed., Chere B. Estrin. Gaithersburg, MD: Aspen Publications, 1996.

The Paralegal's Guide to U.S. Government Jobs: How to Land a Job in 140 Law-Related Careers, 7th ed. Washington, DC: Federal Reports, 1997.

The Professional Paralegal Job Search: A Guide for Launching Your Legal Career, Christofer Ulmont French. Boston: Little, Brown and Company, 1995.

Resumes for Law Careers, the editors of VGM Career Horizons. Lincolnwood, IL: VGM Career Horizons, 1995.

So You Want to Be a Lawyer: A Practical Guide to Law as a Career, The Law School Admission Council. New York: Broadway Books, 1998.

Working in Law and Justice, Mary Lee Davis. Minneapolis, MN: Lerner Publications, 1998.

Audiovisual Materials

Innerview: Legal. Video. Fresno, CA: Edgepoint Productions.

Paralegal. Video. Calhoun, KY: NIMCO, Inc.

Paralegal (Day in a Career series). Video. Charleston, WV: Cambridge Educational.

Paralegal (Vocational Visions series). Video. Charleston, WV: Cambridge Educational.

Public, Civil, and Social Services

Books

Applying for Federal Jobs: A Guide to Writing Successful Applications and Resumes for the Job You Want in Government, Patricia B. Wood. Chicago: Login Publications Consortium, 1995.

Career Advancement for Women in the Federal Service: An Annotated Bibliography and Resource Book, Lynn C. Ross. New York: Garland Publishing, 1993.

Careers in Government, Mary Elizabeth Pitz. Lincolnwood, IL: VGM Career Horizons, 1994.

Careers in International Affairs, Maria Pinto Carland and Michael Trucano, eds. Washington, DC: Georgetown University Press, 1996.

Careers in Social Work, Leon H. Ginsberg. Needham Heights, MA: Allyn & Bacon, 1997.

Directory of Colleges and Universities With Accredited Social Work Degree Programs. Alexandria, VA: Council on Social Work Education, 1994.

Federal Applications That Get Results: From SF 171s to Federal-Style Resumes, Russ Smith. Kirkwood, MO: Impact Christian Books, 1996.

Federal Civil Service Jobs: The Complete Guide, Hy Hammer. New York: Macmillan, 1995.

Federal Personnel Guide: An Annual Publication, Kenneth D. Whitehead, ed. Chevy Chase, MD: Key Communications Group, annual.

Find a Federal Job Fast: How to Cut the Red Tape and Get Hired, 4th ed., Ronald L. Krannich and Caryl R. Krannich, eds. Manassas Park, VA: Impact Publications, 1998.

Government Jobs: The New Employment Manual, 3rd rev. ed., Richard M. Zink. Dearborn, MI: Zinks International Career Guidance, 1994.

Guide to Careers in World Affairs, Foreign Policy Association staff and Pamela Gerard, eds. Manassas Park, VA: Impact Publications, 1993.

Opportunities in Counseling and Development Careers, Neale J. Baxter, Mark U. Toch, and Philip A. Perry. Lincolnwood, IL: VGM Career Horizons, 1997.

Opportunities in Federal Government Careers, 2nd ed., Neale J. Baxter. Lincolnwood, IL: VGM Career Horizons, 1994.

Opportunities in Gerontology and Aging Services Careers, Ellen Williams. Lincolnwood, IL: VGM Career Horizons, 1995.

Opportunities in Social Work Careers, Renee Wittenberg and Donald W. Beless. Lincolnwood, IL: VGM Career Horizons, 1997.

The Peace Corps and More: 175 Ways to Work, Study and Travel at Home and Abroad, Medea Benjamin and Miya Rodolfo-Sioson. Santa Ana, CA: Seven Locks Press, 1997.

Resumes for Government Careers. Lincolnwood, IL: VGM Career Horizons, 1996.

Resumes for Social Service Careers. Lincolnwood, IL: VGM Career Horizons, 1995.

Social Work Career Development: A Handbook for Job Hunting and Career Planning, Carol Doelling. Washington, DC: National Association of Social Workers, 1997.

Summary Information on Master of Social Work Programs. Alexandria, VA: Council on Social Work Education, annual.

Take Charge of Your Own Career: A Guide to Federal Employment, Donna J. Moore and Susan Vanderwey. Lutz, FL: Psychological Assessment Resources, 1994.

United States Government Manual, Office of the Federal Register, National Archives and Records Administration staff, ed. Lanham, MD: Bernan Press, annual.

VGM's Handbook of Government and Public Service Careers, Annette Selden, ed. Lincolnwood, IL: VGM Career Horizons, 1994.

What Social Workers Do, Margaret Gibelman. Washington, DC: National Association of Social Workers, 1995.

Working for Your Uncle: Complete Guide to Finding a Job With the Federal Government, 2nd ed., Federal Jobs Digest staff. Ossining, NY: Breakthrough Publications, 1998.

Audiovisual Materials

Innerview: Federal Government. Video. Fresno, CA: Edgepoint Productions.

Innerview: Fire Fighting. Video. Fresno, CA: Edgepoint Productions.

Innerview: Local Government. Video. Fresno, CA: Edgepoint Productions.

Innerview: Public Social Services. Video. Fresno, CA: Edgepoint Productions.

Letter Carrier (*Vocational Visions* series). Video. Charleston, WV: Cambridge Educational.

Opportunities and Challenges. Video series with segment on firefighter. Bloomington, IL: Meridian Education Corp.

Social Worker. Video. Calhoun, KY: NIMCO, Inc.

Social Worker (*Day in a Career* series). Video. Charleston, WV: Cambridge Educational.

Religious Careers

Books

Careers for Women as Clergy, Julie F. Parker. New York: The Rosen Publishing Group, 1993.

Considering a Church Career? Discovering God's Plan for Your Life, Philip Bickel and Curtis Deterding. St Louis, MO: Concordia Publishing House, 1996.

Opportunities in Religious Service Careers, John O. Nelson and Mark Rowh. Lincolnwood, IL: VGM Career Horizons, 1998.

Teaching and Library Science

Books

Careers for Bookworms and Other Literary Types, Marjorie Eberts and Margaret Gisler. Lincolnwood, IL: VGM Career Horizons, 1995.

Careers in Education, 3rd ed., Roy A. Edelfelt. Lincolnwood, IL: VGM Career Horizons, 1997.

Careers in Teaching, rev. ed., Robert Shockley and Glenn W. Cutlip. New York: The Rosen Publishing Group, 1997.

Directory of Programs for Preparing Individuals for Careers in Special Education, Council for Exceptional Children staff. Reston, VA: Council for Exceptional Children, 1997.

Extending the Librarian's Domain: A Survey of Emerging Occupational Opportunities for Librarians and Information Professionals. Washington, DC: Special Libraries Association, 1994.

How to Get a Job in Education, 2nd ed., Joel Levin. Boston: Adams Media Corp., 1995.

Opportunities in Library and Information Science Careers, Kathleen De La Pena McCook and Margaret Myers. Lincolnwood, IL: VGM Career Horizons, 1996.

Opportunities in Special Education Careers, Robert Connelly. Lincolnwood, IL: VGM Career Horizons, 1995.

Opportunities in Teaching Careers, Janet Fine. Lincolnwood, IL: VGM Career Horizons, 1996.

Opportunities in Technical Education Careers, Robert Connelly. Lincolnwood, IL: VGM Career Horizons, 1997.

Petersons Guide to Colleges for Careers in Teaching. Princeton, NJ: Petersons Guides, revised regularly.

Resumes for Education, the editors of VGM Career Horizons. Lincolnwood, IL: VGM Career Horizons, 1992.

Scaling the Ivory Tower: Merits and Its Limits in Academic Careers, Lionel S. Lewis. New Brunswick, NJ: Transaction Publishers, 1998.

Teach Abroad: The Complete International Guide to Teaching Opportunities Overseas, Central Bureau staff. London: Kuperard, 1993.

Teaching, Marjorie Eberts and Margaret Gisler. Lincolnwood, IL: VGM Career Horizons, 1995.

Writing Resumes That Work: A How-To-Do-It Manual for Librarians, Robert R. Newlen. New York: Neal-Schuman Publishers, 1998.

Audiovisual Materials

Education and Communication Specialists. Video. Calhoun, KY: NIMCO, Inc.

Education, Cooperative Extension, and Communication Careers. Video. Calhoun, KY: NIMCO, Inc.

Education (*Video Career Library* series). Video. Bloomington, IL: Meridian Education Corp.

Information Science and Technology (*Career Encounters* series). Video. Charleston, WV: Cambridge Educational.

Innerview: Education. Video. Fresno, CA: Edgepoint Productions.

Innerview: Special Education. Video. Fresno, CA: Edgepoint Productions.

Innerview: University Level Education. Video. Fresno, CA: Edgepoint Productions.

Teaching (*Career Encounters* series). Video. Charleston, WV: Cambridge Educational.

Directory — Institutions Offering Career Training

The information in this directory was generated from the IPEDS (Integrated Postsecondary Education Data System) database of the U.S. Department of Education. It includes only regionally or nationally accredited institutions offering postsecondary occupational training in administration, business, and the office. Because college catalogs and directories of colleges and universities are readily available elsewhere, this directory does not include institutions that offer only bachelor's and advanced degrees.

Armed Services

ALABAMA

John C Calhoun State Community
College
P.O. Box 2216
Decatur 35609-2216

TEXAS

Wayland Baptist University
1900 West Seventh
Plainview 79072

WEST VIRGINIA

The University of Charleston
2300 MacCorkle Ave. SE
Charleston 25304

Custodial Services

CALIFORNIA

Center for Employment Training,
Gilroy
7800 Arroyo Circle
Gilroy 95020

Center for Employment Training,
Spring St.
426 Spring St.
Los Angeles 90013

Center for Employment Training,
Vernon
2947 East 44th St.
Vernon 90058

Center for Employment Training,
Salinas
330 Griffin St.
Salinas 93901

Center for Employment Training, Santa
Ana
120 West Fifth St.
Santa Ana 92701

ILLINOIS

Illinois Valley Community College
2578 East 350th Rd.
Oglesby 61348

MINNESOTA

Minnesota Riverland Technical College,
Faribault Campus
1225 Southwest Third St.
Faribault 55021

Northeast Metro Technical College
3300 Century Ave. N
White Bear Lake 55110

PENNSYLVANIA

Philadelphia Elwyn Institute
4040 Market St.
Philadelphia 19104-3003

Fire Control Technology

ALABAMA

Chattahoochee Valley Community
College
2602 College Dr.
Phenix City 36869

Community College of the Air Force
Maxwell Air Force Base
Montgomery 36112

Jefferson State Community College
2601 Carson Rd.
Birmingham 35215-3098

ALASKA

University of Alaska, Anchorage
3211 Providence Dr.
Anchorage 99508

University of Alaska, Fairbanks
Signers Hall
Fairbanks 99775

ARIZONA

Glendale Community College
6000 West Olive Ave.
Glendale 85302

Mesa Community College
1833 West Southern Ave.
Mesa 85202

Phoenix College
1202 West Thomas Rd.
Phoenix 85013

Pima Community College
2202 West Anklam Rd.
Tucson 85709-0001

Yavapai College
1100 East Sheldon St.
Prescott 86301

ARKANSAS

Black River Technical College
Hwy. 304
P.O. Box 468
Pocahontas 72455

CALIFORNIA

Allan Hancock College
800 South College Dr.
Santa Maria 93454

American River College
4700 College Oak Dr.
Sacramento 95841

Bakersfield College
1801 Panorama Dr.
Bakersfield 93305-1299

Butte College
3536 Butte Campus Dr.
Oroville 95965

Cabrillo College
6500 Soquel Dr.
Aptos 95003

Chabot College
25555 Hesperian Blvd.
Hayward 94545

College of San Mateo
1700 West Hillsdale Blvd.
San Mateo 94402

Columbia College, Columbia
P.O. Box 1849
Columbia 95310

Crafton Hills College
11711 Sand Canyon Rd.
Yucaipa 92399-1799

El Camino College
16007 Crenshaw Blvd.
Torrance 90506

Fresno City College
1101 East University Ave.
Fresno 93741

Long Beach City College
4901 East Carson St.
Long Beach 90808

Merced College
3600 M St.
Merced 95348-2898

Mission College
3000 Mission College Blvd.
Santa Clara 95054-1897

Monterey Peninsula College
980 Fremont Blvd.
Monterey 93940-4799

Mount San Antonio College
1100 North Grand
Walnut 91789

Oxnard College
4000 South Rose Ave.
Oxnard 93033

Rancho Santiago College
17th at Bristol
Santa Ana 92706

Rio Hondo College
3600 Workman Mill Rd.
Whittier 90601-1699

San Diego Miramar College
10440 Black Mountain Rd.
San Diego 92126-2999

Santa Rosa Junior College
1501 Mendocino Ave.
Santa Rosa 95401-4395

Shasta College
P.O. Box 496006
Redding 96049

Sierra College
5000 Rocklin Rd.
Rocklin 95677

COLORADO

Aims Community College
P.O. Box 69
Greeley 80632

Arapahoe Community College
2500 West College Dr.
Littleton 80160-9002

Red Rocks Community College
13300 West Sixth Ave.
Golden 80401

FLORIDA

Broward Community College
225 East Las Olas Blvd.
Fort Lauderdale 33301

Daytona Beach Community College
1200 Volusia Ave.
Daytona Beach 32114

Edison Community College
8099 College Pkwy. SW
Fort Myers 33906-6210

Florida Community College at
Jacksonville
501 West State St.
Jacksonville 32202

Indian River Community College
3209 Virginia Ave.
Fort Pierce 34981

Lake County Area Vocational-Technical
Center
2001 Kurt St.
Eustis 32726

Lewis M Lively Area Vocational-
Technical Center
500 North Appleyard Dr.
Tallahassee 32304

Miami-Dade Community College
300 Northeast Second Ave.
Miami 33132

Palm Beach Community College
4200 Congress Ave.
Lake Worth 33461

Pasco-Hernando Community College
36727 Blanton Rd.
Dade City 33525-7599

Sarasota County Technical Institute
4748 Beneva Rd.
Sarasota 34233-1798

Seminole Community College
100 Weldon Blvd.
Sanford 32773-6199

South Technical Education Center
1300 Southwest 30th Ave.
Boynton Beach 33426-9099

William T McFatter Vocational
Technical Center
6500 Nova Dr.
Davie 33317

GEORGIA

Dekalb College
3251 Panthersville Rd.
Decatur 30034

HAWAII

Honolulu Community College
874 Dillingham Blvd.
Honolulu 96817

ILLINOIS

City College of Chicago, Chicago City-
Wide College
226 West Jackson Blvd.
Chicago 60606-6997

College of Du Page
Lambert Rd. and 22nd St.
Glen Ellyn 60137

Illinois Central College
One College Dr.
East Peoria 61635

Investigations Institute
2155 Stonington Ave.
Hoffman Estates 60195-2057

Joliet Junior College
1216 Houbolt Ave.
Joliet 60436

Lincoln Land Community College
Shepherd Rd.
Springfield 62194-9256

Moraine Valley Community College
10900 South 88th Ave.
Palos Hills 60465-0937

Prairie State College
202 Halsted St.
Chicago Heights 60411

Southeastern Illinois College
3575 College Rd.
Harrisburg 62946

INDIANA

Indiana Vocational Technical College,
Central Indiana
One West 26th St.
Indianapolis 46206-1763

IOWA

Des Moines Community College
2006 Ankeny Blvd.
Ankeny 50021

Kirkwood Community College
P.O. Box 2068
Cedar Rapids 52406

KANSAS

Johnson County Community College
12345 College Blvd.
Overland Park 66210-1299

LOUISIANA

Delgado Community College
615 City Park Ave.
New Orleans 70119

Louisiana State University, Eunice
P.O. Box 1129
Eunice 70535

MAINE

Southern Maine Technical College
Fort Rd.
South Portland 04106

MASSACHUSETTS

Bristol Community College
777 Elsbree St.
Fall River 02720

Middlesex Community College
Springs Rd.
Bedford 01730

North Shore Community College
One Ferncroft Rd.
Danvers 01923

Tad Technical Institute
45 Spruce St.
Chelsea 02150

MICHIGAN

Delta College
University Center 48710

Henry Ford Community College
5101 Evergreen Rd.
Dearborn 48128

Lansing Community College
419 North Capitol Ave.
Lansing 48901-7210

Macomb Community College
14500 Twelve Mile Rd.
Warren 48093-3896

MINNESOTA

Duluth Technical College
2101 Trinity Rd.
Duluth 55811

MISSOURI

Saint Louis Community College, Forest
Park
5600 Oakland Ave.
Saint Louis 63110

NEBRASKA

Southeast Community College, Lincoln
Campus
8800 O St.
Lincoln 68520

NEVADA

Community College of Southern
Nevada
3200 East Cheyenne Ave.
Las Vegas 89030

Truckee Meadows Community College
7000 Dandini Blvd.
Reno 89512

NEW HAMPSHIRE

New Hampshire Technical College at
Laconia
Prescott Hill Rte. 106
Laconia 03246

NEW JERSEY

Mercer County Community College
1200 Old Trenton Rd.
Trenton 08690

NEW YORK

Corning Community College
Spencer Hill
Corning 14830

Monroe Community College
1000 East Henrietta Rd.
Rochester 14623

Onondaga Community College
Rte. 173
Syracuse 13215

Suffolk County Community College,
Ammerman Campus
533 College Rd.
Selden 11784

NORTH CAROLINA

Central Piedmont Community College
P.O. Box 35009
Charlotte 28235

Guilford Technical Community College
P.O. Box 309
Jamestown 27282

OHIO

Columbus State Community College
550 East Spring St., P.O. Box 1609
Columbus 43216

Lakeland Community College
7700 Clocktower Dr.
Mentor 44060-7594

Lawrence County Joint Vocational
School
Rte. 2 Getaway
Chesapeake 45619

University of Akron, Main Campus
302 Buchtel Common
Akron 44325-4702

OKLAHOMA

Oklahoma State University, Oklahoma
City
900 North Portland
Oklahoma City 73107

OREGON

Chemeketa Community College
P.O. Box 14007
Salem 97309-7070

Portland Community College
P.O. Box 19000
Portland 97280-0990

RHODE ISLAND

Community College of Rhode Island
400 East Ave.
Warwick 02886-1805

Providence College
River Ave. and Eaton St.
Providence 02918

TEXAS

Austin Community College
5930 Middle Fiskville Rd.
Austin 78752

Collin County Community College
2200 West University
McKinney 75070

Houston Community College System
22 Waugh Dr.
P.O. Box 7849
Houston 77270-7849

San Antonio College
1300 San Pedro Ave.
San Antonio 78284

Tarrant County Junior College District
1500 Houston St.
Fort Worth 76102

WASHINGTON

Bates Technical College
1101 South Yakima Ave.
Tacoma 98405

Spokane Community College
North 1810 Greene Ave.
Spokane 99207

WISCONSIN

Blackhawk Technical College
P.O. Box 5009
Janesville 53547

Fox Valley Technical College
1825 North Bluemound Dr.
Appleton 54913-2277

Milwaukee Area Technical College
700 West State St.
Milwaukee 53233

Northeast Wisconsin Technical College
2740 West Mason St.
P.O. Box 19042
Green Bay 54307-9042

Wisconsin Area Vocational Training
and Adult Education System District
Number Four
3550 Anderson St.
Madison 53704

Legal Services Technology

ALABAMA

Gadsden State Community College
P.O. Box 227
Gadsden 35902-0227

George C Wallace State Community
College, Hanceville
801 Main St. NW
P.O. Box 2000
Hanceville 35077-2000

James H. Faulkner State Community
College
1900 U.S. Hwy. 30 S
Bay Minette 36507

John C Calhoun State Community
College
P.O. Box 2216
Decatur 35609-2216

Phillips Junior College
4900 Corporate Dr.
Huntsville 35805

Samford University
800 Lakeshore Dr.
Birmingham 35229

ALASKA

Alaska Junior College
800 East Dimond Blvd.
Anchorage 99515

Charter College
2221 East Northern Lights Blvd.
Anchorage 99508

University of Alaska, Anchorage
3211 Providence Dr.
Anchorage 99508

ARIZONA

Academy Business College
3320 West Cheryl Dr.
Phoenix 85051

American Institute of Court Reporting
3443 North Central Ave.
Phoenix 85012

Lamson Business College
6367 East Tanque Verde Rd.
Tucson 85715

Lamson Junior College
1980 West Main
Mesa 85201

Lamson Junior College
2701 West Bethany Home Rd.
Phoenix 85017

Paralegal Institute
3602 West Thomas Rd.
Phoenix 85061-1408

Phoenix College
1202 West Thomas Rd.
Phoenix 85013

Pima Community College
2202 West Anklam Rd.
Tucson 85709-0001

Sterling School, Inc.
801 East Indian School Rd.
Phoenix 85014

ARKANSAS

Westark Community College
P.O. Box 3649
Fort Smith 72913

CALIFORNIA

American River College
4700 College Oak Dr.
Sacramento 95841

Catherine College, Inc.
8155 Van Nuys Blvd.
Panorama 91402

Century Business College
3325 Wilshire Blvd.
Los Angeles 90010

Century Schools
2665 Fifth Ave.
San Diego 92103

Cerritos College
11110 Alondra Blvd.
Norwalk 90650

City College of San Francisco
50 Phelan Ave.
San Francisco 94112

Coastline Community College
11460 Warner Ave.
Fountain Valley 92708

College of the Redwoods
7351 Tompkins Hill Rd.
Eureka 95501-9302

College of the Sequoias
915 South Mooney Blvd.
Visalia 93277

De Anza College
21250 Stevens Creek Blvd.
Cupertino 95014

El Camino College
16007 Crenshaw Blvd.
Torrance 90506

Fresno City College
1101 East University Ave.
Fresno 93741

Fullerton College
321 East Chapman Ave.
Fullerton 92632-2095

Humphreys College
3600 Sisk Rd.
Modesto 95356

Kensington College
2428 North Grand Ave.
Santa Ana 92701

Merit College
7101 Sepulveda Blvd.
Van Nuys 91405

Napa Valley College
2277 Napa Vallejo Hwy.
Napa 94558

Newbridge College
700 El Camino Real
Tustin 92680

Pasadena City College
1570 East Colorado Blvd.
Pasadena 91106

Phillips College, Inland Empire Campus
4300 Central Ave.
Riverside 92506

Phillips Junior College
8520 Balboa Blvd.
Northridge 91325

Phillips Junior College L A South
One Civic Plaza
Carson 90745

Phillips Junior College, Condie Campus
One West Campbell Ave.
Campbell 95008

Platt College, Ontario
2920 Inland Empire Blvd.
Ontario 91764

Rancho Santiago College
17th at Bristol
Santa Ana 92706

Rio Hondo College
3600 Workman Mill Rd.
Whittier 90601-1699

Saint Mary's College of California
P.O. Box 3554
Moraga 94575

San Joaquin College of Law
3385 East Shields Ave.
Fresno 93726

Sawyer College at Ventura
2101 East Gonzales Rd.
Oxnard 93030

Skyline College
3300 College Dr.
San Bruno 94066

Southern California College of Business
and Law
595 West Lambert Rd.
Brea 92621

Southwestern College
900 Otay Lakes Rd.
Chula Vista 92010

University of Northern California,
Lorenzo Patino School Law
727-1/2 J St.
Sacramento 95814-2501

University of San Francisco
2130 Fulton St.
San Francisco 94117-1080

University of West Los Angeles
1155 West Arbor Vitae St.
Inglewood 90301

Watterson College
1165 East Colorado Blvd.
Pasadena 91106

Watterson College Pacific
2030 University Dr.
Vista 92083

Watterson College Pacific
815 North Oxnard Blvd.
Oxnard 93030

West Los Angeles College
4800 Freshman Dr.
Culver 90230

West Valley College
14000 Fruitvale Ave.
Saratoga 95070

COLORADO

Arapahoe Community College
2500 West College Dr.
Littleton 80160-9002

Blair Junior College
828 Wooten Rd.
Colorado Springs 80915

College of the Canons
Forge Rd. Industrial Park, P.O. Box 1180
Canon City 81212

Community College of Aurora
16000 East Centre Tech Pkwy.
Aurora 80011-9036

Community College of Denver
P.O. Box 173363
Denver 80217

Denver Paralegal Institute
1401 19th St.
Denver 80202-1213

Denver Paralegal Institute, Colorado
Springs
105 East Vermijo Ave.
Colorado Springs 80903

Pikes Peak Community College
5675 South Academy Blvd.
Colorado Springs 80906-5498

CONNECTICUT

Branford Hall Career Institute
Nine Business Park Dr.
Branford 06405

Briarwood College
2279 Mount Vernon Rd.
Southington 06489

Connecticut Institute for Paralegal
Studies
26 Sixth St.
Stamford 06905

Huntington Institute, Inc.
193 Broadway
Norwich 06360

Manchester Community College
60 Bidwell St., P.O. Box 1045
Manchester 06040-1046

Mattatuck Community College
750 Chase Pkwy.
Waterbury 06708

Morse School of Business
275 Asylum St.
Hartford 06103

Norwalk Community Technical College
188 Richards Ave.
Norwalk 06854

Sacred Heart University
5151 Park Ave.
Fairfield 06432-1023

Teikyo Post University
800 Country Club Rd., P.O. Box 2540
Waterbury 06723-2540

The Corporate Education Center, Inc.
2A Ives St.
Danbury 06810

University of Bridgeport
380 University Ave.
Bridgeport 06601

University of Hartford
200 Bloomfield Ave.
West Hartford 06117

DELAWARE

Delaware Technical and Community
College, Southern Campus
P.O. Box 610
Georgetown 19947

The Career Institute
711 Market St. Mall
Wilmington 19801

FLORIDA

American Institute for Paralegal
Studies, Inc., Tampa
University of Tampa
Tampa 33606

Broward Community College
225 East Las Olas Blvd.
Fort Lauderdale 33301

Daytona Beach Community College
1200 Volusia Ave.
Daytona Beach 32114

Florida Community College at
Jacksonville
501 West State St.
Jacksonville 32202

Gulf Coast Community College
5230 West Hwy. 98
Panama City 32401

Hillsborough Community College
P.O. Box 31127
Tampa 33631-3127

Indian River Community College
3209 Virginia Ave.
Fort Pierce 34981

International College
2654 Tamiami Trail E
Naples 33962

Jones College, Jacksonville
5353 Arlington Expwy.
Jacksonville 32211

Keiser College of Technology
1500 Northwest 49th St.
Fort Lauderdale 33309

Legal Career Institute
7289 Garden Rd.
Riviera Beach 33404

Legal Career Institute
5225 West Broward Blvd.
Fort Lauderdale 33317

Manatee Community College
5840 26th St. W
Bradenton 34207

Miami-Dade Community College
300 Northeast Second Ave.
Miami 33132

Okaloosa-Walton Community College
100 College Blvd.
Niceville 32578

Orlando College
5500-5800 Diplomat Circle
Orlando 32810

Palm Beach Community College
4200 Congress Ave.
Lake Worth 33461

Paralegal Careers, Inc.
1211 North Westshore
Tampa 33607

Pensacola Junior College
1000 College Blvd.
Pensacola 32504

Saint Petersburg Junior College
P.O. Box 13489
Saint Petersburg 33733

Santa Fe Community College
3000 Northwest 83rd St.
Gainesville 32601

Seminole Community College
100 Weldon Blvd.
Sanford 32773-6199

South College
1760 North Congress Ave.
West Palm Beach 33409

Southern College
5600 Lake Underhill Rd.
Orlando 32807

Tallahassee Community College
444 Appleyard Dr.
Tallahassee 32304-2895

Tampa College
3319 West Hillsborough Ave.
Tampa 33614

Tampa College, Lakeland
1200 U.S. Hwy. 98 S
Lakeland 33801

Tampa College, Pinellas
15064 U.S. Hwy. 19 N
Clearwater 34624

Valencia Community College
P.O. Box 3028
Orlando 32802

Webster College, Inc.
5623 U.S. Hwy. 19 S
New Port Richey 34652

GEORGIA

Athens Area Technical Institute
U.S. Hwy. 29 N
Athens 30610-0399

HAWAII

Kapiolani Community College
4303 Diamond Head Rd.
Honolulu 96816

IDAHO

Lewis-Clark State College
Eighth Ave. and Sixth St.
Lewiston 83501

New Careers College of Business and
Technology
2410 Bank Dr.
Boise 83705

ILLINOIS

Elgin Community College
1700 Spartan Dr.
Elgin 60123

Illinois Central College
One College Dr.
East Peoria 61635

MacCormac College
506 South Wabash
Chicago 60605

Midstate College
244 Southwest Jefferson
Peoria 61602

Robert Morris College
180 North Lasalle St.
Chicago 60601

Sanford-Brown College
3237 West Chain of Rocks Rd.
Granite 62040

South Suburban College
15800 South State St.
South Holland 60473

William Rainey Harper College
1200 West Algonquin Rd.
Palatine 60067-7398

Woodridge Business Institute
1310 Mercantile Dr.
Highland 62249

INDIANA

Ball State University
2000 University Ave.
Muncie 47306

Indiana Vocational Technical College,
Central Indiana
One West 26th St.
Indianapolis 46206-1763

Professional Career Institute
2611 Waterfront Pkwy. & East Dr.
Indianapolis 46214-2028

Sawyer College, Hammond
6040 Hohman Ave.
Hammond 46320

Sawyer College, Merrillville Branch
3803 East Lincoln Hwy.
Merrillville 46410

University of Indianapolis
1400 East Hanna Ave.
Indianapolis 46227

Vincennes University
1002 North First St.
Vincennes 47591

IOWA

American Institute of Commerce
2302 West First St.
Cedar Falls 50613

Des Moines Community College
2006 Ankeny Blvd.
Ankeny 50021

Kirkwood Community College
P.O. Box 2068
Cedar Rapids 52406

Teikyo Marycrest University
1607 West 12th St.
Davenport 52804-4096

KANSAS

Johnson County Community College
12345 College Blvd.
Overland Park 66210-1299

Kansas City Kansas Community College
7250 State Ave.
Kansas City 66112

The Brown Mackie College
8000 West 110th St.
Overland Park 66210

The Brown Mackie College
126 South Santa Fe St.
Salina 67402-1787

Washburn University of Topeka
1700 College Ave.
Topeka 66621

Wichita State University
1845 Fairmount
Wichita 67260

KENTUCKY

Eastern Kentucky University
Lancaster Ave.
Richmond 40475

Kentucky Career Institute
8095 Connector Dr., P.O. Box 143
Florence 41022-0143

Midway College
512 Stephens St.
Midway 40347-1120

Sullivan College
3101 Bardstown Rd.
Louisville 40205

University of Louisville
South Third St.
Louisville 40292-0001

LOUISIANA

Baton Rouge College
2834 South Sherwood Forest
Baton Rouge 70816

Jefferson College
12 Westbank Expwy.
Gretna 70053

McNeese State University
4100 Ryan Rd.
Lake Charles 70609

Nicholls State University
University Station
Thibodaux 70310

Phillips Junior College
822 South Clearview Pkwy.
New Orleans 70123

Southern Technical College
303 Rue Louis XIV
Lafayette 70508

Tulane University of Louisiana
6823 Saint Charles Ave.
New Orleans 70118

MAINE

Beal College
629 Main St.
Bangor 04401

Casco Bay College
477 Congress St.
Portland 04101

MARYLAND

Abbie Business Institute
5310 Spectrum Dr.
Frederick 21701

Anne Arundel Community College
101 College Pkwy.
Arnold 21012

Baltimore City Community College
2901 Liberty Heights Ave.
Baltimore 21215

Dundalk Community College
7200 Sollers Point Rd.
Dundalk 21222

Frederick Community College
7932 Opossumtown Pike
Frederick 21702

Hagerstown Business College
18618 Crestwood Dr.
Hagerstown 21742

Montgomery College of Takoma Park
Takoma Ave. and Fenton St.
Takoma Park 20912

Prince Georges Community College
301 Largo Rd.
Largo 23701-1243

Villa Julie College
Green Spring Valley Rd.
Stevenson 21153

MASSACHUSETTS

Aquinas College at Milton
303 Adams St.
Milton 02186

Bay Path College
588 Longmeadow St.
Longmeadow 01106

Becker College, Worcester
61 Sever St.
Worcester 01615-0071

Fisher College
118 Beacon St.
Boston 02116

Kinyon-Campbell Business School
59 Linden St.
New Bedford 02740

Kinyon-Campbell Business School
1041 Pearl St.
Brockton 02401

Massachusetts Bay Community College
50 Oakland St.
Wellesley Hills 02181

Middlesex Community College
Springs Rd.
Bedford 01730

Mount Ida College
777 Dedham St.
Newton Centre 02159

North Shore Community College
One Ferncroft Rd.
Danvers 01923

Northern Essex Community College
Elliott Way
Haverhill 01830-2399

Quincy College
34 Coddington St.
Quincy 02169

Stonehill College
Washington St.
North Easton 02357

MICHIGAN

Academy of Court Reporting
26111 Evergreen Rd.
Southfield 48076-4481

American Education Centers
26075 Woodward Ave.
Huntington Woods 48070

American Institute for Paralegal
Studies, Inc.
17515 West Nine Mile Rd.
Southfield 48075

Delta College
University Center 48710

Ferris State University
901 South State St.
Big Rapids 49307

Gogebic Community College
East 4946 Jackson Rd.
Ironwood 49938

Great Lakes Junior College of Business
310 South Washington Ave.
Saginaw 48607

Henry Ford Community College
5101 Evergreen Rd.
Dearborn 48128

Jackson Community College
2111 Emmons Rd.
Jackson 49201

Kellogg Community College
450 North Ave.
Battle Creek 49017

Lansing Community College
419 North Capitol Ave.
Lansing 48901-7210

Macomb Community College
14500 Twelve Mile Rd.
Warren 48093-3896

Montcalm Community College
2800 College Dr.
Sidney 48885

Mott Community College
1401 East Court St.
Flint 48503

Northwestern Michigan College
1701 East Front St.
Traverse City 49684

Oakland Community College
2480 Opdyke Rd.
Bloomfield Hills 48304-2266

Oakland University
Rochester Hills 48309-4401

Professional Careers Institute
23300 Greenfield Ave.
Oak Park 48237

Southwestern Michigan College
58900 Cherry Grove Rd.
Dowagiac 49047-9793

University of Detroit, Mercy
P.O. Box 19900
Detroit 48219-0900

MINNESOTA

Inver Hills Community College
5445 College Trail
Inver Grove Heights 55076

North Hennepin Community College
7411 85th Ave. N
Brooklyn Park 55445

Northland Community College
Hwy. 1 E
Thief River Falls 56701

MISSISSIPPI

Mississippi Gulf Coast Community
College
Central Office, P.O. Box 67
Perkinston 39573

Phillips Junior College
2680 Insurance Center Dr.
Jackson 39216

Phillips Junior College
942 Beach Dr.
Gulfport 39507

MISSOURI

Drury College
900 North Benton Ave.
Springfield 65802

Missouri Western State College
4525 Downs Dr.
Saint Joseph 64507

Northwest Missouri Community
College
4315 Pickett Rd.
Saint Joseph 64503-1635

Penn Valley Community College
3201 Southwest Trafficway
Kansas City 64111

Phillips Junior College
1010 West Sunshine
Springfield 65807

Rockhurst College
1100 Rockhurst Rd.
Kansas City 64110

Saint Louis Community College, Forest
  Park
5600 Oakland Ave.
Saint Louis 63110

Sanford-Brown Business College
12006 Manchester Rd.
Des Peres 63131

Vattenott College
3925 Industrial Dr.
Saint Ann 63074

Watterson College, Saint Louis Missouri
3323 South Kings Hwy.
Saint Louis 63139

Webster University
470 East Lockwood
Saint Louis 63119

William Jewell College
500 College Hill
Liberty 64068

MONTANA

College of Great Falls
1301 Twentieth St. S
Great Falls 59405-4996

May Technical College
P.O. Box 127
Billings 59103

May Technical College, Great Falls
1807 Third St. NW
Great Falls 59404

Missoula Vocational Technical Center
909 South Ave. W
Missoula 59801

NEBRASKA

College of Saint Mary
1901 South 72nd St.
Omaha 68124

Institute of Computer Science
808 South 74th Place
Omaha 68114

Metropolitan Community College Area
P.O. Box 3777
Omaha 68103

Nebraska College of Business
3636 California St.
Omaha 68131

NEVADA

Community College of Southern
  Nevada
3200 East Cheyenne Ave.
Las Vegas 89030

Morrison College/Reno Business
  College
140 Washington St.
Reno 89503

NEW HAMPSHIRE

Hesser College
Three Sundial Ave.
Manchester 03103

McIntosh College
23 Cataract Ave.
Dover 03820

New Hampshire Technical College at
  Nashua
505 Amherst St.
Nashua 03061-2052

New Hampshire Technical Institute
11 Institute Dr.
Concord 03301

NEW JERSEY

Bergen Community College
400 Paramus Rd.
Paramus 07652

Brookdale Community College
Newman Springs Rd.
Lincroft 07738-1599

Burlington County College
Rte. 530
Pemberton 08068

Cittone Institute
523 Fellowship Rd.
Mount Laurel 08054

Cumberland County College
College Dr., P.O. Box 517
Vineland 08360

Horizon Institute of Paralegal Studies
453 North Wood Ave.
Linden 07036

Katharine Gibbs School
80 Kingsbridge Rd.
Piscataway 08854

Mercer County Community College
1200 Old Trenton Rd.
Trenton 08690

Middlesex County College
155 Mill Rd., P.O. Box 3050
Edison 08818-3050

Omega Institute
Rte. 130 South Cinnaminson Mall
Cinnaminson 08077

Sussex County Community College
  Commission
College Hill
Newton 07860

NEW MEXICO

Albuquerque Career Institute
111 Wyoming NE
Albuquerque 87123

Albuquerque Technical-Vocational
  Institute
525 Buena Vista SE
Albuquerque 87106

San Juan College
4601 College Blvd.
Farmington 87402

Santa Fe Community College
South Richards Ave. P.O. Box 4187
Santa Fe 87502-4187

NEW YORK

Betty Owen Schools, Inc.
350 Fifth Ave.
New York 10118

Broome Community College
P.O. Box 1017
Binghamton 13902

Corning Community College
Spencer Hill
Corning 14830

Erie Community College, City Campus
121 Ellicott St.
Buffalo 14203

Herkimer County Community College
Reservoir Rd.
Herkimer 13350-1598

Nassau Community College
One Education Dr.
Garden City 11530

National Academy for Paralegal Studies,
  Inc.
28 Industrial Dr.
P.O. Box 907
Middletown 10940

Rennert Bilingual
Two West 45th St.
New York 10036

Schenectady County Community
  College
Washington Ave.
Schenectady 12305

Suffolk County Community College,
  Western Campus
Crooked Hill Rd.
Brentwood 11717

Suffolk County Community College,
  Ammerman Campus
533 College Rd.
Selden 11784

The Sobelsohn School
370 Seventh Ave.
New York 10001

Tompkins-Cortland Community
  College
170 North St.
Dryden 13053

NORTH CAROLINA

Cape Fear Community College
411 North Front St.
Wilmington 28401

Carteret Community College
3505 Arendell St.
Morehead City 28557

Central Carolina Community College
1105 Kelly Dr.
Sanford 27330

Central Piedmont Community College
P.O. Box 35009
Charlotte 28235

Coastal Carolina Community College
444 Western Blvd.
Jacksonville 28546-6877

Davidson County Community College
P.O. Box 1287
Lexington 27293

Durham Technical Community College
1637 Lawson St.
Durham 27703

Fayetteville Technical Community
  College
2201 Hull Rd.
Fayetteville 28303

Forsyth Technical Community College
2100 Silas Creek Pkwy.
Winston-Salem 27103

Guilford Technical Community College
P.O. Box 309
Jamestown 27282

Johnston Community College
P.O. Box 2350
Smithfield 27577-2350

Kings College
322 Lamar Ave.
Charlotte 28204

Pitt Community College
Hwy. 11 S
P.O. Drawer 7007
Greenville 27835-7007

Rockingham Community College
P.O. Box 38
Wentworth 27375-0038

Southwestern Community College
275 Webster Rd.
Sylva 28779

Western Piedmont Community College
1001 Burkemont Ave.
Morganton 28655-9978

NORTH DAKOTA

Interstate Business College
520 East Main Ave.
Bismarck 58501

OHIO

Academy of Court Reporting, Columbus
630 East Broad St.
Columbus 43215

Academy of Court Reporting, Akron
2930 West Market St.
Akron 44333

Academy of Court Reporting
614 Superior Ave. NW
Cleveland 44113

American Institute for Paralegal
  Studies, Inc.
400 East Second St.
Dayton 45401

American Institute for Paralegal
  Studies, Inc.
3200 Chagrin Blvd.
Pepper Pike 44124-5974

American Institute for Paralegal
  Studies, Inc.
1216 Sunburg Rd.
Columbus 43219

American Institute for Paralegal
  Studies, Inc.
2020 Easton St.
Canton 44720

American Institute for Paralegal
  Studies, Inc.
1231 West Kemper Rd.
Cincinnati 45240

American Institute for Paralegal
  Studies, Inc.
16699 Bagley Rd.
Cleveland 44130

American School of Technology
2100 Morse Rd.
Columbus 43229

Columbus Para Professional
  Institute
1077 Lexington Ave.
Columbus 43201

Columbus State Community College
550 East Spring St.
P.O. Box 1609
Columbus 43216

Dyke College
112 Prospect Ave.
Cleveland 44115

Lakeland Community College
7700 Clocktower Dr.
Mentor 44060-7594

Lawrence County Joint Vocational
  School
Rte. 2 Getaway
Chesapeake 45619

Lima Technical College
4240 Campus Dr.
Lima 45804

Muskingum Area Technical College
1555 Newark Rd.
Zanesville 43701

Raedel College and Industrial Welding
  School
137 Sixth St. NE
Canton 44702

Sawyer College of Business
3150 Mayfield Rd.
Cleveland Heights 44118

Sawyer College of Business, West
13027 Lorain Ave.
Cleveland 44111

Sinclair Community College
444 West Third St.
Dayton 45402

Technology Education Center
288 South Hamilton Rd.
Columbus 43213

Tri-County Vocational School
15675 St. Rte. 691
Nelsonville 45764

University of Akron, Main Campus
302 Buchtel Common
Akron 44325-4702

University of Cincinnati, Main Campus
2624 Clifton Ave.
Cincinnati 45221-0127

University of Toledo
2801 West Bancroft
Toledo 43606

OKLAHOMA

City College, Inc.
1370 North Interstate Dr.
Norman 73072

Oklahoma Junior College of Business
and Technology
3232 Northwest 65th
Oklahoma City 73116

Rogers State College
Will Rogers and College Hill
Claremore 74017

Rose State College
6420 Southeast 15th
Midwest City 73110

OREGON

College of Legal Arts
52M Southwest Hall
Portland 97201

Pioneer Pacific College
25195 Southwest Parkway Ave.
Wilsonville 97070

Portland Community College
P.O. Box 19000
Portland 97280-0990

Western Business College
505 Southwest Sixth Ave.
Portland 97204

PENNSYLVANIA

Academy of Medical Arts and Business
279 Boas St.
Harrisburg 17102

American Center for Technical Arts
and Sciences
100 East Lancaster Ave.
Wayne 19087

American Center for Technical Arts
1930 Chestnut St.
Philadelphia 19103

Central Pennsylvania Business School
107 College Hill Rd.
Summerdale 17093-0309

Community College of Allegheny
County
800 Allegheny Ave.
Pittsburgh 15233-1895

Duffs Business Institute
110 Ninth St.
Pittsburgh 15222

Gannon University
109 West Sixth St.
Erie 16541

Harrisburg Area Community College,
Harrisburg Campus
One Hacc Dr.
Harrisburg 17110

Liberty Academy of Business
511 North Broad St.
Philadelphia 19123

Luzerne County Community College
1333 South Prospect St.
Nanticoke 18634

Manor Junior College
700 Fox Chase Rd.
Jenkintown 19046

Mount Aloysius College
One College Dr.
Cresson 16630-1999

Peirce Junior College
1420 Pine St.
Philadelphia 19102

Pennsylvania College of Technology
One College Ave.
Williamsport 17701

Pennsylvania State University, Main
Campus
201 Old Main
University Park 16802

Robert Morris College
Narrows Run Rd.
Coraopolis 15108-1189

Star Technical Institute, Kingston
212 Wyoming Ave.
Kingston 18704

Star Technical Institute, Whitehall
1541 Alta Dr.
Whitehall 18052

The Career Institute
1825 J F Kennedy Blvd.
Philadelphia 19103

The PJA School
7900 West Chester Pike
Upper Darby 19082

Western School of Health & Business
Careers
Rte. 22 and 3824 Northern Pike
Monroeville 15146

Western School of Health & Business
Careers
411 Seventh Ave.
Pittsburgh 15219

Westmoreland County Community
College
Youngwood 15697-1895

RHODE ISLAND

Johnson and Wales University
Abbott Park Place
Providence 02903-3376

Katharine Gibbs School
178 Butler Ave.
Providence 02906

SOUTH CAROLINA

Florence-Darlington Technical College
P.O. Box 100548
Florence 29501-0548

Greenville Technical College
Station B
P.O. Box 5616
Greenville 29606-5616

Midlands Technical College
P.O. Box 2408
Columbia 29202

Trident Technical College
P.O. Box 118067
Charleston 29423-8067

SOUTH DAKOTA

Kilian Community College
1600 South Menlo Ave.
Sioux Falls 57105

National College
321 Kansas City St.
Rapid City 57701

Nettleton Junior College
100 South Spring Ave.
Sioux Falls 57104

TENNESSEE

Chattanooga State Technical
Community College
4501 Amnicola Hwy.
Chattanooga 37406

Cleveland State Community College
P.O. Box 3570
Cleveland 37320-3570

Memphis State University
Memphis 38152

Pellissippi State Technical Community
College
P.O. Box 22990
Knoxville 37933-0990

State Technical Institute of Memphis
5983 Macon Cove
Memphis 38134

TEXAS

Austin Community College
5930 Middle Fiskville Rd.
Austin 78752

Center for Advanced Legal Studies
3910 Kirby
Houston 77098

Collin County Community College
2200 West University
McKinney 75070

Cooke County College
1525 West California
Gainesville 76240

Del Mar College
101 Baldwin
Corpus Christi 78404-3897

El Centro College
Main and Lamar
Dallas 75202

El Paso Community College
P.O. Box 20500
El Paso 79998

Grayson County College
6101 Grayson Dr.
Denison 75020

Houston Community College System
22 Waugh Dr., P.O. Box 7849
Houston 77270-7849

Midland College
3600 North Garfield
Midland 79705

National Career Institute
1209 Seventh St.
Harlingen 78550

North Harris Montgomery Community
College District
250 North Sam Houston Pkwy. E
Houston 77060

Phillips School of Business & Technology
119 West Eighth St.
Austin 78701

San Antonio College
1300 San Pedro Ave.
San Antonio 78284

San Antonio Court Reporting Institute,
Inc.
5430 Fredericksburg Rd.
San Antonio 78229

Southern Career Institute, Inc.
2301 South Congress
Austin 78704

Southern Methodist University
6425 Boaz St.
Dallas 75275-0221

Southwestern Institutes
4888 Loop Central Dr.
Houston 77081

Tarrant County Junior College District
1500 Houston St.
Fort Worth 76102

Texas School of Business, Inc.
711 Airtex Dr.
Houston 77073

Texas School of Business, Southwest, Inc.
10250 Bissonnet
Houston 77036

Tyler Junior College
P.O. Box 9020
Tyler 75711

UTAH

Phillips Junior College, Salt Lake City
3098 Highland Dr.
Salt Lake City 84106

Utah Valley Community College
800 West, 1200 South
Orem 84058

Westminster College of Salt Lake City
1840 South, 1300 East
Salt Lake City 84105

VERMONT

Champlain College
163 South Willard St.
Burlington 05401

VIRGINIA

Commonwealth College
4160 Virginia Beach Blvd.
Virginia Beach 23452

Para-Legal Institute
95 24-A Lee Hwy.
Fairfax 22031

University of Richmond
Maryland Hall
Richmond 23173

WASHINGTON

Clark College
1800 East McLoughlin Blvd.
Vancouver 98663

Edmonds Community College
20000 68th Ave. W
Lynnwood 98036

Highline Community College
P.O. Box 98000
Des Moines 98198-9800

Phillips Junior College
North 1101 Fancher
Spokane 99212-1204

Pierce College
9401 Farwest Dr. SW
Tacoma 98498

Spokane Community College
North 1810 Greene Ave.
Spokane 99207

WEST VIRGINIA

Marshall University
400 Hal Greer Blvd.
Huntington 25755

The College of West Virginia
609 South Kanawha
Beckley 25802

The University of Charleston
2300 MacCorkle Ave. SE
Charleston 25304

West Virginia Business College
1052 Main St.
Wheeling 26003

West Virginia Business College
215 West Main St.
Clarksburg 26301

West Virginia Career College
148 Willey St.
Morgantown 26505

WISCONSIN

Chippewa Valley Technical College
620 West Clairemont Ave.
Eau Claire 54701

Lakeshore Vocational Training and
Adult Education System District
1290 North Ave.
Cleveland 53015

MBTI Business Training Institute
820 North Plankinton Ave.
Milwaukee 53203

Milwaukee Area Technical College
700 West State St.
Milwaukee 53233

Northeast Wisconsin Technical College
2740 West Mason St., P.O. Box 19042
Green Bay 54307-9042

WYOMING

Casper College
125 College Dr.
Casper 82601

Laramie County Community College
1400 East College Dr.
Cheyenne 82007

Library Assistant Technology

CALIFORNIA

Foothill College
12345 El Monte Rd.
Los Altos Hills 94022

Fresno City College
1101 East University Ave.
Fresno 93741

Palomar College
1140 West Mission
San Marcos 92069-1487

Sacramento City College
3835 Freeport Blvd.
Sacramento 95822

CONNECTICUT

Mohegan Community College
Mahan Dr., P.O. Box 629
Norwich 06360

ILLINOIS

City College of Chicago, Wright College
4300 North Narragansett
Chicago 60634

College of Du Page
Lambert Rd. and 22nd St.
Glen Ellyn 60137

NEW HAMPSHIRE

School for Lifelong Learning
25 Concord Rd., Dunlap Center
Durham 03824

Police Science and Law Enforcement Technology

ALABAMA

Community College of the Air Force
Maxwell Air Force Base
Montgomery 36112

Gadsden State Community College
P.O. Box 227
Gadsden 35902-0227

George C Wallace State Community
College, Hanceville
801 Main St. NW, P.O. Box 2000
Hanceville 35077-2000

John C Calhoun State Community
College
P.O. Box 2216
Decatur 35609-2216

ALASKA

University of Alaska, Southeast
11120 Glacier Hwy.
Juneau 99801

ARIZONA

Arizona Institute of Business and
Technology
925 South Gilbert Rd.
Mesa 85204

Arizona Western College
P.O. Box 929
Yuma 85366

Central Arizona College
8470 North Overfield Rd.
Coolidge 85228-9778

Glendale Community College
6000 West Olive Ave.
Glendale 85302

Mesa Community College
1833 West Southern Ave.
Mesa 85202

Phoenix College
1202 West Thomas Rd.
Phoenix 85013

Pima Community College
2202 West Anklam Rd.
Tucson 85709-0001

ARKANSAS

Capital City Junior College of Business
7723 Asher Ave.
Little Rock 72214

East Arkansas Community College
Newcastle Rd.
Forrest City 72335

Garland County Community College
100 College Dr.
Hot Springs 71913

CALIFORNIA

American Institute of Specialized
Studies
8345 Reseda Blvd.
Northridge 91324

American Technical College for Career
Training
191 South East St.
San Bernardino 92401

California Career Schools
392 West Cerritos Ave.
Anaheim 92805

California Security Training School
2458 West Lomita Blvd.
Lomita 90717

Center for Employment Training, San
Jose-McGinness
1212 McGinness Ave.
San Jose 95127

Century Business College
3325 Wilshire Blvd.
Los Angeles 90010

Century Schools
2665 Fifth Ave.
San Diego 92103

Chaffey Community College
5885 Haven Ave.
Rancho Cucamonga 91737-3002

City College of San Francisco
50 Phelan Ave.
San Francisco 94112

Contra Costa College
2600 Mission Bell Dr.
San Pablo 94806

De Anza College
21250 Stevens Creek Blvd.
Cupertino 95014

Fresno City College
1101 East University Ave.
Fresno 93741

Fullerton College
321 East Chapman Ave.
Fullerton 92632-2095

Imperial Valley College
P.O. Box 158
Imperial 92251-0158

Lassen College
Hwy. 139, P.O. Box 3000
Susanville 96130

Martial Arts Security Service, Inc.
2024 North Broadway
Santa Ana 92706-2622

Mount San Antonio College
1100 North Grand
Walnut 91789

Napa Valley College
2277 Napa Vallejo Hwy.
Napa 94558

Palomar College
1140 West Mission
San Marcos 92069-1487

Professional Investigators Training
School
620 North Kenwood Place
Glendale 91206

Rancho Santiago College
17th at Bristol
Santa Ana 92706

Rio Hondo College
3600 Workman Mill Rd.
Whittier 90601-1699

Rouse School of Special Detective
Training
3410 G West McArthur Blvd.
Santa Ana 92704

Royal Security Training Academy
237 West Gage Ave.
Los Angeles 90003

Sacramento City College
3835 Freeport Blvd.
Sacramento 95822

Safety First Security Training Academy
156 North West Ave.
Fresno 93728

San Diego Miramar College
10440 Black Mountain Rd.
San Diego 92126-2999

San Joaquin Valley College
8400 West Mineral King Ave.
Visalia 93291

San Joaquin Valley College
201 New Stine Rd.
Bakersfield 93309

San Joaquin Valley College
3333 North Bond
Fresno 93726

Santa Rosa Junior College
1501 Mendocino Ave.
Santa Rosa 95401-4395

Shasta College
P.O. Box 496006
Redding 96049

Sierra College
5000 Rocklin Rd.
Rocklin 95677

Solano County Community College
District
4000 Suisun Valley Rd.
Suisun 94585

Southwestern College
900 Otay Lakes Rd.
Chula Vista 92010

Victor Valley College
18422 Bear Valley Rd.
Victorville 92392-9699

COLORADO

Aims Community College
P.O. Box 69
Greeley 80632

Colorado Mountain College
P.O. Box 10001
Glenwood Springs 81602

Delta-Montrose Area Vocational
Technical Center
1765 U.S. Hwy. 50
Delta 81416

Denver Business College
7350 North Broadway
Denver 80221

Morgan Community College
17800 County Rd. 20
Fort Morgan 80701

Nakazono Security Training
1780 South Bellaire St.
Denver 80222

Trinidad State Junior College
600 Prospect St.
Trinidad 81082

CONNECTICUT

Housatonic Community College
510 Barnum Ave.
Bridgeport 06608

Manchester Community College
60 Bidwell St., P.O. Box 1045
Manchester 06040-1046

Mattatuck Community College
750 Chase Pkwy.
Waterbury 06708

Mohegan Community College
Mahan Dr., P.O. Box 629
Norwich 06360

Northwestern Connecticut Community
College
Park Place E
Winsted 06098

Norwalk Community Technical College
188 Richards Ave.
Norwalk 06854

Tunxis Community College
Rtes. 6 and 177
Farmington 06032

DELAWARE

Delaware Technical and Community
College, Southern Campus
P.O. Box 610
Georgetown 19947

Delaware Technical Community
College Stanton-Wilmington
400 Stanton-Christiana Rd.
Newark 19702

DISTRICT OF COLUMBIA

PTC Career Institute
529 14th St. NW
Washington 20004

FLORIDA

Brevard Community College
1519 Clearlake Rd.
Cocoa 32922

Career City College
1317 Northeast Fourth Ave.
Fort Lauderdale 33304

Central Florida Community College
P.O. Box 1388
Ocala 34478

Chipola Junior College
3094 Indian Circle
Marianna 32446

Daytona Beach Community College
1200 Volusia Ave.
Daytona Beach 32114

Florida Community College at
Jacksonville
501 West State St.
Jacksonville 32202

Indian River Community College
3209 Virginia Ave.
Fort Pierce 34981

Lake City Community College
Rte. 3, P.O. Box 7
Lake City 32055

Lake County Area Vocational-Technical
Center
2001 Kurt St.
Eustis 32726

Lewis M Lively Area Vocational-
Technical Center
500 North Appleyard Dr.
Tallahassee 32304

Manatee Vocational-Technical Center
5603 34th St. W
Bradenton 34210

Miami-Dade Community College
300 Northeast Second Ave.
Miami 33132

North Florida Junior College
Turner Davis Dr.
Madison 32340

Palm Beach Community College
4200 Congress Ave.
Lake Worth 33461

Pasco-Hernando Community College
36727 Blanton Rd.
Dade City 33525-7599

Santa Fe Community College
3000 Northwest 83rd St.
Gainesville 32601

Sarasota County Technical Institute
4748 Beneva Rd.
Sarasota 34233-1798

Seminole Community College
100 Weldon Blvd.
Sanford 32773-6199

South Florida Community College
600 West College Dr.
Avon Park 33825

William T McFatter Vocational
Technical Center
6500 Nova Dr.
Davie 33317

Withlacoochee Technical Institute
1201 West Main St.
Inverness 32650

GEORGIA

Columbus College
4225 University Ave.
Columbus 31907-5645

Floyd College
P.O. Box 1864
Rome 30162-1864

Georgia Military College, Fort Gordon
Center
P.O. Box 7258
Fort Gordon 30905

Georgia Military College, Main Campus
201 East Greene St.
Milledgeville 31061-3398

Interactive Learning Systems
200 Cleveland Rd.
Bogart 30622

Interactive Learning Systems
2191 Northlake Pkwy.
Tucker 30084

Interactive Learning Systems
4814 Old National Hwy.
College Park 30337

PTC Career Institute
44 Broad St. NW
Atlanta 30303

HAWAII

Hawaii Community College
200 West Kawili St.
Hilo 96720-4091

Honolulu Community College
874 Dillingham Blvd.
Honolulu 96817

IDAHO

College of Southern Idaho
P.O. Box 1238
Twin Falls 83301

Eastern Idaho Technical College
1600 South, 2500 East
Idaho Falls 83404

Idaho State University
741 South Seventh Ave.
Pocatello 83209

North Idaho College
1000 West Garden Ave.
Coeur D'Alene 83814

Ricks College
Rexburg 83460-4107

ILLINOIS

Belleville Area College
2500 Carlyle Rd.
Belleville 62221

Black Hawk College, Quad-Cities
6600 34th Ave.
Moline 61265

City College of Chicago, Wright College
4300 North Narragansett
Chicago 60634

City College of Chicago, Harold
Washington
30 East Lake St.
Chicago 60601

City College of Chicago, Richard J
Daley College
7500 South Pulaski Rd.
Chicago 60652

College of Du Page
Lambert Rd. and 22nd St.
Glen Ellyn 60137

College of Lake County
19351 West Washington St.
Gray's Lake 60030-1198

Danville Area Community College
2000 East Main St.
Danville 61832

Illinois Central College
One College Dr.
East Peoria 61635

Illinois Valley Community College
2578 East 350th Rd.
Oglesby 61348

John A Logan College
Carterville 62918

Joliet Junior College
1216 Houbolt Ave.
Joliet 60436

Kankakee Community College
P.O. Box 888
Kankakee 60901

Kaskaskia College
27210 College Rd.
Centralia 62801

Lake Land College
5001 Lake Land Blvd.
Mattoon 61938

Lewis and Clark Community College
5800 Godfrey Rd.
Godfrey 62035

Lincoln Land Community College
Shepherd Rd.
Springfield 62194-9256

Moraine Valley Community College
10900 South 88th Ave.
Palos Hills 60465-0937

Morton College
3801 South Central Ave.
Cicero 60650

Northwestern University
633 Clark St.
Evanston 60208

Oakton Community College
1600 East Golf Rd.
Des Plaines 60016

Parkland College
2400 West Bradley Ave.
Champaign 61821

Pathfinder Enterprises, Inc.
19 East 21st St.
Chicago 60616

PTC Career Institute
11 East Adams St.
Chicago 60603

Rend Lake College
Rte. 1
Ina 62846

Richland Community College
One College Park
Decatur 62521

Rock Valley College
3301 North Mulford Rd.
Rockford 61114

Sauk Valley Community College
173 Rte. 2
Dixon 61021

Shawnee Community College
Shawnee College Rd.
Ullin 62992

South Suburban College
15800 South State St.
South Holland 60473

Southeastern Illinois College
3575 College Rd.
Harrisburg 62946

Southern Illinois University, Carbondale
Carbondale 62901

Triton College
2000 Fifth Ave.
River Grove 60171

Waubonsee Community College
Rte. 47 at Harter Rd.
Sugar Grove 60554-0901

William Rainey Harper College
1200 West Algonquin Rd.
Palatine 60067-7398

INDIANA

Indiana State University
210 North Seventh St.
Terre Haute 47809

Indiana University at Kokomo
2300 South Washington
Kokomo 46902

Indiana University at South Bend
1700 Mishawaka Ave.
South Bend 46615

Indiana University, Purdue University
at Fort Wayne
2101 Coliseum Blvd. E
Fort Wayne 46805

Sawyer College, Merrillville Branch
3803 East Lincoln Hwy.
Merrillville 46410

Vincennes University
1002 North First St.
Vincennes 47591

IOWA

Des Moines Community College
2006 Ankeny Blvd.
Ankeny 50021

Hawkeye Institute of Technology
1501 East Orange Rd.
Waterloo 50704

Indian Hills Community College
525 Grandview
Ottumwa 52501

Iowa Lakes Community College
19 South Seventh St.
Estherville 51334

Iowa Valley Community College
P.O. Box 536
Marshalltown 50158

Iowa Western Community College
2700 College Rd.
P.O. Box 4C
Council Bluffs 51502

Kirkwood Community College
P.O. Box 2068
Cedar Rapids 52406

North Iowa Area Community College
500 College Dr.
Mason City 50401

Western Iowa Technical Community
College
4647 Stone Ave., P.O. Box 265
Sioux City 51102-0265

KANSAS

Barton County Community College
Rte. 3
P.O. Box 136Z
Great Bend 67530

Butler County Community College
901 South Haverhill Rd.
El Dorado 67042

Cowley County Community College
125 South Second St.
Arkansas City 67005

Garden City Community College
801 Campus Dr.
Garden City 67846

Hutchinson Community College
1300 North Plum St.
Hutchinson 67501

Johnson County Community College
12345 College Blvd.
Overland Park 66210-1299

Seward County Community College
P.O. Box 1137
Liberal 67905-1137

KENTUCKY

Eastern Kentucky University
Lancaster Ave.
Richmond 40475

Hopkinsville Community College
North Dr.
Hopkinsville 42240

Northern Kentucky University
University Dr.
Highland Heights 41099

University of Louisville
South Third St.
Louisville 40292-0001

LOUISIANA

Bossier Parish Community College
2719 Airline Dr. N
Bossier City 71111

Delgado Community College
615 City Park Ave.
New Orleans 70119

Delta Career College
4358 Hwy. 84 W
Vidalia 71373

Delta Career College
1900 Cameron St.
Lafayette 70506-1608

Delta Career College, Medical Support
Division
1702 Hudson Ln.
Monroe 71201

Grambling State University
100 Main St., P.O. Drawer 607
Grambling 71245

Jefferson College
12 Westbank Expwy.
Gretna 70053

Louisiana State University, Eunice
P.O. Box 1129
Eunice 70535

Nicholls State University
University Station
Thibodaux 70310

Orleans Security Institute
Louisiana Superdome, P.O. Box 8383
New Orleans 70182

Southern University and A & M College
at Baton Rouge
404 South Clark Building
Baton Rouge 70813

MAINE

Southern Maine Technical College
Fort Rd.
South Portland 04106

University of Maine at Augusta
University Heights
Augusta 04330-9410

University of Maine
Office of Institutional Studies
Orono 04469

MARYLAND

Allegany Community College
Willowbrook Rd.
Cumberland 21502

Anne Arundel Community College
101 College Pkwy.
Arnold 21012

Catonsville Community College
800 South Rolling Rd.
Catonsville 21228

Chesapeake College
P.O. Box 8
Wye Mills 21679-0008

Essex Community College
7201 Rossville Blvd.
Baltimore 21237

Hagerstown Junior College
11400 Robinwood Dr.
Hagerstown 21742-6590

Harford Community College
401 Thomas Run Rd.
Bel Air 21015

Investigative Training Institute
621 Ridgely Ave.
Annapolis 21401

Montgomery College of Rockville
51 Mannakee St.
Rockville 20850

Prince Georges Community College
301 Largo Rd.
Largo 23701-1243

PTC Career Institute
201 East Baltimore St.
Baltimore 21202

Wor-Wic Community College
1409 Wesley Dr.
Salisbury 21801-7131

MASSACHUSETTS

Becker College, Worcester
61 Sever St.
Worcester 01615-0071

Berkshire Community College
1350 West St.
Pittsfield 01201-5786

Bunker Hill Community College
New Rutherford Ave.
Boston 02129

Cape Cod Community College
Rte. 132
West Barnstable 02668

Dean Junior College
99 Main St.
Franklin 02038

Greenfield Community College
One College Dr.
Greenfield 01301-9739

Holyoke Community College
303 Homestead Ave.
Holyoke 01040

Massachusetts Bay Community College
50 Oakland St.
Wellesley Hills 02181

Massasoit Community College
One Massasoit Blvd.
Brockton 02402

Middlesex Community College
Springs Rd.
Bedford 01730

Mount Wachusett Community College
444 Green St.
Gardner 01440

North Shore Community College
One Ferncroft Rd.
Danvers 01923

Northeastern University
360 Huntington Ave.
Boston 02115

Northern Essex Community College
Elliott Way
Haverhill 01830-2399

Quincy College
34 Coddington St.
Quincy 02169

Quinsigamond Community College
670 West Boylston St.
Worcester 01606

Springfield Technical Community
College
Armory Square
Springfield 01105

MICHIGAN

Alpena Community College
666 Johnson St.
Alpena 49707

Delta College
University Center 48710

Grand Rapids Community College
143 Bostwick Ave. NE
Grand Rapids 49505

Jackson Community College
2111 Emmons Rd.
Jackson 49201

Kalamazoo Valley Community College
6767 West O Ave.
Kalamazoo 49009

Kellogg Community College
450 North Ave.
Battle Creek 49017

Kirtland Community College
10775 North Saint Helen Rd.
Roscommon 48653

Lake Michigan College
2755 East Napier
Benton Harbor 49022

Lake Superior State University
Sault Sainte Marie 49783

Lansing Community College
419 North Capitol Ave.
Lansing 48901-7210

Macomb Community College
14500 Twelve Mile Rd.
Warren 48093-3896

Madonna University
36600 Schoolcraft Rd.
Livonia 48150

Montcalm Community College
2800 College Dr.
Sidney 48885

Mott Community College
1401 East Court St.
Flint 48503

Muskegon Community College
221 South Quarterline Rd.
Muskegon 49442

Northern Michigan University
1401 Presque Isle
Marquette 49855

Northwestern Michigan College
1701 East Front St.
Traverse City 49684

Oakland Community College
2480 Opdyke Rd.
Bloomfield Hills 48304-2266

Schoolcraft College
18600 Haggerty Rd.
Livonia 48152

Suomi College
601 Quincy St.
Hancock 49930

Washtenaw Community College
P.O. D1
Ann Arbor 48016

West Shore Community College
3000 North Stiles
Scottville 49454

MINNESOTA

Alexandria Technical College
1601 Jefferson St.
Alexandria 56308

Fond Du Lac Community College
Center
2101 14th St.
Cloquet 55720

Hibbing Community College
1515 East 25th St.
Hibbing 55746

Inver Hills Community College
5445 College Trail
Inver Grove Heights 55076

Lakewood Community College
3401 Century Ave. N
White Bear Lake 55110

Mankato State University
South Rd. and Ellis Ave.
Mankato 56001

Normandale Community College
9700 France Ave. S
Bloomington 55431

North Hennepin Community College
7411 85th Ave. N
Brooklyn Park 55445

Northland Community College
Hwy. 1 E
Thief River Falls 56701

Range Technical College, Hibbing
Campus
2900 East Beltline
Hibbing 55746

Rochester Community College
851 30th Ave. SE
Rochester 55904-4999

Willmar Community College
P.O. Box 797
Willmar 56201-0797

MISSISSIPPI

Mississippi Gulf Coast Community
College
Central Office
P.O. Box 67
Perkinston 39573

Queen City College
800 Hwy. 1 S
Greenville 38701

MISSOURI

Jefferson College
1000 Viking Dr.
Hillsboro 63050

Missouri Southern State College
3950 East Newman Rd.
Joplin 64801-1595

Missouri Western State College
4525 Downs Dr.
Saint Joseph 64507

Penn Valley Community College
3201 Southwest Trafficway
Kansas City 64111

Saint Louis Community College, Forest
Park
5600 Oakland Ave.
Saint Louis 63110

Three Rivers Community College
Three Rivers Blvd.
Poplar Bluff 63901

MONTANA

Dawson Community College
300 College Dr.
Glendive 59330

NEBRASKA

Metropolitan Community College Area
P.O. Box 3777
Omaha 68103

Northeast Community College
801 East Benjamin, P.O. Box 469
Norfolk 68702-0469

NEVADA

Community College of Southern
Nevada
3200 East Cheyenne Ave.
Las Vegas 89030

Truckee Meadows Community College
7000 Dandini Blvd.
Reno 89512

Western Nevada Community College
2201 West Nye Ln.
Carson City 89703

NEW HAMPSHIRE

Hesser College
Three Sundial Ave.
Manchester 03103

NEW JERSEY

Atlantic Community College
5100 Black Horse Pike
Mays Landing 08330-2699

Barclay Career School
28 South Harrison St.
East Orange 07017

Bergen Community College
400 Paramus Rd.
Paramus 07652

Brookdale Community College
Newman Springs Rd.
Lincroft 07738-1599

Burlington County College
Rte. 530
Pemberton 08068

Camden County College
P.O. Box 200
Blackwood 08012

County College of Morris
214 Center Grove Rd.
Randolph 07869

Essex County College
303 University Ave.
Newark 07102

Gloucester County College
Tanyard Rd. & RR 4, P.O. Box 203
Sewell 08080

Mercer County Community College
1200 Old Trenton Rd.
Trenton 08690

Middlesex County College
155 Mill Rd., P.O. Box 3050
Edison 08818-3050

Ocean County College
College Dr.
Toms River 08753

Passaic County Community College
College Blvd.
Paterson 07509

PTC Career Institute, University
 Heights
200 Washington St.
Newark 07102

Raritan Valley Community College
P.O. Box 3300
Somerville 08876

Union County College
1033 Springfield Ave.
Cranford 07016

NEW MEXICO

Albuquerque Technical-Vocational
 Institute
525 Buena Vista SE
Albuquerque 87106

New Mexico State University, Main
 Campus
P.O. Box 30001
Las Cruces 88003

Santa Fe Community College
South Richards Ave.
P.O. Box 4187
Santa Fe 87502-4187

University of New Mexico, Gallup
 Branch
200 College Rd.
Gallup 87301

NEW YORK

Adirondack Community College
Bay Rd.
Queensbury 12804

Broome Community College
P.O. Box 1017
Binghamton 13902

Canisius College
2001 Main St.
Buffalo 14208

Cayuga County Community College
Franklin St.
Auburn 13021

Clinton Community College
RR 3, P.O. Box 8A
Plattsburgh 12901

Columbia-Greene Community College
P.O. Box 1000
Hudson 12534

CUNY John Jay College Criminal
 Justice
899 Tenth Ave.
New York 10019

Dutchess Community College
Pendell Rd.
Poughkeepsie 12601

Erie Community College, North
 Campus
Main St. and Youngs Rd.
Williamsville 14221

Hilbert College
5200 South Park Ave.
Hamburg 14075-1597

Jamestown Community College
525 Falconer St.
Jamestown 14701

Marist College
290 North Rd.
Poughkeepsie 12601

Monroe Community College
1000 East Henrietta Rd.
Rochester 14623

Orange County Community College
115 South St.
Middletown 10940

Rockland Community College
145 College Rd.
Suffern 10901

Suffolk County Community College,
 Eastern Campus
Speonk Riverhead Rd.
Riverhead 11901

Suffolk County Community College,
 Western Campus
Crooked Hill Rd.
Brentwood 11717

Suffolk County Community College,
 Ammerman Campus
533 College Rd.
Selden 11784

Sullivan County Community College
Le Roy Rd., P.O. Box 4002
Loch Sheldrake 12759-4002

SUNY College of Technology at Canton
Canton 13617

SUNY College of Technology at
 Farmingdale
Melville Rd.
Farmingdale 11735

SUNY Westchester Commmunity
 College
75 Grasslands Rd.
Valhalla 10595

Superior Career Institute, Inc.
116 West 14th St.
New York 10011

Tompkins-Cortland Community
 College
170 North St.
Dryden 13053

NORTH CAROLINA

Alamance Community College
P.O. Box 8000
Graham 27253

American Institute of Applied Science
P.O. Box 639
Youngsville 27596

Asheville-Buncombe Technical
 Community College
340 Victoria Rd.
Asheville 28801

Beaufort County Community College
P.O. Box 1069
Washington 27889

Brunswick Community College
P.O. Box 30
Supply 28462

Cape Fear Community College
411 North Front St.
Wilmington 28401

Carteret Community College
3505 Arendell St.
Morehead City 28557

Catawba Valley Community College
2550 Hwy. 70 SE
Hickory 28602-0699

Central Carolina Community College
1105 Kelly Dr.
Sanford 27330

Central Piedmont Community College
P.O. Box 35009
Charlotte 28235

Cleveland Community College
137 South Post Rd.
Shelby 28150

Coastal Carolina Community College
444 Western Blvd.
Jacksonville 28546-6877

College of the Albemarle
P.O. Box 2327, 1208 North Road St.
Elizabeth City 27906-2327

Craven Community College
800 College Ct.
New Bern 28562

Davidson County Community College
P.O. Box 1287
Lexington 27293

Durham Technical Community College
1637 Lawson St.
Durham 27703

Fayetteville Technical Community
 College
2201 Hull Rd.
Fayetteville 28303

Forsyth Technical Community College
2100 Silas Creek Pkwy.
Winston-Salem 27103

Gaston College
Hwy. 321
Dallas 28034

Guilford Technical Community College
P.O. Box 309
Jamestown 27282

Halifax Community College
P.O. Drawer 809
Weldon 27890

Haywood Community College
Freedlander Dr.
Clyde 28721

James Sprunt Community College
P.O. Box 398
Kenansville 28349

Johnston Community College
P.O. Box 2350
Smithfield 27577-2350

Mayland Community College
P.O. Box 547
Spruce Pine 28777

Mitchell Community College
500 West Broad
Statesville 28677

Montgomery Community College
P.O. Box 787
Troy 27371

Pitt Community College
Hwy. 11 S, P.O. Drawer 7007
Greenville 27835-7007

Randolph Community College
P.O. Box 1009
Asheboro 27204

Richmond Community College
P.O. Box 1189
Hamlet 28345

Robeson Community College
P.O. Box 1420
Lumberton 28359

Rowan-Cabarrus Community College
P.O. Box 1595
Salisbury 28145-1595

Southeastern Community College
P.O. Box 151
Whiteville 28472

Stanly Community College
141 College Dr.
Albemarle 28001

Vance-Granville Community College
State Rd. 11, P.O. Box 917
Henderson 27536

Wake Technical Community College
9101 Fayetteville Rd.
Raleigh 27603-5696

Wayne Community College
P.O Box 8002
Goldsboro 27533-8002

Western Piedmont Community College
1001 Burkemont Ave.
Morganton 28655-9978

Wilson Technical Community College
902 Herring Ave.
Wilson 27893

NORTH DAKOTA

Minot State University
500 University Ave. W
Minot 58707

United Tribes Technical College
3315 University Dr.
Bismarck 58501

University of North Dakota, Lake Region
North College Dr.
Devils Lake 58301

OHIO

Brentley Institute, Inc.
11750 Shaker Blvd.
Cleveland 44120

Butler County JVS District, D Russel
 Lee Career Center
3603 Hamilton Middletown Rd.
Hamilton 45011

Central Ohio Technical College
1179 University Dr.
Newark 43055-1767

Columbus State Community College
550 East Spring St., P.O. Box 1609
Columbus 43216

Cuyahoga Community College District
700 Carnegie Ave.
Cleveland 44115-2878

Delaware Joint Vocational School
 District
1610 Rte. 521
Delaware 43015

Eastland Career Center
4465 South Hamilton Rd.
Groveport 43125

Edison State Community College
1973 Edison Dr.
Piqua 45356

Gallia Jackson Vinton JUSD
P.O. Box 157
Rio Grande 45674

Hocking Technical College
3301 Hocking Pkwy.
Nelsonville 45764

Jefferson Technical College
4000 Sunset Blvd.
Steubenville 43952-3598

Lakeland Community College
7700 Clocktower Dr.
Mentor 44060-7594

Lawrence County Joint Vocational
 School
Rte. 2 Getaway
Chesapeake 45619

Lima Technical College
4240 Campus Dr.
Lima 45804

Lorain County Community College
1005 North Abbe Rd.
Elyria 44035

Midwest Technical Schools, Inc.
7009 Taylorsville Rd.
Huber Heights 45424

Muskingum Area Technical College
1555 Newark Rd.
Zanesville 43701

North Central Technical College
2441 Kenwood Circle, P.O. Box 698
Mansfield 44901

Ohio University, Chillicothe Branch
P.O. Box 629
Chillicothe 45601

Owens Technical College, Findlay
 Campus
300 Davis St.
Findlay 45840

Owens Technical College
30335 Oregon Rd., P.O. Box 10000
Toledo 43699-1947

PTC Career Institute
1140 Euclid Ave.
Cleveland 44115

Sinclair Community College
444 West Third St.
Dayton 45402

Southern Hills Joint Vocational School
District
9193 Hamer Rd.
Georgetown 45121

Terra Technical College
2830 Napoleon Rd.
Fremont 43420

University of Akron, Main Campus
302 Buchtel Common
Akron 44325-4702

University of Cincinnati, Main Campus
2624 Clifton Ave.
Cincinnati 45221-0127

University of Toledo
2801 West Bancroft
Toledo 43606

Youngstown State University
410 Wick Ave.
Youngstown 44555

OKLAHOMA

Cameron University
2800 Gore Blvd.
Lawton 73505

Central Oklahoma Area Vocational
Technical School
1720 South Main
Sapulpa 74030

Central Oklahoma Area Vocational
Technical School
Three Court Circle
Drumright 74030

Connors State College
Rte. 1
P.O. Box 1000
Warner 74469

Northeastern Oklahoma Agricultural
and Mechanical College
200 Eye St. NE
Miami 74354

Northern Oklahoma College
P.O. Box 310
Tonkawa 74653

Oklahoma State University, Oklahoma
City
900 North Portland
Oklahoma City 73107

Platt College
6125 West Reno
Oklahoma City 73127

Platt College
4821 South 72nd East Ave.
Tulsa 74145

Redland Community College
1300 South Country Club Rd.
P.O. Box 370
El Reno 73036

Rogers State College
Will Rogers and College Hill
Claremore 74017

Rose State College
6420 Southeast 15th
Midwest City 73110

Tulsa Junior College
6111 East Skelly Dr.
Tulsa 74135

OREGON

Blue Mountain Community College
P.O. Box 100
Pendleton 97801

Clackamas Community College
19600 Molalla Ave.
Oregon City 97045

Lane Community College
4000 East 30th Ave.
Eugene 97405

Linn-Benton Community College
6500 Southwest Pacific Blvd.
Albany 97321

Pioneer Pacific College
25195 Southwest Parkway Ave.
Wilsonville 97070

Rogue Community College
3345 Redwood Hwy.
Grants Pass 97527

Southwestern Oregon Community
College
1988 Newmark Ave.
Coos Bay 97420

Treasure Valley Community College
650 College Blvd.
Ontario 97914

PENNSYLVANIA

Advanced Career Training
McClatchy Fl Southwest Corner 69th &
Market
Upper Darby 19082

American Center for Technical Arts
1930 Chestnut St.
Philadelphia 19103

Bucks County Community College
Swamp Rd.
Newtown 18940

Community College of Allegheny
County
800 Allegheny Ave.
Pittsburgh 15233-1895

Community College of Beaver County
One Campus Dr.
Monaca 15061

Community College of Philadelphia
1700 Spring Garden St.
Philadelphia 19130

Delaware County Community College
901 South Media Line Rd.
Media 19063

Delaware County Institute of Training
615 Ave. of the States
Chester 19013

Harrisburg Area Community College,
Harrisburg Campus
One Hacc Dr.
Harrisburg 17110

Lackawanna Junior College
901 Prospect Ave.
Scranton 18505

Lehigh County Community College
4525 Education Park Dr.
Schnecksville 18078-2598

Lion Investigation Academy
434 Clearfield St.
Freemansburg 18017

Luzerne County Community College
1333 South Prospect St.
Nanticoke 18634

Mercyhurst College
501 East 38th St.
Erie 16546

Montgomery County Community
College
340 Dekalb Pike
Blue Bell 19422

PTC Career Institute
40 North Second St.
Philadelphia 19106

Suburban Academy of Law
Enforcement
3550 William Penn Hwy.
Pittsburgh 15235

Westmoreland County Community
College
Youngwood 15697-1895

York College Pennsylvania
Country Club Rd.
York 17405-7199

RHODE ISLAND

Community College of Rhode Island
400 East Ave.
Warwick 02886-1805

SOUTH CAROLINA

Central Carolina Technical College
506 North Guignard Dr.
Sumter 29150

Florence-Darlington Technical College
P.O. Box 100548
Florence 29501-0548

Horry-Georgetown Technical College
P.O. Box 1966
Conway 29526

Midlands Technical College
P.O. Box 2408
Columbia 29202

Orangeburg-Calhoun Technical College
3250 Saint Matthews Rd.
Orangeburg 29115

Piedmont Technical College
P.O. Drawer 1467
Greenwood 29648

Tri-County Technical College
P.O. Box 587
Pendleton 29670

Trident Technical College
P.O. Box 118067
Charleston 29423-8067

SOUTH DAKOTA

Western Dakota Vocational Technical
Institute
1600 Sedivy
Rapid City 57701

TENNESSEE

East Tennessee State University
P.O. Box 70716
Johnson City 37614

Roane State Community College
Patton Ln.
Harriman 37748

Shelby State Community College
P.O. Box 40568
Memphis 38174-0568

Tennessee Technological University
Dixie Ave.
Cookeville 38505

Walters State Community College
500 South Davy Crockett Pkwy.
Morristown 37813-6899

TEXAS

Alvin Community College
3110 Mustang Rd.
Alvin 77511

Austin Community College
5930 Middle Fiskville Rd.
Austin 78752

Bee County College
3800 Charco Rd.
Beeville 78102

Central Texas College
P.O. Box 1800
Killeen 76540-9990

Chenier
2816 Loop 306
San Angelo 76904

Chenier
6300 Richmond
Houston 77057

Cooke County College
1525 West California
Gainesville 76240

Del Mar College
101 Baldwin
Corpus Christi 78404-3897

El Centro College
Main and Lamar
Dallas 75202

El Paso Community College
P.O. Box 20500
El Paso 79998

Grayson County College
6101 Grayson Dr.
Denison 75020

Kilgore College
1100 Broadway
Kilgore 75662-3299

Lamar University, Beaumont
4400 Mlk
P.O. Box 10001
Beaumont 77710

Laredo Junior College
West End Washington St.
Laredo 78040

McLennan Community College
1400 College Dr.
Waco 76708

Navarro College
3200 West Seventh
Corsicana 75110

Northeast Texas Community College
P.O. Box 1307
Mount Pleasant 75456

Odessa College
201 West University
Odessa 79764

San Antonio College
1300 San Pedro Ave.
San Antonio 78284

San Jacinto College, Central Campus
8060 Spencer Hwy.
Pasadena 77505

San Jacinto College, North Campus
5800 Uvalde
Houston 77049

South Plains College
1401 College Ave.
Levelland 79336

Southwest Texas Junior College
2401 Garner Field Rd.
Uvalde 78801

Tarrant County Junior College
District
1500 Houston St.
Fort Worth 76102

Texas Security Officers Institute
6906 Atwell
Houston 77081

Texas Southmost College
80 Fort Brown
Brownsville 78520

Trinity Valley Community College
500 South Prairieville
Athens 75751

Tyler Junior College
P.O. Box 9020
Tyler 75711

Wayland Baptist University
1900 West Seventh
Plainview 79072

Weatherford College
308 East Park Ave.
Weatherford 76086

UTAH

Bridgerland Applied Technology Center
1301 North, 600 West
Logan 84321

Salt Lake Community College
P.O. Box 30808
Salt Lake City 84130

Southern Utah University
351 West Center
Cedar City 84720

Weber State University
3750 Harrison Blvd.
Ogden 84408

VERMONT

Champlain College
163 South Willard St.
Burlington 05401

VIRGINIA

Central Virginia Community College
3506 Wards Rd.
Lynchburg 24502

Danville Community College
1008 South Main St.
Danville 24541

Germanna Community College
P.O. Box 339
Locust Grove 22508

J Sargeant Reynolds Community College
P.O. Box 85622
Richmond 23285-5622

John Tyler Community College
13101 Jefferson Davis Hwy.
Chester 23831-5399

Mountain Empire Community College
P.O. Drawer 700
Big Stone Gap 24219

New River Community College
P.O. Drawer 1127
Dublin 24084

Northern Virginia Community College
4001 Wakefield Chapel Rd.
Annandale 22003

Paul D Camp Community College
100 North College Dr., P.O. Box 737
Franklin 23851

Southside Virginia Community College
Rte. 1, P.O. Box 60
Alberta 23821

Southwest Virginia Community College
P.O. Box SVCC
Richlands 24641

Thomas Nelson Community College
P.O. Box 9407
Hampton 23670

Tidewater Community College
Rte. 135
Portsmouth 23703

Virginia Highlands Community College
P.O. Box 828
Abingdon 24210

Virginia School of Polygraph
7909 Brookfield Rd.
Norfolk 23518

Virginia Western Community College
3095 Colonial Ave.
Roanoke 24015

Wytheville Community College
1000 East Main St.
Wytheville 24382

WASHINGTON

Bellevue Community College
3000 Landerholm Circle SE
Bellevue 98007-6484

Columbia Basin College
2600 North 20th Ave.
Pasco 99301

Everett Community College
801 Wetmore Ave.
Everett 98201

Green River Community College
12401 Southeast 320th St.
Auburn 98002

Olympic College
1600 Chester Ave.
Bremerton 98310-1699

Shoreline Community College
16101 Greenwood Ave. N
Seattle 98133

Spokane Community College
North 1810 Greene Ave.
Spokane 99207

WEST VIRGINIA

Bluefield State College
219 Rock St.
Bluefield 24701

Fairmont State College
1201 Locust Ave.
Fairmont 26554

Southern West Virginia Community
College
P.O. Box 2900
Logan 25601

West Virginia State College
Rte. 25
Institute 25112

WISCONSIN

Blackhawk Technical College
P.O. Box 5009
Janesville 53547

Chippewa Valley Technical College
620 West Clairemont Ave.
Eau Claire 54701

Fox Valley Technical College
1825 North Bluemound Dr.
Appleton 54913-2277

Gateway Technical College
3520 30th Ave.
Kenosha 53144-1690

Good, Armstrong, and Associates, Ltd.
2142 South 55th St.
Milwaukee 53219

Lakeshore Vocational Training and
Adult Education System District
1290 North Ave.
Cleveland 53015

Mid-State Technical College, Main
Campus
500 32nd St. N
Wisconsin Rapids 54494

Milwaukee Area Technical College
700 West State St.
Milwaukee 53233

Nicolet Vocational Training and Adult
Education System District
P.O. Box 518
Rhinelander 54501

North Central Technical College
1000 Campus Dr.
Wausau 54401-1899

Northeast Wisconsin Technical College
2740 West Mason St., P.O. Box 19042
Green Bay 54307-9042

Waukesha County Technical College
800 Main St.
Pewaukee 53072

Western Wisconsin Technical College
304 North Sixth St., P.O. Box 908
La Crosse 54602-0908

Wisconsin Area Vocational Training
and Adult Education System District
Number Four
3550 Anderson St.
Madison 53704

Wisconsin Area Vocational Training
and Adult Education System,
Moraine Park
235 North National Ave., P.O. Box 1940
Fond Du Lac 54936-1940

WYOMING

Casper College
125 College Dr.
Casper 82601

Sheridan College
P.O. Box 1500
Sheridan 82801

Public Administration Technology

ARIZONA

Phoenix College
1202 West Thomas Rd.
Phoenix 85013

CALIFORNIA

Allan Hancock College
800 South College Dr.
Santa Maria 93454

Antelope Valley College
3041 West Ave. K
Lancaster 93534

Butte College
3536 Butte Campus Dr.
Oroville 95965

Cabrillo College
6500 Soquel Dr.
Aptos 95003

Cerritos College
11110 Alondra Blvd.
Norwalk 90650

Chabot College
25555 Hesperian Blvd.
Hayward 94545

Citrus College
1000 West Foothill Blvd.
Glendora 91741-1899

College of Marin
Kentfield 94904

College of San Mateo
1700 West Hillsdale Blvd.
San Mateo 94402

College of the Sequoias
915 South Mooney Blvd.
Visalia 93277

College of the Canyons
26455 North Rockwell Canyon Rd.
Santa Clarita 91355

College of the Redwoods
7351 Tompkins Hill Rd.
Eureka 95501-9302

College of the Desert
43-500 Monterey St.
Palm Desert 92260

Cosumnes River College
8401 Center Pkwy.
Sacramento 95823-5799

Cuesta College
P.O. Box 8106
San Luis Obispo 93403-8106

Diablo Valley College
321 Golf Club Rd.
Pleasant Hill 94523

El Camino College
16007 Crenshaw Blvd.
Torrance 90506

Fresno City College
1101 East University Ave.
Fresno 93741

Fullerton College
321 East Chapman Ave.
Fullerton 92632-2095

Golden West College
15744 Golden West
Huntington Beach 92647

Grossmont College
8800 Grossmont College Dr.
El Cajon 92020

Hartnell College
156 Homestead Ave.
Salinas 93901

Long Beach City College
4901 East Carson St.
Long Beach 90808

Los Angeles Southwest College
1600 West Imperial Hwy.
Los Angeles 90047

Los Angeles Valley College
5800 Fulton Ave.
Van Nuys 91401

Mendocino College
P.O. Box 3000
Ukiah 95482

Merced College
3600 M St.
Merced 95348-2898

Merritt College
12500 Campus Dr.
Oakland 94619

Modesto Junior College
435 College Ave.
Modesto 95350-9977

Monterey Peninsula College
980 Fremont Blvd.
Monterey 93940-4799

Moorpark College
7075 Campus Rd.
Moorpark 93021

Mount San Jacinto College
1499 North State St.
San Jacinto 92383-2399

Pasadena City College
1570 East Colorado Blvd.
Pasadena 91106

Porterville College
100 East College Ave.
Porterville 93257

Rancho Santiago College
17th at Bristol
Santa Ana 92706

Riverside Community College
4800 Magnolia Ave.
Riverside 92506-1299

San Joaquin Delta College
5151 Pacific Ave.
Stockton 95207

Santa Monica College
1900 Pico Blvd.
Santa Monica 90405-1628

Southwestern College
900 Otay Lakes Rd.
Chula Vista 92010

Ventura College
4667 Telegraph Rd.
Ventura 93003

West Los Angeles College
4800 Freshman Dr.
Culver 90230

West Valley College
14000 Fruitvale Ave.
Saratoga 95070

Yuba College
2088 North Beale Rd.
Marysville 95901

COLORADO

Aims Community College
P.O. Box 69
Greeley 80632

Arapahoe Community College
2500 West College Dr.
Littleton 80160-9002

Colorado Northwestern Community
College
500 Kennedy Dr.
Rangely 81648-3598

Pikes Peak Community College
5675 South Academy Blvd.
Colorado Springs 80906-5498

Pueblo Community College
900 West Orman Ave.
Pueblo 81004

Red Rocks Community College
13300 West Sixth Ave.
Golden 80401

Trinidad State Junior College
600 Prospect St.
Trinidad 81082

CONNECTICUT

Connecticut Institute of Technology
Two Elizabeth St.
West Haven 06516

DELAWARE

Delaware Technical Community
College Stanton-Wilmington
400 Stanton-Christiana Rd.
Newark 19702

FLORIDA

Edison Community College
8099 College Pkwy. SW
Fort Myers 33906-6210

Florida Community College at
Jacksonville
501 West State St.
Jacksonville 32202

Indian River Community College
3209 Virginia Ave.
Fort Pierce 34981

Miami-Dade Community College
300 Northeast Second Ave.
Miami 33132

Pensacola Junior College
1000 College Blvd.
Pensacola 32504

Polk Community College
999 Ave. H NE
Winter Haven 33881

Seminole Community College
100 Weldon Blvd.
Sanford 32773-6199

HAWAII

Honolulu Community College
874 Dillingham Blvd.
Honolulu 96817

Maui Community College
310 Kaahumanu Ave.
Kahului 96732

IDAHO

Idaho State University
741 South Seventh Ave.
Pocatello 83209

ILLINOIS

Lake Land College
5001 Lake Land Blvd.
Mattoon 61938

INDIANA

Indiana University, Purdue University
at Indianapolis
355 North Lansing
Indianapolis 46202

Indiana University, Purdue University
at Fort Wayne
2101 Coliseum Blvd. E
Fort Wayne 46805

IOWA

Iowa Western Community College
2700 College Rd.
P.O. Box 4C
Council Bluffs 51502

KENTUCKY

Kentucky Technical, West Kentucky
State Vocational Technical School
P.O. Box 7408
Paducah 42002-7408

LOUISIANA

Delgado Community College
615 City Park Ave.
New Orleans 70119

T H Harris Technical Institute
337 East South St.
P.O. Box 713
Opelousas 70570

MAINE

University of Maine
Office of Institutional Studies
Orono 04469

MASSACHUSETTS

Hebrew College
43 Hawes St.
Brookline 02146

Lincoln Institute of Land Policy
113 Brattle St.
Cambridge 02138

Massasoit Community College
One Massasoit Blvd.
Brockton 02402

Quinsigamond Community College
670 West Boylston St.
Worcester 01606

Springfield Technical Community
College
Armory Square
Springfield 01105

University of Massachusetts at Lowell
One University Ave.
Lowell 01854

Wentworth Institute of Technology
550 Huntington Ave.
Boston 02115

MICHIGAN

Alpena Community College
666 Johnson St.
Alpena 49707

Ferris State University
901 South State St.
Big Rapids 49307

Grand Rapids Community College
143 Bostwick Ave. NE
Grand Rapids 49505

Henry Ford Community College
5101 Evergreen Rd.
Dearborn 48128

Lansing Community College
419 North Capitol Ave.
Lansing 48901-7210

Michigan Technological University
1400 Townsend Dr.
Houghton 49931-1295

MINNESOTA

Duluth Technical College
2101 Trinity Rd.
Duluth 55811

Saint Paul Technical College
235 Marshall Ave.
Saint Paul 55102

MISSISSIPPI

Northeast Mississippi Community
College
Cunningham Blvd.
Booneville 38829

MISSOURI

Mineral Area College
P.O. Box 1000
Flat River 63601

Park College
87 River Park Dr.
Parkville 64152-3795

MONTANA

College of Great Falls
1301 Twentieth St. S
Great Falls 59405-4996

NEW HAMPSHIRE

New Hampshire Technical Institute
11 Institute Dr.
Concord 03301

University of New Hampshire, Main
Campus
Thompson Hall
Durham 03824

NEW JERSEY

Mercer County Community College
1200 Old Trenton Rd.
Trenton 08690

Middlesex County College
155 Mill Rd.
P.O. Box 3050
Edison 08818-3050

Ocean County College
College Dr.
Toms River 08753

Thomas A Edison State College
101 West State St.
Trenton 08608-1176

NEW MEXICO

Albuquerque Technical-Vocational
Institute
525 Buena Vista SE
Albuquerque 87106

NEW YORK

Broome Community College
P.O. Box 1017
Binghamton 13902

Columbia-Greene Community College
P.O. Box 1000
Hudson 12534

Corning Community College
Spencer Hill
Corning 14830

CUNY Bronx Community College
West 181st St. & University Ave.
Bronx 10453

CUNY College of Staten Island
2800 Victory Blvd.
Staten Island 10314

CUNY Hostos Community College
500 Grand Concourse
Bronx 10451

CUNY New York City Technical College
300 Jay St.
Brooklyn 11201

Erie Community College, City Campus
121 Ellicott St.
Buffalo 14203

Erie Community College, North
Campus
Main St. and Youngs Rd.
Williamsville 14221

Finger Lakes Community College
4355 Lake Shore Dr.
Canandaigua 14424

Fulton-Montgomery Community
College
2805 State Hwy. 67
Johnstown 12095

Genesee Community College
One College Rd.
Batavia 14020

Herkimer County Community College
Reservoir Rd.
Herkimer 13350-1598

Hudson Valley Community College
80 Vandenburgh Ave.
Troy 12180

Jefferson Community College
Outer Coffeen St.
Watertown 13601

Mater Dei College
Riverside Dr.
Ogdensburg 13669

Mohawk Valley Community College
1101 Sherman Dr.
Utica 13501

Monroe Community College
1000 East Henrietta Rd.
Rochester 14623

Nassau Community College
One Education Dr.
Garden City 11530

Niagara County Community College
3111 Saunders Settlement Rd.
Sanborn 14132

North Country Community College
20 Winona Ave.
P.O. Box 89
Saranac Lake 12983

Onondaga Community College
Rte. 173
Syracuse 13215

Paul Smith's College of Arts and Science
New York 12970

Rochester Institute of Technology
One Lamb Memorial Dr.
Rochester 14623-0887

Saint John's University
8000 Utopia Pkwy.
Jamaica 11439

Schenectady County Community
College
Washington Ave.
Schenectady 12305

SUNY College of Technology at
Farmingdale
Melville Rd.
Farmingdale 11735

SUNY College of Technology at Canton
Canton 13617

SUNY Ulster County Community
College
Cottekill Rd.
Stone Ridge 12484

SUNY Westchester Commmunity
College
75 Grasslands Rd.
Valhalla 10595

NORTH CAROLINA

Central Piedmont Community College
P.O. Box 35009
Charlotte 28235

Gaston College
Hwy. 321
Dallas 28034

Guilford Technical Community College
P.O. Box 309
Jamestown 27282

Wake Technical Community College
9101 Fayetteville Rd.
Raleigh 27603-5696

NORTH DAKOTA

North Dakota State College of Science
800 North Sixth St.
Wahpeton 58076

OHIO

Cincinnati Technical College
3520 Central Pkwy.
Cincinnati 45223

Clark State Community College
570 East Leffel Ln.
Springfield 45505

Columbus State Community College
550 East Spring St., P.O. Box 1609
Columbus 43216

Ohio University, Eastern Campus
National Rd. W
Saint Clairsville 43950

Ohio University, Ironton Branch
1804 Liberty Ave.
Ironton 45638

Ohio University, Main Campus
Athens 45701

Sinclair Community College
444 West Third St.
Dayton 45402

Stark Technical College
6200 Frank Ave. NW
Canton 44720

University of Akron, Wayne College
10470 Smucker Rd.
Orrville 44667

University of Akron, Main Campus
302 Buchtel Common
Akron 44325-4702

University of Cincinnati, Main Campus
2624 Clifton Ave.
Cincinnati 45221-0127

University of Toledo
2801 West Bancroft
Toledo 43606

Urbana University
College Way
Urbana 43078

OKLAHOMA

Platt College
4821 South 72nd East Ave.
Tulsa 74145

OREGON

Blue Mountain Community College
P.O. Box 100
Pendleton 97801

Clackamas Community College
19600 Molalla Ave.
Oregon City 97045

Oregon Institute of Technology
3201 Campus Dr.
Klamath Falls 97601-8801

PENNSYLVANIA

Bucks County Community College
Swamp Rd.
Newtown 18940

Harrisburg Area Community College,
Harrisburg Campus
One Hacc Dr.
Harrisburg 17110

Lehigh County Community College
4525 Education Park Dr.
Schnecksville 18078-2598

Pennsylvania College of Technology
One College Ave.
Williamsport 17701

Pennsylvania Institute of Technology
800 Manchester Ave.
Media 19063

Westmoreland County Community
College
Youngwood 15697-1895

RHODE ISLAND

Roger Williams University
One Old Ferry Rd.
Bristol 02809-2923

SOUTH CAROLINA

Florence-Darlington Technical College
P.O. Box 100548
Florence 29501-0548

Horry-Georgetown Technical College
P.O. Box 1966
Conway 29526

Spartanburg Methodist College
1200 Textile Dr.
Spartanburg 29301-0009

Spartanburg Technical College
Hwy. I-85
P.O. Drawer 4386
Spartanburg 29305

Trident Technical College
P.O. Box 118067
Charleston 29423-8067

University of South Carolina at Aiken
171 University Pkwy.
Aiken 29801

University of South Carolina at
Lancaster
P.O. Box 889
Lancaster 29720

TENNESSEE

Pellissippi State Technical Community
College
P.O. Box 22990
Knoxville 37933-0990

TEXAS

San Antonio College
1300 San Pedro Ave.
San Antonio 78284

Tarrant County Junior College District
1500 Houston St.
Fort Worth 76102

Texarkana College
2500 North Robison Rd.
Texarkana 75501

VERMONT

Southern Vermont College
Monument Rd.
Bennington 05201

Vermont Technical College
Randolph Center 05061

VIRGINIA

J Sargeant Reynolds Community College
P.O. Box 85622
Richmond 23285-5622

New River Community College
P.O. Drawer 1127
Dublin 24084

Thomas Nelson Community College
P.O. Box 9407
Hampton 23670

Tidewater Community College
Rte. 135
Portsmouth 23703

WASHINGTON

Bates Technical College
1101 South Yakima Ave.
Tacoma 98405

Centralia College
600 West Locust St.
Centralia 98531

Spokane Community College
North 1810 Greene Ave.
Spokane 99207

Spokane Falls Community College
West 3410 Fort George Wright Dr.
Spokane 99204

Walla Walla Community College
500 Tausick Way
Walla Walla 99362

Yakima Valley Community College
P.O. Box 1647
Yakima 98907

WEST VIRGINIA

Bluefield State College
219 Rock St.
Bluefield 24701

WISCONSIN

Mid-State Technical College, Main
Campus
500 32nd St. N
Wisconsin Rapids 54494

Northeast Wisconsin Technical College
2740 West Mason St., P.O. Box 19042
Green Bay 54307-9042

Wisconsin Area Vocational Training
and Adult Education System District
Number Four
3550 Anderson St.
Madison 53704

Wisconsin Area Vocational Training
and Adult Education System,
Moraine Park
235 North National Ave., P.O. Box 1940
Fond Du Lac 54936-1940

WYOMING

Laramie County Community College
1400 East College Dr.
Cheyenne 82007

Public Service Technology

ALABAMA

Samford University
800 Lakeshore Dr.
Birmingham 35229

CALIFORNIA

Phillips Junior College
8520 Balboa Blvd.
Northridge 91325

COLORADO

Parks Junior College
9065 Grant St.
Denver 80229

CONNECTICUT

Manchester Community College
60 Bidwell St., P.O. Box 1045
Manchester 06040-1046

FLORIDA

Daytona Beach Community College
1200 Volusia Ave.
Daytona Beach 32114

Valencia Community College
P.O. Box 3028
Orlando 32802

HAWAII

Denver Business College, Honolulu
1916 Young St.
Honolulu 96826

INDIANA

Indiana University, Purdue University
at Indianapolis
355 North Lansing
Indianapolis 46202

IOWA

Des Moines Community College
2006 Ankeny Blvd.
Ankeny 50021

Iowa Valley Community College
P.O. Box 536
Marshalltown 50158

Kirkwood Community College
P.O. Box 2068
Cedar Rapids 52406

MAINE

University of Maine
Office of Institutional Studies
Orono 04469

MASSACHUSETTS

Berkshire Community College
1350 West St.
Pittsfield 01201-5786

Holyoke Community College
303 Homestead Ave.
Holyoke 01040

Lincoln Institute of Land Policy
113 Brattle St.
Cambridge 02138

Quinsigamond Community College
670 West Boylston St.
Worcester 01606

MICHIGAN

Delta College
University Center 48710

MINNESOTA

Minneapolis Community College
1501 Hennepin Ave.
Minneapolis 55403

North Hennepin Community College
7411 85th Ave. N
Brooklyn Park 55445

NEW MEXICO

University of New Mexico, Gallup Branch
200 College Rd.
Gallup 87301

NEW YORK

Cazenovia College
Cazenovia 13035

Corning Community College
Spencer Hill
Corning 14830

Fulton-Montgomery Community
College
2805 State Hwy. 67
Johnstown 12095

Genesee Community College
One College Rd.
Batavia 14020

Herkimer County Community College
Reservoir Rd.
Herkimer 13350-1598

Hilbert College
5200 South Park Ave.
Hamburg 14075-1597

Hudson Valley Community College
80 Vandenburgh Ave.
Troy 12180

Jamestown Community College
525 Falconer St.
Jamestown 14701

Jefferson Community College
Outer Coffeen St.
Watertown 13601

Mater Dei College
Riverside Dr.
Ogdensburg 13669

Medaille College
18 Agassiz Circle
Buffalo 14214

Mohawk Valley Community College
1101 Sherman Dr.
Utica 13501

Monroe Community College
1000 East Henrietta Rd.
Rochester 14623

Niagara County Community College
3111 Saunders Settlement Rd.
Sanborn 14132

Onondaga Community College
Rte. 173
Syracuse 13215

Rochester Institute of Technology
One Lamb Memorial Dr.
Rochester 14623-0887

Schenectady County Community
College
Washington Ave.
Schenectady 12305

Suffolk County Community College,
Ammerman Campus
533 College Rd.
Selden 11784

SUNY College of Technology at Alfred
Alfred 14802

SUNY Empire State College
Two Union Ave.
Saratoga Springs 12866

SUNY Ulster County Community
College
Cottekill Rd.
Stone Ridge 12484

SUNY Westchester Commmunity
College
75 Grasslands Rd.
Valhalla 10595

Tompkins-Cortland Community
College
170 North St.
Dryden 13053

Touro College
27-33 West 23rd St.
New York 10010

OHIO

Vocational Guidance Services
2239 East 55th St.
Cleveland 44103

OKLAHOMA

Kiamichi AVTS SD #7, Hugo Campus
107 South 15th, P.O. Box 699
Hugo 74743

Metro Tech Vocational Technical Center
1900 Springlake Dr.
Oklahoma City 73111

PENNSYLVANIA

Community College of Philadelphia
1700 Spring Garden St.
Philadelphia 19130

Sawyer School
717 Liberty Ave.
Pittsburgh 15222

TENNESSEE

Morristown State Area Vocational-
Technical School
821 West Louise Ave.
Morristown 37813

Shelby State Community College
P.O. Box 40568
Memphis 38174-0568

TEXAS

Avalon Vocational Technical Institute
1407 Texas St.
Fort Worth 76102

Houston Community College System
22 Waugh Dr., P.O. Box 7849
Houston 77270-7849

WISCONSIN

Milwaukee Area Technical College
700 West State St.
Milwaukee 53233

Religious Occupations

CALIFORNIA

Booker T Crenshaw Christian College &
School Ministry, Inc.
3134 Franklin Ave.
San Diego 92113

Golden Gate Baptist Seminary
Strawberry Point
Mill Valley 94941

International School of Theology
24600 Arrowhead Springs Rd.
San Bernardino 92414

Pacific Coast Baptist Bible College
1100 South Valley Center
San Dimas 91773

San Jose Christian College
790 South 12th St., P.O. Box 1090
San Jose 95108

The Master's College
21726 Placerita Cyn Rd.
Santa Clarita 91322-0878

The Salvation Army School for Officers'
Training
30840 Hawthorne Blvd.
Rancho Palos Ve 90274

Trinity Life Bible College
5225 Hillsdale at Madison
Sacramento 95842

COLORADO

Nazarene Bible College
1111 Chapman Dr., P.O. Box 15749
Colorado Springs 80935

FLORIDA

Florida Baptist Theological College
5400 College Dr.
Graceville 32440

Florida Bible College
1701 Poinciana Blvd.
Kissimmee 34758

Florida Christian College, Inc.
1011 Bill Beck Blvd.
Kissimmee 34744

Gospel Crusade Institute of Ministry
1200 Glory Way Blvd., Rte. 2
P.O. Box 279
Bradenton 34202

United Bible College & Seminary
P.O. Box 585284
Orlando 32858

Zoe College, Inc.
9570 One Regency Square Blvd.
Jacksonville 32225

GEORGIA

Beulah Heights Bible College
892-906 Berne St. SE
Atlanta 30316

IDAHO

Boise Bible College
8695 Marigold St.
Boise 83714

Northwest Nazarene College
623 Holly
Nampa 83686-5897

ILLINOIS

Lincoln Christian College and
Seminary
100 Campus View Dr.
Lincoln 62656-2111

Moody Bible Institute
820 North Lasalle Blvd.
Chicago 60610

INDIANA

Indiana Wesleyan University
4201 South Washington St.
Marion 46953

IOWA

Emmaus Bible College
2570 Asbury Rd.
Dubuque 52001

KANSAS

Hesston College
P.O. Box 3000
Hesston 67062

Manhattan Christian College
1415 Anderson Ave.
Manhattan 66502

KENTUCKY

Clear Creek Baptist Bible College
300 Clear Creek Rd.
Pineville 40977

Kentucky Mountain Bible College
P.O. Box 10
Vancleve 41385

Southern Baptist Theological Seminary
2825 Lexington Rd.
Louisville 40280

LOUISIANA

New Orleans Baptist Theological
Seminary
3939 Gentilly Blvd.
New Orleans 70126

World Evangelism Bible College and
Seminary
P.O. Box 38000
Baton Rouge 70806

MARYLAND

Ner Israel Rabbinical College
Mount Wilson Ln.
Baltimore 21208

Washington Bible College
6511 Princess Garden Pkwy.
Lanham 20706

MASSACHUSETTS

Baptist Bible College East
950 Metropolitan Ave.
Hyde Park 02136

Gordon-Conwell Theological Seminary
130 Essex St.
South Hamilton 01982

MICHIGAN

Reformed Bible College
3333 East Beltline NE
Grand Rapids 49505

Sacred Heart Major Seminary
2701 Chicago Blvd.
Detroit 48206

MINNESOTA

Association Free Lutheran Bible School
3110 East Medicine Lake Blvd.
Plymouth 55441-3099

North Central Bible College
910 Elliot Ave.
Minneapolis 55404

Oak Hills Bible College
1600 Oak Hills Rd. SW
Bemidji 56601

MISSISSIPPI

Southeastern Baptist College
4229 Hwy. 15 N
Laurel 39440

MISSOURI

Baptist Bible College
628 East Kearney
Springfield 65803

Berean College
1445 Boonville Ave.
Springfield 65802

Central Bible College
3000 North Grant
Springfield 65803

Midwestern Baptist Theological
Seminary
5001 North Oak St. Trafficway
Kansas City 64118

Ozark Christian College
1111 North Main St.
Joplin 64801

NEBRASKA

Grace College of the Bible
Ninth and Williams
Omaha 68108

Platte Valley Bible College
305 East 16th St., P.O. Box 1227
Scottsbluff 69361

NEW JERSEY

College of Saint Elizabeth
Two Convent Rd.
Morristown 07960-6989

NEW MEXICO

Nazarene Indian Bible College
2315 Markham Rd. SW, P.O. Box 12295
Albuquerque 87195

NEW YORK

Elim Bible Institute
7245 College St.
Lima 14485

Practical Bible Training School
400 Riverside Dr., P.O. Box 601
Bible School Park 13737-0601

Word of Life Bible Institute
Rte. 9
Pottersville 12860

NORTH CAROLINA

East Coast Bible College
6900 Wilkinson Blvd.
Charlotte 28214

Roanoke Bible College
714 First St.
Elizabeth City 27909-3926

Southeastern Baptist Theological
Seminary
P.O. Box 1889
Wake Forest 27588-1889

OHIO

Cincinnati Bible College & Seminary
2700 Glenway Ave.
Cincinnati 45204-3200

Circleville Bible College
1476 Lancaster Pike
Circleville 43113

OKLAHOMA

Hillsdale Free Will Baptist College
P.O. Box 7208
Moore 73153

Oklahoma Baptist University
500 West University
Shawnee 74801

Southwestern College of Christian
Ministries
P.O. Box 340
Bethany 73008

OREGON

Eugene Bible College
2155 Bailey Hill Rd.
Eugene 97405

Multnomah School of Bible
8435 Northeast Glisan St.
Portland 97220

Portland Bible College
9201 Northeast Fremont
Portland 97220

Western Baptist College
5000 Deer Park Dr. SE
Salem 97301

PENNSYLVANIA

Baptist Bible College and Seminary
538 Venard Rd.
Clarks Summit 18411

Lancaster Bible College
901 Eden Rd.
Lancaster 17601

Saint Charles Borromeo Seminary
1000 East Wynnewood Rd.
Overbrook 19096

Valley Forge Christian College
Charlestown Rd.
Phoenixville 19460

RHODE ISLAND

Zion Bible Institute
27 Middle Hwy.
Barrington 02806

SOUTH CAROLINA

Bob Jones University
Greenville 29614

Columbia Bible College and Seminary
7435 Monticello Rd.
P.O. Box 3122
Columbia 29230

TENNESSEE

Emmanuel Bible College
610 Boscobel St.
Nashville 37206

Memphis School of Preaching
4400 Knight Arnold Rd.
Memphis 38118

Mid America Baptist Seminary
1255 Poplar Ave.
Memphis 38104

Tennessee Temple University
1815 Union Ave.
Chattanooga 37404

United Theological Seminary, Scarritt-
Bennett Center
19th Ave. S
Nashville 37203

TEXAS

International Christian Institute &
Graduate School
P.O. Box 720405
Houston 71727

Texas Bible College
816 Evergreen
Houston 77023

VIRGINIA

Eastern Mennonite College and
Seminary
1200 Park Rd.
Harrisonburg 22801-2462

The Catholic Home Study Institute
Nine Loudoun St. SE
Leesburg 22075-3012

WASHINGTON

Lutheran Bible Institute of Seattle
4221 228th SE
Issaquah 98027

Puget Sound Christian College
410 Fourth Ave. N
Edmonds 98020-3171

WEST VIRGINIA

Appalachian Bible College
P.O. Box ABC
Bradley 25818

Social Work and Recreation Technology

ALABAMA

Community College of the Air Force
Maxwell Air Force Base
Montgomery 36112

Lawson State Community College
3060 Wilson Rd. SW
Birmingham 35221

ARIZONA

Pima Community College
2202 West Anklam Rd.
Tucson 85709-0001

CALIFORNIA

Alexander Training Institute of San
Francisco
30 Grant Ave.
San Francisco 94108

Allan Hancock College
800 South College Dr.
Santa Maria 93454

Diablo Valley College
321 Golf Club Rd.
Pleasant Hill 94523

Fresno City College
1101 East University Ave.
Fresno 93741

Imperial Valley College
P.O. Box 158
Imperial 92251-0158

COLORADO

Aims Community College
P.O. Box 69
Greeley 80632

FLORIDA

Charlotte Vocational-Technical Center
18300 Toledo Blade Blvd.
Port Charlotte 33948-3399

IDAHO

Ricks College
Rexburg 83460-4107

ILLINOIS

City College of Chicago, Kennedy-King
6800 South Wentworth Ave.
Chicago 60621

College of Du Page
Lambert Rd. and 22nd St.
Glen Ellyn 60137

Elgin Community College
1700 Spartan Dr.
Elgin 60123

Rock Valley College
3301 North Mulford Rd.
Rockford 61114

South Suburban College
15800 South State St.
South Holland 60473

INDIANA

Indiana University East
2325 Chester Blvd.
Richmond 47374

KANSAS

Allen County Community College
1801 North Cottonwood
Iola 66749

Cloud County Community College
2221 Campus Dr., P.O. Box 1002
Concordia 66901-1002

Colby Community College
1255 South Range
Colby 67701

Kansas City Area Vocational Technical
School
2220 North 59th St.
Kansas City 66104

Kaw Area Vocational-Technical School
5724 Huntoon
Topeka 66604

Neosho County Community College
1000 South Allen
Chanute 66720

North Central Kansas Area Vocational
Technical School
Hwy. 24, P.O. Box 507
Beloit 67420

Salina Area Vocational Technical School
2562 Scanlan Ave.
Salina 67401

Wichita Area Vocational Technical School
428 South Broadway
Wichita 67202-3910

KENTUCKY

Hopkinsville Community College
North Dr.
Hopkinsville 42240

Jefferson Community College
109 East Broadway
Louisville 40202

Owensboro Community College
4800 New Hartford Rd.
Owensboro 42303

MASSACHUSETTS

Dean Junior College
99 Main St.
Franklin 02038

Massasoit Community College
One Massasoit Blvd.
Brockton 02402

Mount Ida College
777 Dedham St.
Newton Centre 02159

MICHIGAN

Delta College
University Center 48710

Grand Rapids Community College
143 Bostwick Ave. NE
Grand Rapids 49505

Macomb Community College
14500 Twelve Mile Rd.
Warren 48093-3896

Mott Community College
1401 East Court St.
Flint 48503

MINNESOTA

Inver Hills Community College
5445 College Trail
Inver Grove Heights 55076

Lakewood Community College
3401 Century Ave. N
White Bear Lake 55110

Willmar Community College
P.O. Box 797
Willmar 56201-0797

MISSISSIPPI

Mississippi Gulf Coast Community
College
Central Office
P.O. Box 67
Perkinston 39573

MISSOURI

Jefferson College
1000 Viking Dr.
Hillsboro 63050

Saint Louis Community College, Forest
Park
5600 Oakland Ave.
Saint Louis 63110

MONTANA

Blackfeet Community College
P.O. Box 819
Browning 59417

NEBRASKA

Metropolitan Community College Area
P.O. Box 3777
Omaha 68103

NEW JERSEY

Brookdale Community College
Newman Springs Rd.
Lincroft 07738-1599

Camden County College
P.O. Box 200
Blackwood 08012

Essex County College
303 University Ave.
Newark 07102

Hudson County Community College
901 Bergen Ave.
Jersey City 07306

Ocean County College
College Dr.
Toms River 08753

NEW MEXICO

Northern New Mexico Community
College
1002 North Onate St.
Espanola 87532

NORTH CAROLINA

Central Piedmont Community College
P.O. Box 35009
Charlotte 28235

Halifax Community College
P.O. Drawer 809
Weldon 27890

Wayne Community College
P.O. Box 8002
Goldsboro 27533-8002

OHIO

Clark State Community College
570 East Leffel Ln.
Springfield 45505

Columbus State Community College
550 East Spring St.
P.O. Box 1609
Columbus 43216

Edison State Community College
1973 Edison Dr.
Piqua 45356

Washington State Community College
710 Colegate Dr.
Marietta 45750

OKLAHOMA

Caddo-Kiowa Area Vocational Technical
School
P.O. Box 190
Fort Cobb 73038

Connors State College
Rte. 1, P.O. Box 1000
Warner 74469

Francis Tuttle Area Vocational-
Technical Center
12777 North Rockwell Ave.
Oklahoma City 73142-2789

Metro Tech Vocational Technical Center
1900 Springlake Dr.
Oklahoma City 73111

OREGON

Chemeketa Community College
P.O. Box 14007
Salem 97309-7070

Lane Community College
4000 East 30th Ave.
Eugene 97405

Portland Community College
P.O. Box 19000
Portland 97280-0990

Rogue Community College
3345 Redwood Hwy.
Grants Pass 97527

PENNSYLVANIA

Community College of Allegheny
County
800 Allegheny Ave.
Pittsburgh 15233-1895

Harrisburg Area Community College,
Harrisburg Campus
One Hacc Dr.
Harrisburg 17110

Keystone Junior College
P.O. Box 50
La Plume 18440-0200

Pennsylvania State University, Main
Campus
201 Old Main
University Park 16802

RHODE ISLAND

Community College of Rhode Island
400 East Ave.
Warwick 02886-1805

SOUTH CAROLINA

Denmark Technical College
P.O. Box 327
Denmark 29042

Florence-Darlington Technical College
P.O. Box 100548
Florence 29501-0548

Midlands Technical College
P.O. Box 2408
Columbia 29202

Piedmont Technical College
P.O. Drawer 1467
Greenwood 29648

Trident Technical College
P.O. Box 118067
Charleston 29423-8067

TEXAS

Austin Community College
5930 Middle Fiskville Rd.
Austin 78752

VERMONT

Champlain College
163 South Willard St.
Burlington 05401

WASHINGTON

Spokane Falls Community College
West 3410 Fort George Wright Dr.
Spokane 99204

WEST VIRGINIA

The College of West Virginia
609 South Kanawha
Beckley 25802

Teacher and Teacher's Aide Training

ALABAMA

Bishop State Community College
351 North Broad St.
Mobile 36690

Community College of the Air Force
Maxwell Air Force Base
Montgomery 36112

Gadsden State Community College
P.O. Box 227
Gadsden 35902-0227

John C Calhoun State Community
College
P.O. Box 2216
Decatur 35609-2216

Shoals Community College
P.O. Box 2545
Muscle Shoals 35662

ARIZONA

Berlitz Language Centers
3333 East Camelback Rd.
Phoenix 85018

Eastern Arizona College
Church St.
Thatcher 85552-0769

Mesa Community College
1833 West Southern Ave.
Mesa 85202

Navajo Community College
Tsaile 86556

Opportunities Industrialization Center,
Phoenix
39 East Jackson St.
Phoenix 85004

Pima Community College
2202 West Anklam Rd.
Tucson 85709-0001

ARKANSAS

Black River Technical College
Hwy. 304, P.O. Box 468
Pocahontas 72455

Quapaw Technical Institute
201 Vo-Tech Dr.
Hot Springs 71913

Red River Technical College
P.O. Box 140
Hope 71801

CALIFORNIA

Allan Hancock College
800 South College Dr.
Santa Maria 93454

Antelope Valley College
3041 West Ave. K
Lancaster 93534

Berlitz Language Centers
323 North Beverly Dr.
Beverly Hills 90210

Berlitz Language Centers
1475 South Bascom Ave.
Campbell 95008

Berlitz Language Centers
2061 Business Center Dr.
Irvine 92715

Berlitz Language Centers
3345 Wilshire Blvd.
Los Angeles 90010

Berlitz Language Centers
430 Cambridge Ave.
Palo Alto 94306

Berlitz Language Centers
600 South Lake Ave.
Pasadena 91106

Berlitz Language Centers
7801 Mission Center Ct.
San Diego 92108

Berlitz Language Centers
660 Market St.
San Francisco 94104

Berlitz Language Centers
501 Santa Monica Blvd.
Santa Monica 90401

Berlitz Language Centers
2355 Crenshaw Blvd., Park Del Amo
Torrance 90501

Berlitz Language Centers
1646 North California Blvd.
Walnut Creek 94596

Berlitz Language Centers
6415 Independence Ave.
Woodland Hills 91367

Bethesda Christian University
14300 Leffingwell Rd.
Whittier 90604

Cerritos College
11110 Alondra Blvd.
Norwalk 90650

Chaffey Community College
5885 Haven Ave.
Rancho Cucamonga 91737-3002

City College of San Francisco
50 Phelan Ave.
San Francisco 94112

College of Alameda
555 Atlantic Ave.
Alameda 94501

College of the Canyons
26455 North Rockwell Canyon Rd.
Santa Clarita 91355

Columbia College, Columbia
P.O. Box 1849
Columbia 95310

Compton Community College
1111 East Artesia Blvd.
Compton 90221

D-Q University
Rd. 31
P.O. Box 409
Davis 95617-0409

El Camino College
16007 Crenshaw Blvd.
Torrance 90506

Golden West College
15744 Golden West
Huntington Beach 92647

Hartnell College
156 Homestead Ave.
Salinas 93901

Imperial Valley College
P.O. Box 158
Imperial 92251-0158

Long Beach City College
4901 East Carson St.
Long Beach 90808

Mira Costa College
One Barnard Dr.
Oceanside 92056-3899

Modesto Junior College
435 College Ave.
Modesto 95350-9977

Monterey Institute of International
Studies
425 Van Buren
Monterey 93940

Montessori Training Center of San
Diego
4544 Pocahontas Ave.
San Diego 92117

Montessori Western Teacher Training
Program
5856 Belgrove
Garden Grove 92645

Mount Saint Mary's College
12001 Chalon Rd.
Los Angeles 90049

Napa Valley College
2277 Napa Vallejo Hwy.
Napa 94558

Pasadena City College
1570 East Colorado Blvd.
Pasadena 91106

Phillips Junior College, Condie Campus
One West Campbell Ave.
Campbell 95008

Rowland Heights Montessori Institute
18760 East Colima Rd.
Rowland Heights 91748

Rudolf Steiner College
9200 Fair Oaks Blvd.
Fair Oaks 95628

San Diego City College
1313 12th Ave.
San Diego 92101

Santa Monica College
1900 Pico Blvd.
Santa Monica 90405-1628

Santa Monica Montessori Institute
1909 Colorado Ave.
Santa Monica 90404

Santa Rosa Junior College
1501 Mendocino Ave.
Santa Rosa 95401-4395

Shasta College
P.O. Box 496006
Redding 96049

Sierra College
5000 Rocklin Rd.
Rocklin 95677

Southwestern College
900 Otay Lakes Rd.
Chula Vista 92010

Saint Giles Language Teaching Center
One Hallidie Plaza
San Francisco 94102

Ventura College
4667 Telegraph Rd.
Ventura 93003

Vista College
2020 Milvia St.
Berkeley 94704-1183

Yuba College
2088 North Beale Rd.
Marysville 95901

COLORADO

Berlitz Language Centers
55 Madison St.
Denver 80206

College of the Canons
Forge Rd. Industrial Park, P.O. Box 1180
Canon City 81212

CONNECTICUT

Berlitz Language Centers
3001 Summer St.
Stamford 06905

Berlitz Language Centers
125 Main St.
Westport 06880

Berlitz Language Centers
61 South Main St.
West Hartford 06107

Manchester Community College
60 Bidwell St.
P.O. Box 1045
Manchester 06040-1046

DELAWARE

Berlitz Language Centers
One Rodney Square
Wilmington 19801

DISTRICT OF COLUMBIA

Berlitz Language Centers
1050 Connecticut Ave. NW
Washington 20036

The Washington Montessori Institute
2119 South St. NW
Washington 20008

FLORIDA

Berlitz Language Centers
396 Alhambra Circle
Coral Gables 33134

Berlitz Language Centers
2455 East Sunrise Blvd.
Fort Lauderdale 33304

Berlitz Language Centers
100 North Biscayne Blvd.
Miami 33132

Berlitz Language Centers
100 West Kennedy Blvd.
Tampa 33602

GEORGIA

Andrew College
College St.
Cuthbert 31740-1395

Berlitz Language Centers
3400 Peachtree Rd. NE
Atlanta 30326

Covered Bridge Montessori School
NCME, Atlanta
2175 Norcross Tucker Rd.
Norcross 30071

Dekalb Technical Institute
495 North Indian Creek Dr.
Clarkston 30021

Reinhardt College
P.O. Box 128
Waleska 30183

South College
709 Mall Blvd.
Savannah 31406

HAWAII

Brigham Young University, Hawaii
Campus
55-220 Kulanui St.
Laie 96762

Hawaii Community College
200 West Kawili St.
Hilo 96720-4091

IDAHO

College of Southern Idaho
P.O. Box 1238
Twin Falls 83301

North Idaho College
1000 West Garden Ave.
Coeur D'Alene 83814

Ricks College
Rexburg 83460-4107

ILLINOIS

Berlitz Language Centers
Two North Lasalle
Chicago 60602

Berlitz Language Centers, Water Tower
Place
845 North Michigan
Chicago 60611

Berlitz Language Centers
201 East Ogden Ave.
Hinsdale 60521

Berlitz Language Centers
1821 Walden Office Square
Schaumburg 60173

Berlitz Language Centers
950 Green Bay Rd.
Winnetka 60093

Montessori Education Center Associated
302 South Grant
Hinsdale 60521

Spanish Coalition for Jobs, Inc.
2011 West Pershing Rd.
Chicago 60609

INDIANA

Ancilla Domini College
P.O. Box 1
Donaldson 46513

Anderson University
1100 East Fifth St.
Anderson 46012-3462

Berlitz Language Centers
8888 Keystone Crossing
Indianapolis 46240

Indiana University, Purdue University
at Fort Wayne
2101 Coliseum Blvd. E
Fort Wayne 46805

Vincennes University
1002 North First St.
Vincennes 47591

IOWA

Kirkwood Community College
P.O. Box 2068
Cedar Rapids 52406

KANSAS

Allen County Community College
1801 North Cottonwood
Iola 66749

Barton County Community College
Rte. 3, P.O. Box 136Z
Great Bend 67530

Butler County Community College
901 South Haverhill Rd.
El Dorado 67042

Cloud County Community College
2221 Campus Dr., P.O. Box 1002
Concordia 66901-1002

Coffeyville Community College
400 West 11th St.
Coffeyville 67337

Colby Community College
1255 South Range
Colby 67701

Cowley County Community College
125 South Second St.
Arkansas City 67005

Dodge City Community College
2501 North 14th Ave.
Dodge City 67801

Fort Scott Community College
2108 South Horton
Fort Scott 66701

Garden City Community College
801 Campus Dr.
Garden City 67846

Highland Community College
P.O. Box 68
Highland 66035-0068

Hutchinson Community College
1300 North Plum St.
Hutchinson 67501

Independence Community College
Brookside Dr. and College Ave.
Independence 67301

Kansas City Kansas Community College
7250 State Ave.
Kansas City 66112

Pratt Community College
Hwy. 61
Pratt 67124

Seward County Community College
P.O. Box 1137
Liberal 67905-1137

KENTUCKY

Midway College
512 Stephens St.
Midway 40347-1120

LOUISIANA

Delgado Community College
615 City Park Ave.
New Orleans 70119

Southern University Shreveport, Bossier
City Campus
3050 Martin L King Dr.
Shreveport 71107

MAINE

University of Maine at Farmington
86 Main St.
Farmington 04938

MARYLAND

Allegany Community College
Willowbrook Rd.
Cumberland 21502

Anne Arundel Community College
101 College Pkwy.
Arnold 21012

Berlitz Language Centers
Two North Charles St.
Baltimore 21201

Berlitz Language Centers
11300 Rockville Pike
Rockville 20852

Catonsville Community College
800 South Rolling Rd.
Catonsville 21228

Chesapeake College
P.O. Box 8
Wye Mills 21679-0008

Dundalk Community College
7200 Sollers Point Rd.
Dundalk 21222

Essex Community College
7201 Rossville Blvd.
Baltimore 21237

Frederick Community College
7932 Opossumtown Pike
Frederick 21702

Hagerstown Junior College
11400 Robinwood Dr.
Hagerstown 21742-6590

Harford Community College
401 Thomas Run Rd.
Bel Air 21015

Howard Community College
Little Patuxent Pkwy.
Columbia 21044

Montgomery College of Rockville
51 Mannakee St.
Rockville 20850

Prince Georges Community College
301 Largo Rd.
Largo 23701-1243

MASSACHUSETTS

Aquinas College at Newton
15 Walnut Park
Newton 02158

Bay Path College
588 Longmeadow St.
Longmeadow 01106

Becker College, Worcester
61 Sever St.
Worcester 01615-0071

Berlitz Language Centers
437 Boylston St.
Boston 02116

Berlitz Language Centers
40 Washington St.
Wellesley Hills 02181

Bristol Community College
777 Elsbree St.
Fall River 02720

Cape Cod Community College
Rte. 132
West Barnstable 02668

Dean Junior College
99 Main St.
Franklin 02038

Endicott College
376 Hale St.
Beverly 01915

Fisher College
118 Beacon St.
Boston 02116

Greenfield Community College
One College Dr.
Greenfield 01301-9739

Hebrew College
43 Hawes St.
Brookline 02146

Lasell College
1844 Commonwealth Ave.
Newton 02166

Middlesex Community College
Springs Rd.
Bedford 01730

Mount Wachusett Community College
444 Green St.
Gardner 01440

North Shore Community College
One Ferncroft Rd.
Danvers 01923

Quinsigamond Community College
670 West Boylston St.
Worcester 01606

Springfield Technical Community
College
Armory Square
Springfield 01105

Wheelock College
200 the Riverway
Boston 02215

MICHIGAN

Alpena Community College
666 Johnson St.
Alpena 49707

Berlitz Language Centers
30700 Telegraph Rd.
Bingham Farms 48025

Delta College
University Center 48710

Ferris State University
901 South State St.
Big Rapids 49307

Gogebic Community College
East 4946 Jackson Rd.
Ironwood 49938

Grand Rapids Community College
143 Bostwick Ave. NE
Grand Rapids 49505

Kalamazoo Valley Community
College
6767 West O Ave.
Kalamazoo 49009

Monroe County Community College
1555 South Raisinville Rd.
Monroe 48161

Muskegon Community College
221 South Quarterline Rd.
Muskegon 49442

Schoolcraft College
18600 Haggerty Rd.
Livonia 48152

Southwestern Michigan College
58900 Cherry Grove Rd.
Dowagiac 49047-9793

MINNESOTA

Berlitz Language Centers
6600 France Ave. S
Minneapolis 55435

College of Saint Catherine, Saint Mary's
Campus
2500 South Sixth St.
Minneapolis 55454

Rochester Community College
851 30th Ave. SE
Rochester 55904-4999

MISSISSIPPI

Coahoma Community College
3240 Friars Point Rd.
Clarksdale 38614

Mary Holmes College
Hwy. 50 W
West Point 39773

Mississippi Gulf Coast Community
College
Central Office, P.O. Box 67
Perkinston 39573

Northeast Mississippi Community
College
Cunningham Blvd.
Booneville 38829

Northwest Mississippi Community
College
Hwy. 51 N
Senatobia 38668

MISSOURI

Berlitz Language Centers
200 South Hanley Rd.
Saint Louis 63105

Crowder College
601 Laclede
Neosho 64850

Saint Charles County Community
College
4601 Mid Rivers Mall Dr.
Saint Peter's 63376

NEBRASKA

Central Community College, Grand
Island
P.O. Box 4903
Grand Island 68802

Northeast Community College
801 East Benjamin, P.O. Box 469
Norfolk 68702-0469

NEW HAMPSHIRE

Hesser College
Three Sundial Ave.
Manchester 03103

NEW JERSEY

Bergen Community College
400 Paramus Rd.
Paramus 07652

Berlitz Language Centers
One Palmer Square
Princeton 08540

Berlitz Language Centers
40 West Ridgewood Ave.
Ridgewood 07450

Berlitz Language Centers
47 Maple St.
Summit 07901

Brookdale Community College
Newman Springs Rd.
Lincroft 07738-1599

Cumberland County College
College Dr., P.O. Box 517
Vineland 08360

Essex County College
303 University Ave.
Newark 07102

Gloucester County College
Tanyard Rd. & RR 4, P.O. Box 203
Sewell 08080

NEW MEXICO

New Mexico Junior College
5317 Lovington Hwy.
Hobbs 88240

University of New Mexico, Gallup
Branch
200 College Rd.
Gallup 87301

NEW YORK

Berlitz Language Centers
41 Mineola Blvd.
Mineola 11501

Berlitz Language Centers
61 Broadway
New York 10006

Berlitz Language Centers
40 West 51st St.
New York 10020

Berlitz Language Centers
36 Main St. W
Rochester 14614

Berlitz Language Centers
One North Broadway
White Plains 10601

Cazenovia College
Cazenovia 13035

CUNY Borough of Manhattan
Community College
199 Chambers St.
New York 10007

CUNY Bronx Community College
West 181st St. & University Ave.
Bronx 10453

CUNY Hostos Community College
500 Grand Concourse
Bronx 10451

CUNY Kingsborough Community
College
2001 Oriental Blvd.
Brooklyn 11235

Iona College
715 North Ave.
New Rochelle 10801

Maria College of Albany
700 New Scotland Ave.
Albany 12208

Mater Dei College
Riverside Dr.
Ogdensburg 13669

Siena College
Rte. 9
Loudonville 12211

Trocaire College
110 Red Jacket Pkwy.
Buffalo 14220

Villa Maria College, Buffalo
240 Pine Ridge Rd.
Buffalo 14225-3999

NORTH CAROLINA

Berlitz Language Centers
5821 Fairview Rd.
Charlotte 28209

Berlitz Language Centers
5974A Six Forks Rd.
Raleigh 27609

Campbell University, Inc.
P.O. Box 97
Buies Creek 27506

Chowan College
Murfreesboro 27855

Isothermal Community College
P.O. Box 804
Spindale 28160

Vance-Granville Community College
State Rd. 1126
P.O. Box 917
Henderson 27536

OHIO

Berlitz Language Centers
156 South Main St.
Akron 44308

Berlitz Languages Centers
503 Race St.
Cincinnati 45202

Berlitz Language Centers
815 Superior
Cleveland 44115

Bowling Green State University,
Firelands
901 Rye Beach Rd.
Huron 44839

Cuyahoga Community College District
700 Carnegie Ave.
Cleveland 44115-2878

Lorain County Community College
1005 North Abbe Rd.
Elyria 44035

Montessori Teacher Education
Collaborative
11424 Bellflower Rd. NE
Cleveland 44106

Sinclair Community College
444 West Third St.
Dayton 45402

University of Akron, Main Campus
302 Buchtel Common
Akron 44325-4702

University of Rio Grande
North College St.
Rio Grande 45674

OKLAHOMA

Bacone College
2299 Old Bacome Rd.
Muskogee 74403-1597

Carl Albert State College
1507 South McKenna
Poteau 74953-5208

Connors State College
Rte. 1, P.O. Box 1000
Warner 74469

Eastern Oklahoma State College
1301 West Main St.
Wilburton 74578

Northeastern Oklahoma Agricultural
and Mechanical College
200 Eye St. NE
Miami 74354

Northern Oklahoma College
P.O. Box 310
Tonkawa 74653

Pontotoc Skill Development Center
601 West 33rd
Ada 74820

Redland Community College
1300 South Country Club Rd.
P.O. Box 370
El Reno 73036

Rogers State College
Will Rogers and College Hill
Claremore 74017

Rose State College
6420 Southeast 15th
Midwest City 73110

Seminole Junior College
P.O. Box 351
Seminole 74868

Tulsa Junior College
6111 East Skelly Dr.
Tulsa 74135

Western Oklahoma State College
2801 North Main St.
Altus 73521-1397

OREGON

Montessori Institute Northwest
P.O. Box 771
Oregon City 97045

Portland Community College
P.O. Box 19000
Portland 97280-0990

PENNSYLVANIA

Berlitz Language Centers
1608 Walnut St.
Philadelphia 19103

Berlitz Language Centers
355 Fifth Ave.
Pittsburgh 15222

Berlitz Language Centers
230 Sugartown Rd.
Wayne 19087

Bucks County Community College
Swamp Rd.
Newtown 18940

Butler County Community College
College Dr. Oak Hills
Butler 16003-1203

Community College of Allegheny
    County
800 Allegheny Ave.
Pittsburgh 15233-1895

Community College of Philadelphia
1700 Spring Garden St.
Philadelphia 19130

Delaware County Community College
901 South Media Line Rd.
Media 19063

Harrisburg Area Community College,
    Harrisburg Campus
One Hacc Dr.
Harrisburg 17110

Keystone Junior College
P.O. Box 50
La Plume 18440-0200

Lehigh County Community College
4525 Education Park Dr.
Schnecksville 18078-2598

Luzerne County Community College
1333 South Prospect St.
Nanticoke 18634

Manor Junior College
700 Fox Chase Rd.
Jenkintown 19046

Montgomery County Community
    College
340 Dekalb Pike
Blue Bell 19422

Northampton County Area Community
    College
3835 Green Pond Rd.
Bethlehem 18017

Reading Area Community College
P.O. Box 1706
Reading 19603

RHODE ISLAND

Community College of Rhode Island
400 East Ave.
Warwick 02886-1805

TENNESSEE

Hiwassee College
225 Hiwassee College Dr.
Madisonville 37354

Jackson State Community College
2046 North Pkwy.
Jackson 38301

TEXAS

Amarillo College
P.O. Box 447
Amarillo 79178

Angelina College
P.O. Box 1768
Lufkin 75902-1768

Berlitz Language Centers
8400 North Mopac
Austin 78759

Berlitz Language Centers
17194 Preston Rd.
Dallas 75248

Berlitz Language Centers
1555 Merrimac Circle
Fort Worth 76107

Berlitz Language Centers
3100 Richmond Ave.
Houston 77098

Berlitz Language Centers
5815 Callahan Rd.
San Antonio 78228

Cisco Junior College
Rte. 3, P.O. Box 3
Cisco 76437

College of the Mainland
1200 Amburn Rd.
Texas City 77591

Del Mar College
101 Baldwin
Corpus Christi 78404-3897

El Paso Community College
P.O. Box 20500
El Paso 79998

Frank Phillips College
P.O. Box 5118
Borger 79008-5118

Galveston College
4015 Ave. Q
Galveston 77550

Grayson County College
6101 Grayson Dr.
Denison 75020

Hill College
P.O. Box 619
Hillsboro 76645

Houston Montessori Center
9601 Katy Fwy.
Houston 77024-1330

Howard County Junior College District
1001 Birdwell Ln.
Big Spring 79720

Kilgore College
1100 Broadway
Kilgore 75662-3299

King's Way Missionary Institute
401 South Kings Hwy.
McAllen 78501

McLennan Community College
1400 College Dr.
Waco 76708

Navarro College
3200 West Seventh
Corsicana 75110

North Harris Montgomery Community
    College District
250 North Sam Houston Pkwy. E
Houston 77060

Panola College
West Panola St.
Carthage 75633

Richland College
12800 Abrams Rd.
Dallas 75243-2199

San Jacinto College,
    Central Campus
8060 Spencer Hwy.
Pasadena 77505

San Jacinto College,
    North Campus
5800 Uvalde
Houston 77049

Southwest Texas Junior College
2401 Garner Field Rd.
Uvalde 78801

Temple Junior College
2600 South First St.
Temple 76504-7435

Texas Southmost College
80 Fort Brown
Brownsville 78520

Trinity Valley Community College
500 South Prairieville
Athens 75751

Tyler Junior College
P.O. Box 9020
Tyler 75711

Weatherford College
308 East Park Ave.
Weatherford 76086

Wharton County Junior College
911 Boling Hwy.
Wharton 77488

UTAH

Dixie College
225 South, 700 East
Saint George 84770

VERMONT

Champlain College
163 South Willard St.
Burlington 05401

Community College of Vermont
P.O. Box 120
Waterbury 05676

VIRGINIA

Berlitz Language Centers
2070 Chain Bridge Rd.
Vienna 22182

J Sargeant Reynolds Community College
P.O. Box 85622
Richmond 23285-5622

Northern Virginia Community College
4001 Wakefield Chapel Rd.
Annandale 22003

Saint Paul's College
406 Windsor Ave.
Lawrenceville 23868

Southern Virginia College for Women
One College Hill Dr.
Buena Vista 24416

Tidewater Community College
Rte. 135
Portsmouth 23703

Virginia Western Community College
3095 Colonial Ave.
Roanoke 24015

WASHINGTON

Berlitz Language Centers
400 112th Ave. NE
Bellevue 98009

Berlitz Language Centers
1525 Fourth Ave.
Seattle 98101

WEST VIRGINIA

Opportunities Industrialization Center,
    North Central West Virginia
120 Jackson St.
Fairmont 26554

WISCONSIN

Berlitz Language Centers
111 East Wisconsin Ave.
Milwaukee 53202

Milwaukee Area Technical College
700 West State St.
Milwaukee 53233

North Central Technical College
1000 Campus Dr.
Wausau 54401-1899

Opportunities Industrialization Center
2835 North 32nd St.
Milwaukee 53210

Waukesha County Technical College
800 Main St.
Pewaukee 53072

WYOMING

Casper College
125 College Dr.
Casper 82601

Central Wyoming College
2660 Peck Ave.
Riverton 82501

Eastern Wyoming College
3200 West C St.
Torrington 82240

Laramie County Community College
1400 East College Dr.
Cheyenne 82007

Northwest Community College
231 West Sixth St.
Powell 82435

Sheridan College
P.O. Box 1500
Sheridan 82801

Western Wyoming Community College
P.O. Box 428
Rock Springs 82902

Index

All jobs mentioned in this volume are listed and cross-referenced in the index. Entries that appear in all capital letters have separate occupational profiles. For example, ADULT EDUCATION WORKER, ARMED SERVICES CAREER, BORDER PATROL AGENT, and so on are profiles in this volume. Entries that are not capitalized refer to jobs that do not have a separate profile but for which information is given.

Under some capitalized entries there is a section entitled "Profile includes." This lists jobs that are mentioned in the profile. For example, in the case of TEACHER, COLLEGE, jobs that are described in the profile are: Assistant professor and Associate professor.

Some entries are followed by a job title in parentheses after the page number on which it can be found. This job title is the occupational profile in which the entry is discussed. For instance, the Assistant professor entry is followed by the profile title (Teacher, college).

Photographic Credits

Earl Dotter 56, 59, 67, 107, 123, 141; Tom Dunham 65; Martha Tabor 29, 32, 41, 43, 44, 46, 48, 50, 54, 61, 62, 71, 75, 80, 82, 85, 89, 92, 93, 97, 100, 102, 105, 111, 115, 118, 125, 128, 130, 133, 135, 137, 148; The Terry Wild Studio 1, 5, 7, 10, 33, 34, 38, 87, 112, 143, 146; Visual Education Corporation 52